Management for Professionals

More information about this series at http://www.springer.com/series/10101

Don K. Mak

Trading Tactics in the Financial Market

Mathematical Methods to Improve Performance

Springer

Don K. Mak
Ottawa, ON, Canada

ISSN 2192-8096 ISSN 2192-810X (electronic)
Management for Professionals
ISBN 978-3-030-70621-0 ISBN 978-3-030-70622-7 (eBook)
https://doi.org/10.1007/978-3-030-70622-7

This Springer imprint is published by the registered company Springer Nature Switzerland AG
The registered company address is: Gewerbestrasse 11, 6330 Cham, Switzerland

Preface

I published the book *Science of Financial Market Trading* in 2003. The idea is to introduce concepts in Physics and techniques in Mathematics to financial market trading, especially in the arena of technical analysis. The book was quickly adopted as a textbook for a graduate course in mathematical finance by a university in USA, and continually used as a reference in various disciplines in institutes and universities worldwide. Thus, we think that we have forged the right approach—that some people would like to see trading concepts to be put on a solid scientific and mathematical ground.

Nevertheless, other than occasional mentions of some of the ideas presented in the book in trading forums, the concepts were basically ignored in the trading community. Trading gurus continue to advocate their trading tactics, and how they would make profits. Traders would continue to believe them, without asking why the tactics would work, i.e., if they work at all.

In this book, we expand some of the earlier ideas, and apply them to analyze trading tactics, which we believe are more relevant to the trading community. We would try to explain, by using Fourier Analysis, why some of the indicators and trading tactics would work better than others and why some indicators and trading tactics would perform poorly and should be steered away from. We will start off applying the trading tactics on some dummy artificial data, and then eventually on real market data.

Chapter 1 is an introduction to Trading Tactics as related to Technical Analysis. Chapter 2, the Market Turning Points, contains the key ideas in the book. It explains why and when a trading tactic is profitable, and how money can be lost. Fourier Analysis would be employed to divide the frequency spectrum of a technical indicator into Profit Zone and Loss Zone. Data sampling also has a substantial effect on profitability, proffering the Profit Zone to be divided into Sure Profit Zone and Unsure Profit Zone. As the timing of data sampling can be critical, a new concept, called skipped convolution, is introduced to better time the market turns. Chapter 3, Simple Moving Average, discusses how market price data can be smoothed to eliminate the high frequency noise using Simple Moving Average (SMA). The popular trading tactic, the crossover of Price with its SMA, is analyzed with Fourier Analysis. The problem of this tactic is that SMA suffers from the disappearance of some signals at certain frequencies. In Chapter 4, Exponential Moving Average (EMA), another smoothing technique, is described. The trading tactic, the crossover of Price with its EMA, is analyzed with Fourier Analysis. In Chapter 5, two popular trading tactics, Awesome Oscillator and Accelerator Oscillator, are examined and their characteristics detailed. The problem with these tactics is that wrapped phases are used by traders, while unwrapped phases should have been used. In Chapter 6, Moving Average Convergence-Divergence (MACD), a popular tool of the trader, together with a related and also popular indicator, the MACD Histogram (MACDH), are mathematically characterized. In Chapter 7, various trading tactics, some popular and some not so popular to traders, are applied to real market data, like S&P500, the Hang Seng Index, the FTSE100, and the CAC40. Performance of different tactics are compared. The results somewhat confirm the outcome of the Fourier Analysis - why some trading tactics have a higher probability of profitability. Chapter 8, Analysis of the Trading Tactics, discusses the tactics that would be recommended, and those that should be avoided. Chapter 9 is the Summary.

The book is written for both traders and academics. Minimal mathematics is used in the main text, which is filled with figures and tables for ease of understanding of the concepts presented. Most of the mathematics is put in the appendices for the academics who may want to comprehend the basis of the ideas. The last appendix contains all the MATLAB programs used in the book. The programs would be useful for readers who would like to see how the characteristics of the trading tactics would change by altering the parameters of the indicators. Also, programs analyzing real market data would allow the data to be analyzed by different trading tactics, as we cannot possibly put all the examples in the book. As well, readers can substitute other real market data in the programs to gauge the profitability of the various trading tactics.

The book basically analyzes tactics that have mostly been used by traders, and have not analyzed some of the new ones proposed (e.g., Mak 2006). These would be left as exercises to the readers.

Hence, for the academics, there are quite a lot of ideas that can be followed up. More research would be needed to substantiate and fine-tune some of the concepts. And for the traders, the current ideas should help them decide what trading tactics to use, and hopefully make more profit.

Ottawa, ON, Canada Don K. Mak

Contents

1 Trading Tactics in Technical Analysis 1
- 1.1 Why Artificial Data? 2
- 1.2 Evidence-Based 3
- 1.3 Science-Based 4
- 1.4 Mathematics-Based 4

2 Market Turning Points 5
- 2.1 Price Data 5
- 2.2 Velocity 6
- 2.3 Velocity Indicators 9
  - 2.3.1 Profit Zone and Loss Zone 12
- 2.4 Sampling 12
  - 2.4.1 Sampling Can Affect the Profitability of a Trade 12
  - 2.4.2 Loss in the Profit Zone 17
  - 2.4.3 Sure Profit Zone and Unsure Profit Zone 19
  - 2.4.4 Skipped Convolution 21
  - 2.4.5 Profit in the Loss Zone 22
  - 2.4.6 Multiple frequencies 23
- 2.5 Acceleration 24
- 2.6 Acceleration Indicators 27

3 Simple Moving Average 29
- 3.1 Simple Moving Average (SMA) 29
  - 3.1.1 Simple Moving Average, N = 10 31
  - 3.1.2 Simple Moving Average, N = 20 39
  - 3.1.3 Simple Moving Average, N = 100 42
- 3.2 Trading Tactics Using Simple Moving Average 45
  - 3.2.1 Price – Simple Moving Average of Price, N = 10 45
  - 3.2.2 Price – Simple Moving Average of Price, N = 20 50
  - 3.2.3 Price – Simple Moving Average of Price, N = 100 53
  - 3.2.4 Comparison of *Price – Simple Moving Average of Price, N = 10, 20 and 100* 55

4 Exponential Moving Average 57
4.1 Exponential Moving Average (EMA) 57
4.2 Trading Tactics Using Exponential Moving Average 61
4.2.1 Price − Exponential Moving Average of Price, M = 3 . . . 61
4.2.2 Price − Exponential Moving Average of Price, M = 6 . . . 64
4.2.3 EMA of Price, M = 3 − EMA of Price, M = 6 67
4.2.4 EMAACCEL 69

5 Awesome Oscillator and Accelerator Oscillator 73
5.1 Awesome Oscillator (AO) 73
5.2 Accelerator Oscillator (AC) 78

6 Moving Average Convergence-Divergence and Its Histogram 85
6.1 Moving Average Convergence-Divergence (MACD) 85
6.2 Moving Average Convergence-Divergence Histogram (MACDH) 88
6.3 MACDH1, MACDH with Price Replacing the Fast EMA 92

7 Trading Tactics in the Real Market 97
7.1 S & P 500 Index 100
7.1.1 MACDH 100
7.1.2 MACD 101
7.1.3 Price − EMA3 102
7.1.4 Fast Fourier Transform and Inverse Fast Fourier Transform of S&P500 Index 103
7.2 Hang Seng Index 105
7.2.1 Price − SMA10 106
7.2.2 Awesome Oscillator 106
7.2.3 Accelerator Oscillator 107
7.2.4 Fast Fourier Transform of the Hang Seng index 108
7.3 FTSE 100 Index 109
7.3.1 Price − EMA6 109
7.3.2 MACDH 110
7.3.3 Fast Fourier Transform of the FTSE 100 index 112
7.4 CAC 40 Index 112
7.4.1 MACDH 113
7.4.2 MACDH1 113
7.4.3 Fast Fourier Transform of CAC 40 index 114
7.5 Comparison of Different Trading Tactics 115

8 Analysis of the Trading Tactics 119
8.1 Profit Zone and Loss Zone 119
8.2 Price − EMA of Price Compared to Price − SMA of Price 119
8.3 Awesome Oscillator (AO) and Moving Average Convergence Divergence (MACD) 122

8.4 Accelerator Oscillator (AC) 122
8.5 MACDH 123
8.6 Recommendations 123

9 Epilogue 125

Appendix A: Sure and Unsure Profit and Loss Zones 127

Appendix B: Simple Moving Average 137

Appendix C: Exponential Moving Average, Moving Average Convergence-Divergence 141

Appendix D: MATLAB Programs 145

Bibliography 263

Index 267

1 Trading Tactics in Technical Analysis

In financial market trading, technical analysis plays a significant role. Technical analysis bases the buy and sell decisions on market behavior such as price and volume, with price being more important (Mak 2003). The data are quite often plotted in charts. Past financial data would be employed to forecast future market movement.

Indicators have been created to operate on series of past financial data. Quite a number of indicators have been developed, all aiming at illustrating what the market situation is, and attempting to forecast what it will be. They are actually equivalent to filters in electrical engineering, or operators in mathematics (Mak 2003). The operator will convolute with the past financial time series to produce another function indicative of the state of the market condition.

The terms velocity indicator and acceleration indicator were introduced in 2003 (Mak 2003), and further explained in 2006 (Mak 2006). These terms are borrowed from the terms velocity and acceleration in Physics. The idea is to apply the concepts and mathematical techniques in Physics to technical analysis in financial market trading, so as to simplify and clarify the terminology and the trading tactics then used. The terms never caught on (googling the terms did not show these items displayed) until about 2017. Even after then, while the terms used by some traders do conform to the meanings in Physics, there are cases where they mean something else. Even worse, sometimes the terms used are totally misleading. In one YouTube video, acceleration is used while velocity should have been employed.

In Physics, velocity measures the rate of change of distance over time, and acceleration measures the rate of change of velocity (these definitions have been simplified, as velocity and acceleration in Physics are vector quantities that have directions). In trading, distance is replaced by price.

When price is plotted against time, the data traces a curve. The rate of change of price on the curve can be called the slope of the curve. We will call the slope the velocity, and the slope of the slope the acceleration. When the velocity is positive,

D. K. Mak, *Trading Tactics in the Financial Market*, Management for Professionals,
https://doi.org/10.1007/978-3-030-70622-7_1

the price is increasing. When the velocity is negative, the price is decreasing. Thus, a simple trading tactic is to buy and hold when the velocity is positive, and sell short and hold when the velocity is negative. The concepts velocity and acceleration, and especially the former, play a significant role in many traders' tactics, even though they may not have realized it.

In 2014, Chan et al. explicitly pointed out that quite a number of technical indicators already used by traders, including the popular Moving Average Convergence Divergence (MACD), are actually velocity indicators, which emulate velocity, and trading tactics have been used to exploit the strategy of buying when velocity is positive, and selling when velocity is negative. They further pointed out that the popular MACD histogram (MACDH) is an acceleration indicator, and some aggressive traders have been using the strategy of buying when acceleration is positive, and selling when acceleration is negative (we will come back later to see whether this strategy makes sense).

In this book, we will try to demonstrate that some trading tactics have a higher probability of winning than others, and some tactics have such a low probability of winning that they should have been avoided. The argument is mathematically based rather than scientifically based, as the former approach is much simpler than the latter. Artificial data would be used in the beginning to substantiate our argument, and eventually real market data would be employed to back up our claims.

1.1 Why Artificial Data?

Someone may wonder why artificial data are used when real market data actually look quite different. The answer is, we need to understand something simple before we can understand something more complicated. This is a common venue taken by scientific research: we first create a simple model.

In science, a model is a representation of a phenomenon, and can be a simplified picture of what reality actually is. To cite an example, Newton's First Law states that an object at rest stays at rest, and an object in motion stays in motion. Force, including frictional force, is not exerted on the object. However, in real life environment, forces almost always exist. In this case, a very simple model is described first, as only after we have grasped something simple should we attempt to apprehend something more complicated. Scientists constantly work on refining and improving models. An improved model can help us understand the behavior of real objects and systems.

Financial market is quite often modeled as waves. In 1900, Charles Dow proposed his wave theory (Pring 1991). He observed that a rising market moves in a series of waves, each rally and correction being higher than its predecessor. When the series of rising peaks and valleys was interrupted, a trend reversal was signaled.

These waves can be modeled as a sum of sine waves (Mak 2003). As described earlier, technical indicators have been created to operate on financial data, in order to gauge the market movement. We would like to point out that, before we can understand the outcome of a technical indicator on the summation of sine waves, we need to understand what the outcome is on a single sine wave. Furthermore, occasionally, real market data can actually be approximated as a single sine wave. If a trading tactic cannot make any profit on a single sine wave, it is highly unlikely that it can make any profit on a summation of sine waves. This easy single sine wave test on tactics would allow us to differentiate the useful from the garbage, as well as understanding the limitations of the useful. We should know that all tools, and scientific theories, are not perfect, and have their domain of application. It is just as important to comprehend their shortcomings as well as their functionalities.

We can never predict how the market would progress, but hopefully we can explain how a trading tactic can make a profit in the past. More importantly, we should try to find out the probability that a tactic can make a profit in the future.

This book would only emphasize on trading tactics that are transparent and objective. Firstly, amateurs and traders should be suspicious of the black box trading programs sold by some gurus. Secondly, tactics that are subjective to individual interpretation, which differs from trader to trader, cannot be depended upon. Thirdly, one should also cast doubt on those so called evidence-based tactics, as one can easily find examples in the market that show evidence that they are profitable.

1.2 Evidence-Based

As the market is random or near-random (Mak 2006), a trader, whatever trading tactics he picks or prefers, can always find evidence that the tactics is profitable in some market data.

Evidence-based practices start off with evidence-based medicine (EBM), which was introduced in 1990. EBM was advocated then as a lot of medical decisions were still based on faith, tradition, intuition, and vehemence. EBM aims to apply the best evidences obtained by the scientific method to medical decision making.

However, evaluating scientific results is extremely complex. A process, called hierarchy of evidence, has been designed to rank the relative strengths of results obtained from scientific research. Typically, systematic reviews and meta-analysis (statistical analysis combining the results of multiple scientific studies) rank at the top. Randomized controlled trials rank above observational studies. And expert opinion and case reports rank at the bottom.

In spite of this undertaking, EBM has been hijacked by some quackery and unqualified practitioners, who would claim that their treatments have some kind of evidences, even though they have little or no scientific plausibility. In 2008, the term science-based medicine (SBM) was coined to combat the limitations of EBM. SBM would emphasize that any treatment needs to be feasible based on some scientific knowledge to begin with. Basic science has to be taken more seriously before any evidences collected.

1.3 Science-Based

Any practice acquired should be compatible with the laws of science. Science should be considered as a necessary starting point as science provides plausibility.

To explain why the market moves, we need to understand the forces behind it. The movement of the market represents the emotions of traders who oscillate between optimism and pessimism, greed and fear. Emotions, in its reality, can be very complicated. Furthermore, each trader has his own thinking, and he can act somewhat independently. The occurrence can be interpreted using a simple model as an approximation. A more complex model can be developed when we understand the phenomenon better, or when new mathematical tools are invented.

As a simple model, one can say that when the interest rate is less than 2%, investors will buy into the stock market, which will rise, and when the interest rate is more than 2%, investors will put their money into term deposits in the bank, and the market will fall. This single parameter, interest rate, of course, cannot explain all the intricate movements of the market. Thus, a more complicated model would accommodate many numeric parameters as input data. A more sophisticated model can involve using neural network, which is trained by repeatedly presented with examples that include both inputs and outputs. The network learns from each example and calculates an output. In addition, genetic algorithm, which is used to solve optimization problem, can help to sort out which parameters are significant. The parameters have to be time-dependent to resolve which direction the market is going. The ongoing collection of all these input information can make the problem quite elaborate.

Thus, we will attempt to take a simpler approach. We will first ensure that our plan is mathematically plausible rather than scientifically plausible, and then we will see whether there are any evidences to sustain our plan.

1.4 Mathematics-Based

Our objective is not to predict the movement of the market, which is probably impossible to predict anyway, but to find a trading tactic that would increase the probability of winning. We will mathematically characterize and compare the various trading tactics that have been employed by traders, and point out which ones are better than others, and which ones should definitely be avoided.

The result of our mathematical deductions needs to be justified by looking into evidences from real market trading. This can be compared to randomized trials as used in evidence-based practices to see whether there are any differences in the outcome of the trials. We can randomly pick any market, and randomly pick any number of days (or bars in any time frame) of trading. The profitability of the trading tactics from each set of market data can then be compared.

In the next chapter, we will describe in more detail what our mathematical approach would be.

Market Turning Points

2

It sure would be nice if the market is always trending up. Investors can simply buy and hold, and sell the stocks when they need money. Unfortunately, the market never behaves as such. One assertion that seems to be certain for the behavior of the market is: the market always goes up, but then again, it will always come down. Thus, traders need to know when the market turns, and hopefully predict the turning points some time ahead. They can go long (buy) when the market goes up, and sell short (sell) when the market comes down. For the forecasting and identification of the turning points, we can turn to a mathematics discipline called Calculus for help. Calculus is the mathematical study of continuous change. It relates to instantaneous rates of change and slopes of curves. It was developed independently by Issac Newton in England and Gottfried Leibniz in Germany in the late seventeenth century.

2.1 Price Data

As explained in Mak (2003), it would be much easier to interpret the ideas of market price movements by choosing some simple waveforms to simulate the market price as a start. We can then progress to more complicated waveforms, and then eventually analyze the real market data.

In 1807, a French mathematician, Joseph Fourier, showed that any practical signal can be expressed as the sum of a number of sine waves. This summation has been called the Fourier series (Broesch 1997; Hubbard 1998). This theorem will allow us to rewrite any financial data as a sum of sine waves.

Thus, to start off with something simple, we will simulate the price with a single sine wave. As an example, we will choose a sine wave of 1.5 cycles, with an amplitude of 1.0, and a period (T) of 40 as shown in Fig. 2.1. (A sine wave can be formed by the projection of a rotating vector of a circle on the vertical axis. Rotating the vector by 360° (=2π radians) will form 1 cycle of the sine wave.) For simplicity

D. K. Mak, *Trading Tactics in the Financial Market*, Management for Professionals,
https://doi.org/10.1007/978-3-030-70622-7_2

of understanding, we can assume that it is a daily chart (i.e., the unit time is 1 day), and the period of 1 cycle is then 40 trading days. Frequency, f, is defined as the reciprocal of a period, and is therefore equal to $1/T = 1/(40$ unit time). Circular frequency, ω, is defined as $2\pi \times$ frequency $= 2\pi f = 2\pi/40$ (radians/unit time).

For this single sine wave, a trader surely would buy at the dip and sell at the peak in order to make maximum profit. Looking at Fig. 2.1, he would go into a short position (sell) on Day 10 (time, $t = 10$), and close his position (buy) on Day 30 ($t = 30$). He would also go into a long position (buy) on Day 30 ($t = 30$), and close his position (sell) on Day 50 ($t = 50$).

But only knowing the past data, and not future data, how is he going to predict that the market is going to turn?

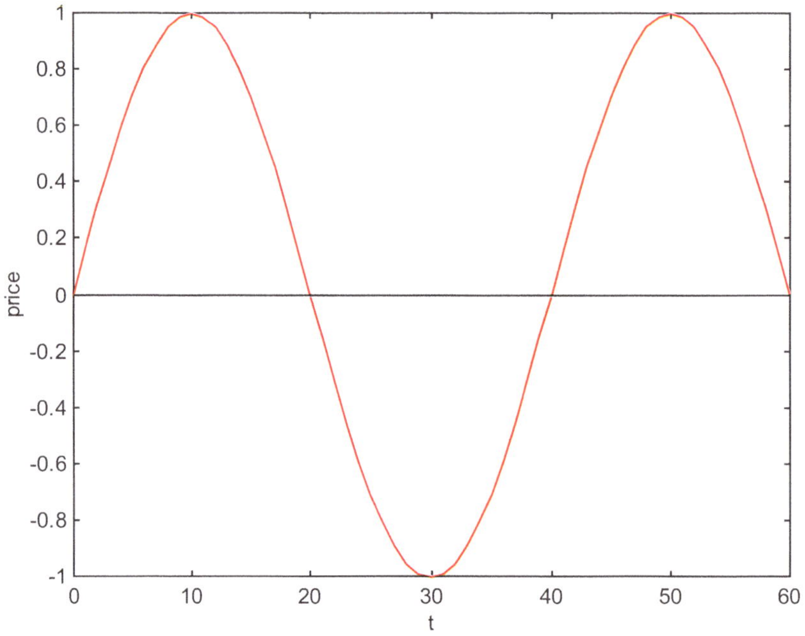

Fig. 2.1 Simulated price data. Price (plotted as a red line) is plotted versus time t, as a sine wave with a period of 40 trading days.

2.2 Velocity

The answer is by simply finding the slope of the curve (Mak 2003). The slope of the curve is the instantaneous rate of change of the curve, and is called first derivative, or simply derivative in Calculus. The derivative of a sine wave is a cosine wave. A cosine wave is actually the same as a sine wave but with 90° added to its phase, and that is why a cosine wave leads the sine wave by 90° ($= \pi/2$ radians). Thus, a cosine wave actually looks exactly like a sine wave but shifted by 90° to the left side. As the period of the wave corresponds to 360°, shifting by 90° would correspond to a shifting of 1/4 of a cycle, i.e., 10 days when the period is 40 days. The cosine wave leads as it cuts the zero-crossing faster by 90° than the sine wave. The slope is plotted in blue color in Fig. 2.2(a). We will borrow a term from Physics and called this slope velocity. In Physics, velocity measures the rate of change of distance over time (this definition has been simplified, as velocity in Physics is a vector quantity that has a direction). In trading terminology here, we replace distance by price.

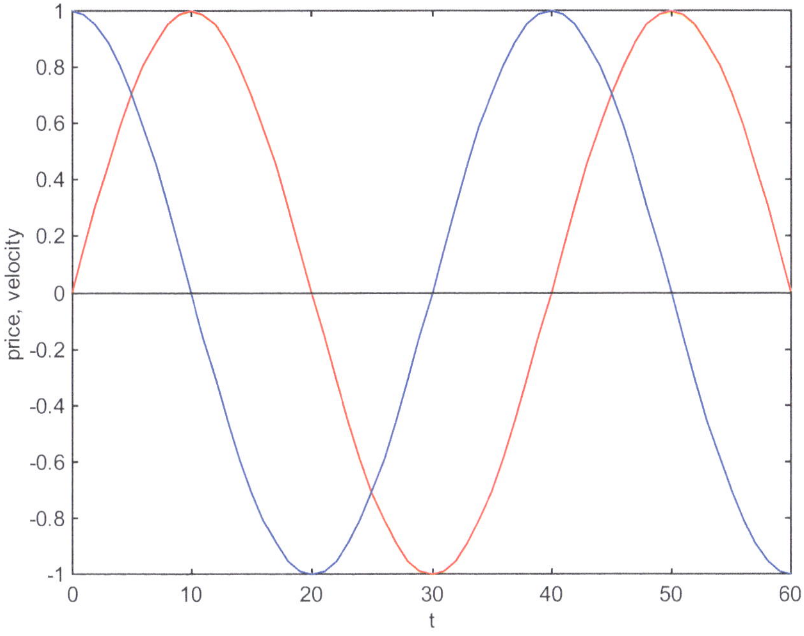

Fig. 2.2(a) Simulated price data. Price (plotted as a red line) is plotted versus time t, as a sine wave with a period of 40 trading days. Velocity is plotted as a blue line. It represents the slope of the price.

It can be noted from Fig. 2.2(a) that, as long as velocity is +ve, e.g., t = 30 to t = 50, price is increasing, and as long as velocity is −ve, e.g., t = 10 to t = 30, price is decreasing. At the peak and trough of the price data (t = 10, 30, 50), the slope or the velocity equals 0. At the peak, e.g., t = 10, velocity goes from +ve to −ve. And at the trough, e.g., t = 30, velocity goes from −ve to +ve.

Thus, when a trader sees that the velocity is approaching from the −ve side to the +ve side, he would predict that the price is bottoming out, and he can go long (buy) at velocity = 0. And as long as the velocity turns positive and holds +ve, he can hold. When a trader sees that the velocity is approaching from the +ve side to the −ve side, he would predict that the price is peaking out, and he can sell short (sell) at velocity = 0. And as long as the velocity turns negative and holds −ve, he can hold. Thus, a simple trading rule can be found in Table 2.1.

Table 2.1 Trading rule using velocity

Velocity	0 (−ve to +ve)	> 0	0 (+ve to −ve)	< 0
Trading rule	Buy	Hold	Sell	Hold

One can simplify the trading rule as: go long when velocity is positive, and sell short when velocity is negative. However, for the sake of clarity, we will only consider the trader going long, and not selling short, even though the ideas in this book can easily be applied to the latter.

The advantage of monitoring the velocity is that the velocity will approach 0 at the turning points. And that is much more noticeable than monitoring the turning of the price data. It should also be noted that if we add a constant to the price data (e.g., constant + sine wave), the velocity would still be the same as if the constant were not added, as the slope (or derivative) of a constant is zero (Fig. 2.2(b)). Real market data can be represented as a constant with cycles of waves riding on top of the constant. The advantage of looking at the slope is that we can simply ignore the constant.

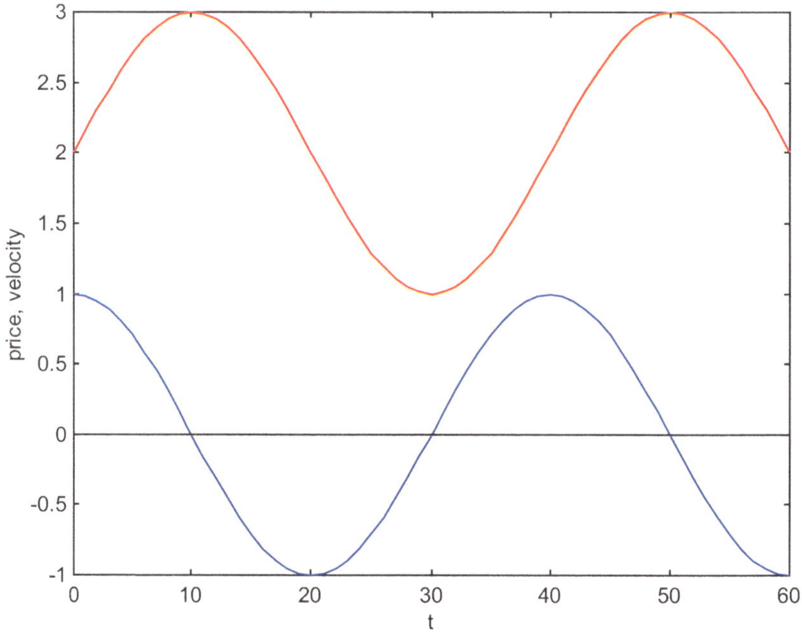

Fig. 2.2(b) Simulated price data. A constant has been added to the price of Fig. 2.2 (a). Price (plotted as a red line) is plotted versus time t, as a sine wave with a period of 40 trading days. Velocity is plotted as a blue line. It represents the slope of the price. The velocity is exactly the same as the velocity shown in Fig. 2.2(a).

Thus, by simply monitoring the velocity, we would know when the market is going to turn. This, of course, sounds too good to be true, and it is. The problem is: how are we going to find the velocity. Price data can be represented as waves of different frequencies, as well as summation of all these waves. It would be difficult to find a velocity that reflects the slopes of all these waves. At best, we can try to create velocity indicators that can emulate velocity. However, as we will soon find out, this is not an easy task.

2.3 Velocity Indicators

In the following chapters, we will describe some existing indicators for simulating the velocity, as well as some new indicators we introduce. Existing indicators are indicators that have been used by traders. As indicators can only use past data for calculation, the velocity indicators would always lag behind the ideal phase lead of $\pi/2$ radians $= 90°$, as shown in Fig. 2.2(a). The lag of the velocity indicator would definitely influence whether the trader makes or loses money.

In Fig. 2.3 (a) – (d) below, we will arbitrarily choose the amplitude of the price signal to be 1 and the amplitude of the velocity indicator signal to be 0.8 so as to show their differences more clearly. The velocity indicators will be drawn with different phase lags from the price, in order to show how phase lag can make or break.

Figures 2.3(a), (b), (c), and (d) shows a velocity indicator having a phase lead of $\pi/2$, 0, $-\pi/2$, and $-\pi$ radians respectively from the price data. Following the trading rule in Table 2.1, the trader will make maximal profit, zero profit, maximal loss, and zero profit respectively.

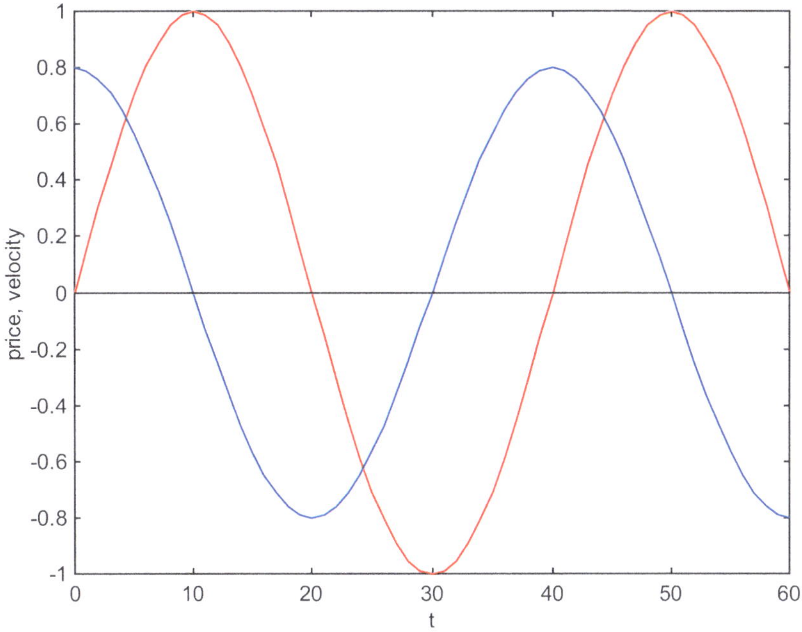

Fig. 2.3(a) Simulated price data. Price (plotted as a red line) is plotted versus time t, as a sine wave with a period of 40 trading days. Velocity indicator of the price data is plotted as a blue line. Here the velocity indicator has an ideal phase lead of $\pi/2$ radians, which is the same as Fig. 2.2(a). Following the trading rule of Table 2.1, maximal profit will be made.

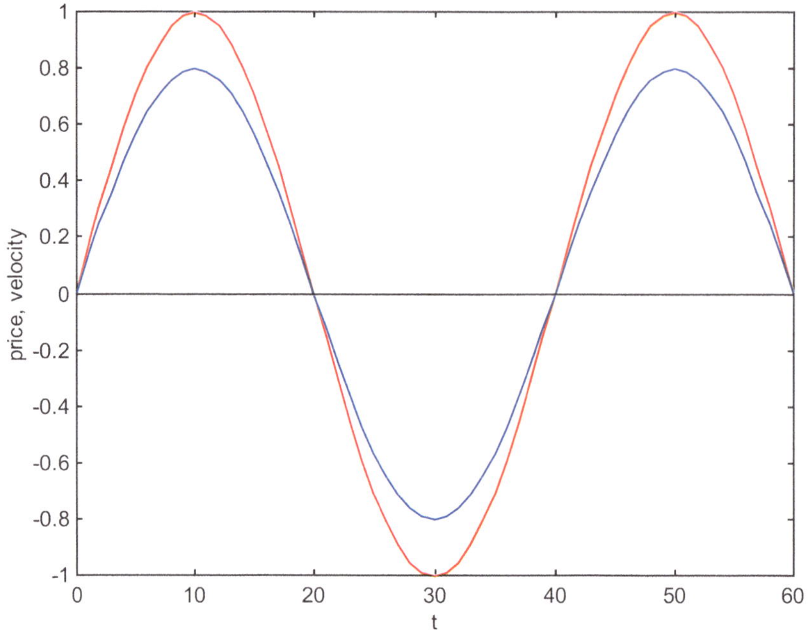

Fig. 2.3(b) Simulated price data. Price (plotted as a red line) is plotted versus time t, as a sine wave with a period of 40 trading days. Velocity indicator of the price data is plotted as a blue line. Here the velocity indicator has a phase lead of 0 radians, i.e., it is totally in phase with the signal. Following the trading rule of Table 2.1, zero profit will be made.

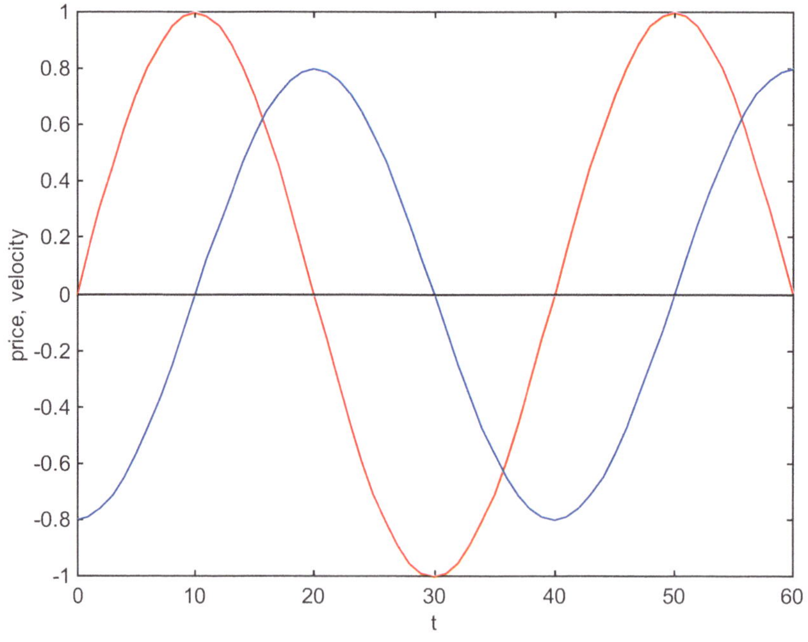

Fig. 2.3(c) Simulated price data. Price (plotted as a red line) is plotted versus time t, as a sine wave with a period of 40 trading days. Velocity indicator of the price data is plotted as a blue line. Here the velocity indicator has a phase lead of $-\pi/2$ radians ($=$a phase lag of $\pi/2$ radians). Following the trading rule of Table 2.1, maximal loss will be made.

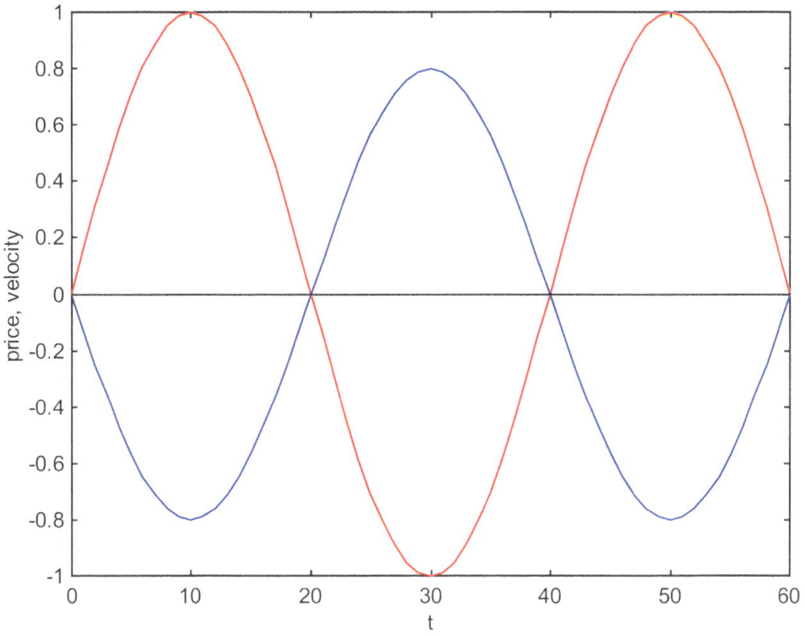

Fig. 2.3(d) Simulated price data. Price (plotted as a red line) is plotted versus time t, as a sine wave with a period of 40 trading days. Velocity indicator of the price data is plotted as a blue line. Here the velocity indicator has a phase lead of $-\pi$ radians (=phase lag of π radians = phase lead of π radians), i.e., it is opposite in phase with the signal. Following the trading rule of Table 2.1, zero profit will be made.

We can create the following table.

Table 2.2 Trading profit made by following the trading rule of Table 2.1. (a)–(d) corresponds to Figs. 2.3(a)–(d)

	(a)	(b)	(c)	(d)
Velocity indicator phase, ϕ, with respect to price signal	$\pi/2$ lead	0 (= 2π)	$-\pi/2$ lead ($\pi/2$ lag = $3\pi/2$ lead)	π lead (=$-\pi$ lead = π lag)
Profit	1	0	-1	0

Thus from Table 2.2, it can be seen that the trader will make maximum profit in (a) and zero profit in (b). He will lose all the money in (c) and make zero profit in (d). In between all these cases, he will either make some profit or lose some money. Profit = 1 in Table 2.2 means the maximum profit the trader can make, i.e., he buys at the bottom, and sells at the top. Profit = -1 would mean he buys at the top, and sells at the bottom.

2.3.1 Profit Zone and Loss Zone

The trading outcome can be described as: if the velocity indicator leads the price signal between 0 and π, the trader will make money; if the velocity indicator leads the price signal between π and 2π (which is equivalent to leading between $-\pi$ and 0 and equivalent to lagging between π and 0), the trader will lose money. Thus, when we design a velocity indicator, we should aim at making it to have a phase lead between 0 and π, and preferably a phase lead of $\pi/2$ radians with respect to the price data, such that maximum profit can be attained. As the phase lead or lag of the velocity indicator of a signal would depend on the frequency of the signal (see, e.g., Chapter 3), it would be challenging to find a velocity indicator that would make a trade profitable for a large range of frequency. We would call the range of frequency ω of a velocity indicator which has a phase lead ϕ, that lies between 0 and π as the Profit Zone for that velocity indicator, while the range of frequency which has a phase lead ϕ, that lies between 0 and $-\pi$ as the Loss Zone. An example will be given in Sections 3.2.1 in Chapter 3.

Other factor also affects the profitability of a trade, as we will show below.

2.4 Sampling

2.4.1 Sampling Can Affect the Profitability of a Trade

As the price signal, and consequently the filtered price signal (price signal after operated on by an indicator), are not continuous, but are sampled, sampling would affect the profitability of a trade. Buy indication occurs when the velocity crosses over from negative to positive, and should trigger a buy when it is exactly at zero. However, as the data are sampled, the buy indication is thus delayed to the next sampled datum when velocity is greater than 0. Similarly, sell indication occurs when the velocity crosses over from positive to negative, and should trigger a sell when it is exactly at zero. However, as the data are sampled, the sell indication is delayed.

Thus, the profitability of a trade would depend upon when the data are sampled. Three examples are shown below, with exactly the same price signal but sampled slightly shifted from the others. A trade using the same velocity indicator, which is arbitrarily phase shifted by the ideal $\pi/2$ lead from the sampled price signals, would produce different profits for the three examples.

The price signal is simulated by a single sine wave of amplitude 1 and circular frequency $\omega = \pi/6$. Had the price signal been continuous, a velocity indicator with a phase lead of $\pi/2$, will buy at the very bottom and sell at the very top, thus making a profit of 2.0. However, as the price signal is sampled, the trade will produce a profit less than 2.0.

Example 2.1

Figure 2.4 plots the price in the top figure, and the filtered price in the middle figure, with

Price = sin (π/6 n), and

Filtered Price = sin (π/6 n + π/2)

The trader will buy at n = 10, which is marked by an * in the bottom figure, and sell at n = 16, which is marked by a + in the bottom figure, thus making a profit of 1.73, which is less than the ideal profit of 2.0. Figure 2.4 can be plotted using the computer program tradeartif, with the parameter tactic set equal to 12, theta0 = 0, and thetashift (= phase lead) set to π/2.

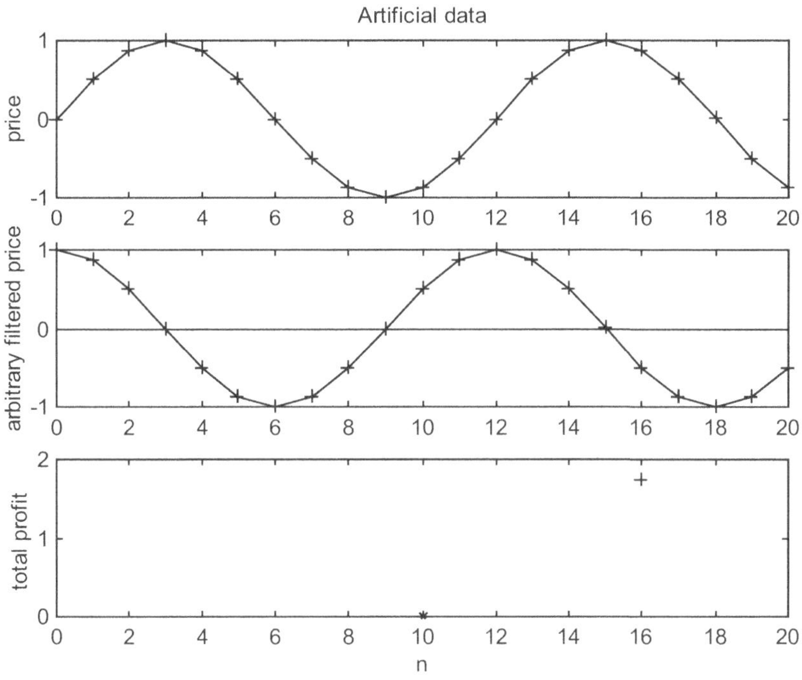

Fig. 2.4 Price is plotted in the top figure, and the filtered price in the middle figure. In the bottom figure, buy indication is marked by an * at n = 10 and sell indication by a + at n = 16, thus making a profit of 1.73, i.e., the profit % is 86.5%.

Example 2.2

Figure 2.5 plots the price in the top figure, and the filtered price in the middle figure, with

Price = sin (π/6 n + π/8), and

Filtered Price = sin (π/6 n + π/8 + π/2)

The trader will buy at n = 9, which is marked by an * in the bottom figure, and sell at n = 15, which is marked by a + in the bottom figure, thus making a profit = 1.85, which is less than the ideal profit of 2.0.

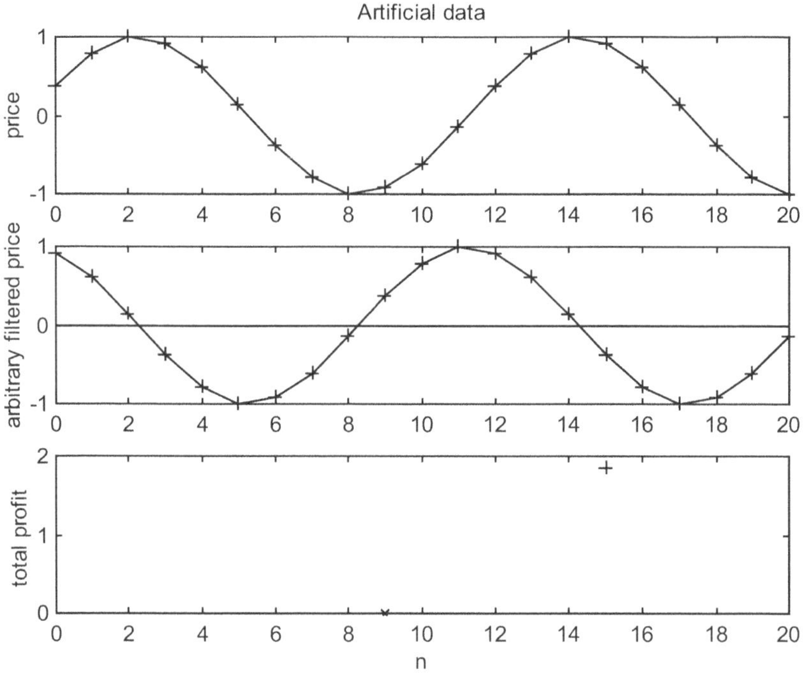

Fig. 2.5 Price is plotted in the top figure, and the filtered price in the middle figure. In the bottom figure, buy indication is marked by an * at n = 9 and sell indication by a + at n = 15, thus making a profit of 1.85, i.e., the profit % is 92.5%.

Example 2.3

Figure 2.6 plots the price in the top figure, and the filtered price in the middle figure, with

Price = sin (π/6 n + π/4), and

Filtered Price = sin (π/6 n + π/4 + π/2)

The trader will buy at n = 8, which is marked by an * in the bottom figure, and sell at n = 14, which is marked by a + in the bottom figure, thus making a profit = 1.93, which is less than the ideal profit of 2.0.

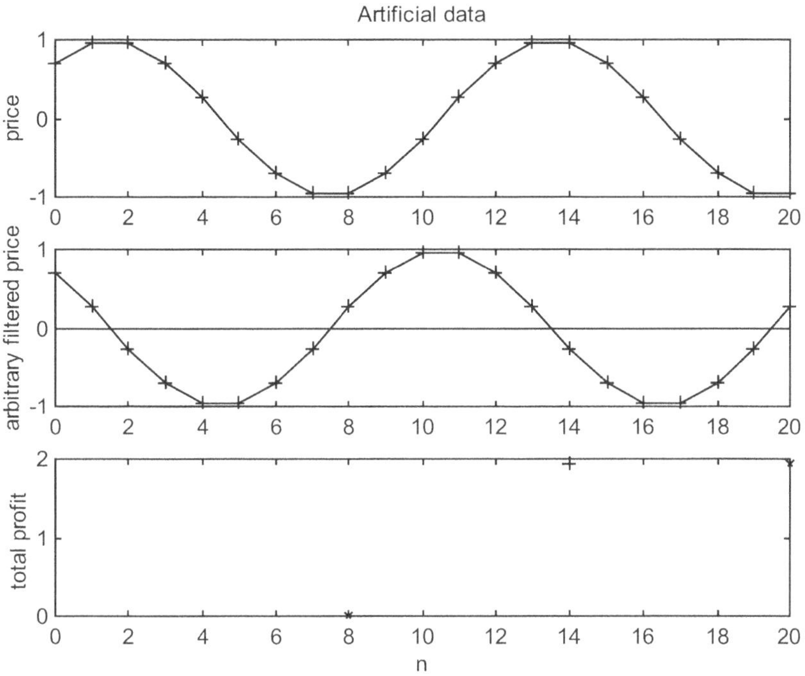

Fig. 2.6 Price is plotted in the top figure, and the filtered price in the middle figure. In the bottom figure, buy indication is marked by an * at n = 8 and sell indication by a + at n = 14, thus making a profit of 1.93, i.e., the profit % is 96.6%.

In each of the examples, the initial phase angle of the price signal is changed to emulate the erratic phase shift of the price signal at the moment when the signal is sampled. It can be seen from the three examples above, that, depending on when the price data are sampled, profit made in a trade can differ, even though the phase lead of the velocity indicator from the price data is exactly the same.

2.4.1.1 Theoretical Calculation of Profit

If the price data is a single sine wave, the Buy Price, Sell Price, and Profit can actually be calculated from

$$\text{nbuy} = \text{Integer}\left((2\pi - \theta_0 - \phi)/\omega\right) + 1 \tag{2.1}$$

$$\text{Buy price} = \sin\ (\text{nbuy} \times \omega + \theta_0) \tag{2.2}$$

$$\text{nsell} = \text{Integer}\left((3\pi - \theta_0 - \phi)/\omega\right) + 1 \tag{2.3}$$

$$\text{Sell price} = \sin\ (\text{nsell} \times \omega + \theta_0) \tag{2.4}$$

Or, as sine wave is an odd function,

$$\text{Sell price} = -\text{Buy price} \tag{2.5}$$

$$\text{Profit} = \text{Sell price} - \text{Buy price} = 2 \times \text{Sell Price} \tag{2.6}$$

$$\text{Profit\%} = \text{Profit}/2 \times 100\% \tag{2.7}$$

where

nbuy = n where the buying indication is triggered

nsell = n where the selling indication is triggered

θ_0 is the initial phase offset of the price signal,

ϕ is the phase lead of the velocity indicator from the price signal

Integer is the integer portion of the argument.

In Eq. (2.7), 2 = peak – valley of the sine wave, whose amplitude equals 1

Equations (2.1)–(2.7) form the basis of the computer program buysellprice.

For Example 2.3

As $\omega = \pi/6$, $\theta_0 = \pi/4$, and $\phi = \pi/2$
nbuy = 8
Buy price = −0.966
nsell = 14
Sell price = 0.966
Profit = 1.93
Profit % = 96.6%

The result of this theoretical calculation agrees with that of the computational calculation described above (Fig. 2.6). The idea of this exercise is that when the circular frequency, and the sampling delay of the price signal simulated as a single sine wave are known, the profit or loss of a trade can be calculated. This is because the phase lead of the velocity indicator acting on the price signal can be pre-determined from the Discrete Time Fourier Transform (DTFT) (see Chapter 3), and the phase lead is given as an input data. However, in real market data or even in artificial data, the computational phase lead of the velocity indicator can have a slight error from the theoretical phase lead calculated, as the computational result uses only limited past data, while DTFT uses infinite past data for some of the velocity indicators. The computational calculation can result in filtered price not an odd function due to minor computational error, causing the Sell price not equal to minus Buy price. In those cases, the computational result can differ from the theoretical calculation.

Not only can sampled data affect profitability, it can also change a trade in the Profit Zone from a profit to a loss, as we will show in the next section.

2.4.2 Loss in the Profit Zone

When the velocity indicator has a phase lead that lies between 0 and π from the price signal, the trade would be profitable. However, as the data are not continuous curves, but are sampled, losses can sometimes occur. Thus, sampled data can cause losses in the Profit Zone where the phase lead of the velocity indicator is greater than or equal to 0, and especially in the neighborhood which is slightly larger than 0.

Example 2.4

Figure 2.7 shows the price signal in the top figure, and the filtered signal in the middle figure. The top figure shows an artificial price data represented by

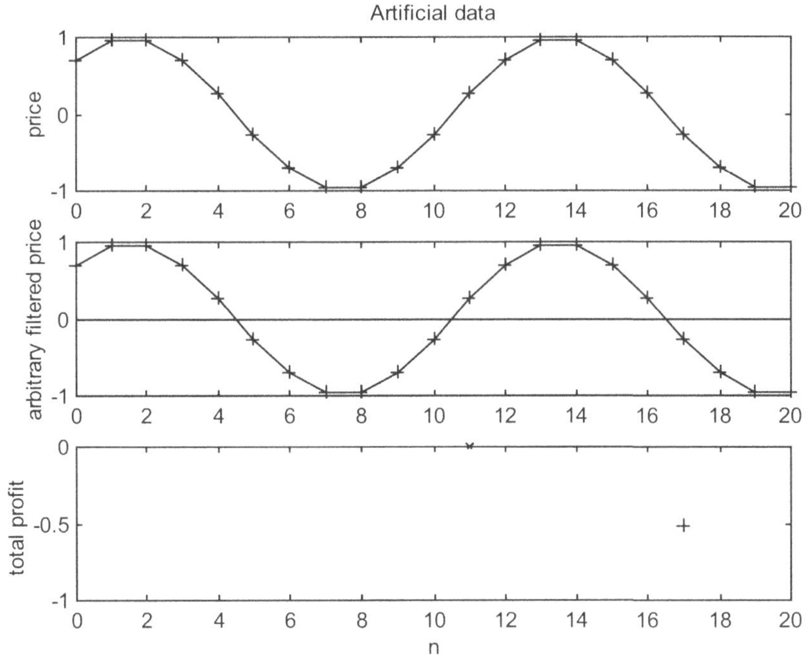

Fig. 2.7 Price is plotted in the top figure, and the filtered price, which is arbitrarily set to be exactly the same as the price signal, is plotted in the middle figure. In the bottom figure, buy indication is marked by an * at $n = 11$ (bought at 0.26) and sell indication by a + at $n = 17$ (sold at -0.26), thus making a loss of 0.52.

Price = sin ($\pi/6$ n + $\pi/4$), where the price has a circular frequency ω of $\pi/6$, and an original phase offset θ_0 of $\pi/4$.

The filtered signal, shown in the middle figure is arbitrarily set to be exactly the same as the price signal, i.e., the phase lead is equal to 0. Had the signal and filtered signal been continuous curves, no profit or loss would be made. However, because the data are sampled, a buy indication is triggered only after the data point crosses 0, i.e., at n = 11, buying at 0.26. Similarly, a sell indication is triggered at n = 17, selling at −0.26, thus contributing a loss of 0.52, as shown in the bottom figure. This computational result agrees with the theoretical calculation using the program buysellprice.

Example 2.5

Figure 2.8 shows the price signal in the top figure, which is the same as the price signal in the top figure of Fig. 2.7. The middle figure of Fig. 2.8 shows that an arbitrary phase lead ϕ of $\pi/12$ is added to the price data, and is then used as filtered price data. The filtered price data would then be

Filtered Price = sin ($\pi/6$ n + $\pi/4$ + $\pi/12$)

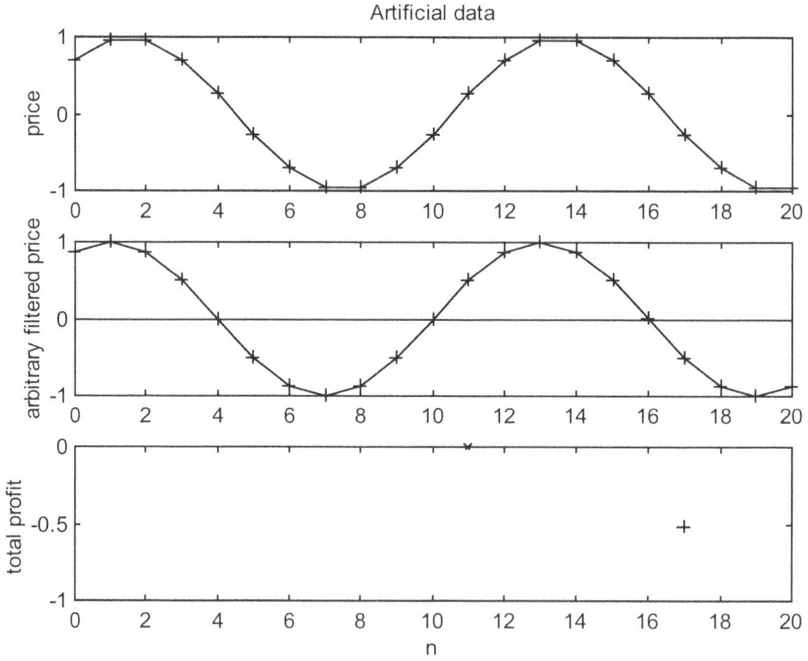

Fig. 2.8 Price is plotted in the top figure, and the filtered price, with a phase lead arbitrarily set to $\pi/12$ from the price, is plotted in the middle figure. In the bottom figure, buy indication is marked by an * at n = 11 (bought at 0.26) and sell indication by a + at n = 17 (sold at −0.26), thus making a loss of 0.52.

As $\pi/12$ lies within the Profit Zone (0 to π), the trade should have been profitable. However, because the data is sampled, the trade actually contributes a loss of 0.52, as shown in the bottom figure. This computational result agrees with the theoretical calculation using the program buysellprice.

2.4.3 Sure Profit Zone and Unsure Profit Zone

For a signal with circular frequency ω, if a velocity indicator has a phase lead between 0 and π, and the phase lead is larger than ω, the trade will surely make a profit. We will define the region of ω where a trade will surely make profit the Sure Profit Zone. If the velocity indicator has a phase lead between 0 and π, but the phase lead is smaller than ω, the trade may or may not make a profit. We will define this region of ω the Unsure Profit Zone. We will define μ to be the phase shift of the price signal caused by sampling delay. In the Unsure Profit Zone, the trade will make a profit if μ is less than the phase lead of the velocity indicator. The trade will lose money if μ is larger than the phase lead of the velocity indicator. The description of the Sure Profit Zone and Unsure Profit Zone is listed in Table 2.3.

Table 2.3 Sure Profit Zone and Unsure Profit Zone

Sure Profit Zone	$\phi > \omega$	always makes a profit
Unsure Profit Zone	$\phi < \omega$	$\mu \leq \phi$ $(\mu > 0)$ makes a profit $\mu > \phi$ $(\mu > 0)$ makes a loss

ϕ is the phase lead of the velocity indicator, and lies between 0 and π. μ is the phase shift of the price signal caused by sampling delay.

More details will be discussed in Appendix A and Section 3.2.1.2 in Chapter 3. Examples for the Unsure Profit Zone are given below:

Example 2.6

$\omega = \pi/6$ and $\phi = \pi/12$. This is an example of Unsure Profit Zone as $\phi < \omega$.
$\mu = \pi/12.01$. As $\mu < \phi$, the trade is supposed to make a profit.
$\theta_0 = \omega - \mu =$ the initial phase offset of the price signal,

Using the program tradeartif with the tactic parameter set to 12, Fig. 2.9 can be drawn, with the Profit % of the trade equals 25.9. This result agrees with the theoretical calculation from the program buysellprice.

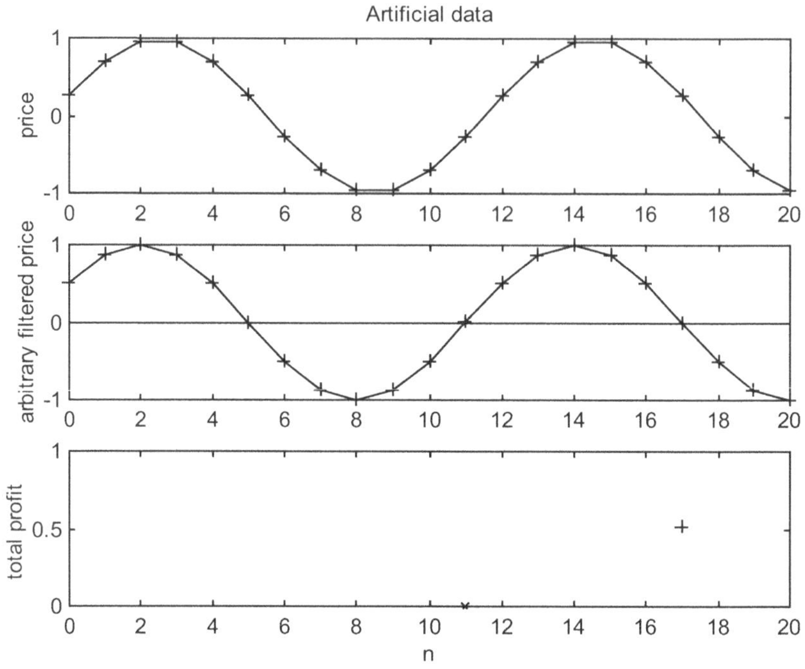

Fig. 2.9 Price is plotted in the top figure, with the initial phase offset $\theta_0 = \omega - \mu = \pi/6 - \pi/12.01$. The filtered price, with a phase lead arbitrarily set to $\pi/12$ from the price, is plotted in the middle figure. In the bottom figure, buy indication is marked by an * at n = 11 (bought at −0.26) and sell indication by a + at n = 17 (sold at 0.26), thus making a profit of 0.52, which is approximately 25.9%.

Example 2.7

$\omega = \pi/6$ and $\phi = \pi/12$. This is an example of Unsure Profit Zone as $\phi < \omega$.
$\mu = \pi/11.99$. As $\mu > \phi$, the trade is supposed to make a loss.
$\theta_0 = \omega - \mu =$ the initial phase offset of the price signal,

Using the program tradeartif with the tactic parameter set to 12, Fig. 2.10 can be drawn, with the Profit % of the trade equals −25.9. This result agrees with the theoretical calculation from the program buysellprice.

Comparing Figs. 2.9 and 2.10, we can see that a slight change in the timing when the original price signal is sampled, can affect whether a trade is profitable or not. These results actually agree with the theoretical calculations shown in Fig A.1 in Appendix A. Figure A.1 also shows that even when a trade is profitable, changes in the sampling timing affects the profitability of a trade, as it has also been shown in Examples 2.1–2.3 above. This would simply mean that the earlier the trader can detect the market turning point, the better the chance that he can make a better profit if the trade is profitable, or avoid a loss, or avoid a larger loss if the trade is losing money. But how is he going to do that? There is actually a trick he can use called skipped convolution, which can be employed to detect market action earlier.

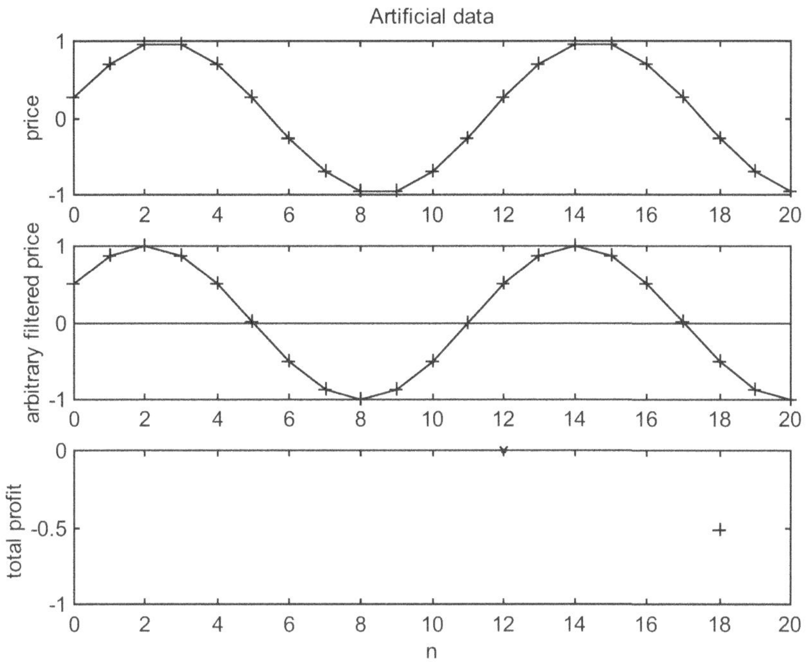

Fig. 2.10 Price is plotted in the top figure, with the initial phase offset $\theta_0 = \omega - \mu = \pi/6 - \pi/11.99$. The filtered price, with a phase lead arbitrarily set to $\pi/12$ from the price, is plotted in the middle figure. In the bottom figure, buy indication is marked by an * at n = 12 (bought at 0.26) and sell indication by a + at n = 18 (sold at −0.26), thus making a loss of 0.52, which is approximately −25.9%.

2.4.4 Skipped Convolution

A technical indicator convolutes with a signal to form a filtered signal. In the case of a velocity indicator, the filtered signal would emulate velocity, which would track the turning points. Traders would definitely like to detect the turning points in the market as early as possible. A new concept, called skipped convolution has been introduced in 2003 to enable earlier detection of market action (Mak 2003, 2006). Let us explain further.

For a trader who makes his decision on the daily chart, he would be looking at the closing price of each day. However, when the market turns south, he probably would like to know at what time during the day the market is turning, rather than waiting to find out at the end of the day. In that case, he can use a chart of lower time frame, e.g., an hourly chart. Assuming there are five trading hours in 1 day, he can create a daily chart from the hourly chart but with more details. A skipped convolution with a skip 5 will be used. Velocity indicator would operate on the closing prices of the first hour of each day, then on the closing prices of the second hour of each day, etc. These details would let the trader know at which hour of the day that the market is turning, rather than for him to find out at the end of the day, where loss would be much larger. He can, of course, use a half-hour chart if more details need to be known. This tactic can possibly cut his losses, or can change his trade from making a loss to making a profit, or a profitable trade to be more profitable. This tactic is particularly important when the market crashes, as a trader would like to get out of the market as soon as he knows when it is going to turn. An example of skipped convolution in real market trading would be given in Chapter 7.

Skipped convolution, of course, has its disadvantages. The trader has to monitor the market more often (unless he has an automated trading system, which lets the computer executes and monitors the trades). A trader who ordinarily monitors the market at the end of the day would have to monitor it at the end of each hour when the market opens, if he chooses hourly skipped convolution. (Of course, if the trader does not want to monitor the market every hour, he can put a stop loss order to his trade to cut his loss in case of market crash). Furthermore, if the market fluctuates during the day, more buy and sell indications can be triggered.

2.4.5 Profit in the Loss Zone

In contrast to loss in the Profit Zone, sampled data can cause profit in the Loss Zone in the neighborhood where the phase lead is larger than $-\pi$.

Example 2.8

Figure 2.11 shows an artificial price data of

$$\text{Price} = \sin(\pi/6\ n + \pi/18)$$

An arbitrary phase lead of the velocity indicator, $-\pi + \pi/12$, is then added to the price data, to form the filtered price data. The filtered price data would then be

$$\text{Filtered Price} = \sin(\pi/6\ n + \pi/18 - \pi + \pi/12)$$

As $-\pi + \pi/12$ lies within the Loss Zone, the trade should have lost money. However, because the data is sampled, the trade actually makes money.

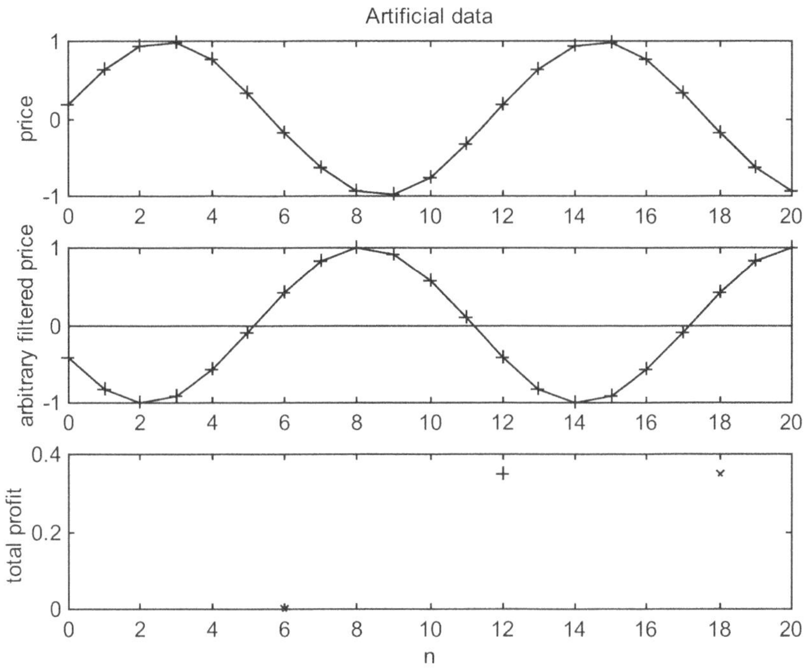

Fig. 2.11 Price is plotted in the top figure, and the filtered price in the middle figure. In the bottom figure, buy indication is marked by an * at n = 6 (bought at −0.17) and sell indication by a + at n = 12 (sold at 0.17), thus making a profit of 0.34.

The Loss Zone can be divided into Sure Loss Zone, where a trade will definitely lose money, and an Unsure Loss Zone, where a trade can make a profit or a lost. This would be detailed in Appendix A. However, as we will see later, velocity indicators having phase lead slightly larger than $-\pi$ will not be used in this book, thus the topic Profit in the Loss Zone will not be explored further.

2.4.6 Multiple frequencies

In Sections 2.4.1, 2.4.2 and 2.4.3, market price data is described as having one single frequency. However, quite often, they are made up of multiple frequencies, each frequency having various phase shifts from others. As velocity indicators have been designed to retain low frequencies as well as high frequencies (as we would see in later chapters), buy/sell indications, and therefore profitability of low frequencies trades can be affected by the presence of high frequency components.

Furthermore, the actual velocity indicators created so far (as we will see in later chapters) lead the price signal by the ideal $\pi/2$ radians only at $\omega = 0$, and lead the price signal by less than $\pi/2$ radians at other ω's. Thus, finding the velocity of the actual real market data is a complicated issue. Hopefully, we can cast some light in solving the real problem by calculating the phase shifts of the velocity indicators across the whole frequency spectrum.

2.5 Acceleration

Another term that we can borrow from Physics is acceleration, which is the rate of change of velocity. We can consider it to be the slope of the slope of the curve, which is called second derivative in Calculus. Assume again that the curve is a sine wave, then the second derivative of a sine wave, according to Calculus, is a minus sine wave, which leads a sine wave by π radians (=180°). It is plotted in Fig. 2.12 as a green curve. Note that when acceleration is +ve (e.g., from t = 20 to 40), the price data is concave up. And when acceleration is −ve (e.g., from t = 40 to 60), the price data is concave down. When acceleration changes from −ve to +ve, the slope of the velocity changes from −ve to +ve. When acceleration changes from +ve to −ve, the slope of the velocity changes from +ve to −ve. This, of course, should be obvious.

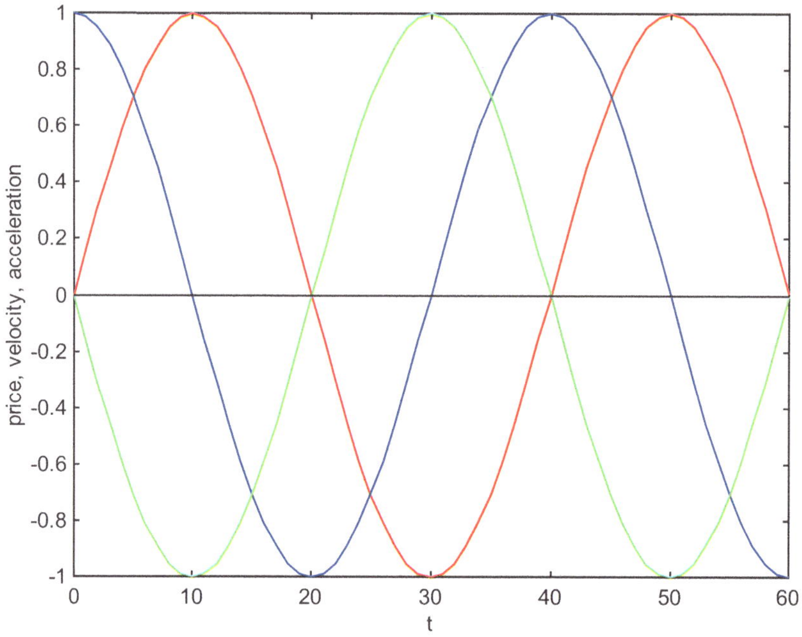

Fig. 2.12 Simulated price data. Price (plotted as a red line) is plotted versus time t, as a sine wave with a period of 40 trading days. Velocity is plotted as a blue line. It represents the slope of the price. Acceleration is plotted as a green line. It represents the slope of the slope of the price.

We can compare velocity and acceleration to driving a car in a straight line. When the car is being driven forward, velocity is +ve. When the car is being reversed or driven backward, velocity is −ve. When the car is driving forward, and the driver steps on the pedal, the car is accelerating. When the driver eases up on the pedal, the car is decelerating, i.e., acceleration is −ve, and velocity is slowing. However, the car is still going forward, and distance is increasing. In trading, that means when acceleration is negative, the price can still go up (e.g., t = 40 to 50). By the same token, when acceleration is positive, the price can still go down (e.g., t = 20 to 30). Thus, acceleration does not play any role in whether market price is going up or down. However, in principle, it can play a role in deciding whether traders would get out of the market or hold their positions, as we will show later.

Acceleration would not be of much use when the price data looks like a sine wave, as the information of velocity is sufficient for the traders to make decision. However, quite often, the price data rises to a local maximum, retraces to a local minimum, and then continues upward (Mak 2003). Figure 2.13 shows such an example, where the price data is simulated by a cubic function. The slope of the price data or velocity would be zero at both turning points. When the market continues in the same direction after the two turning points, the slope of the slope, or acceleration at the two turning points are close to zero and points up. This can be compared with the acceleration pattern of the sine wave when it experiences a major turning point turning down, when acceleration is not close to zero (Fig. 2.12).

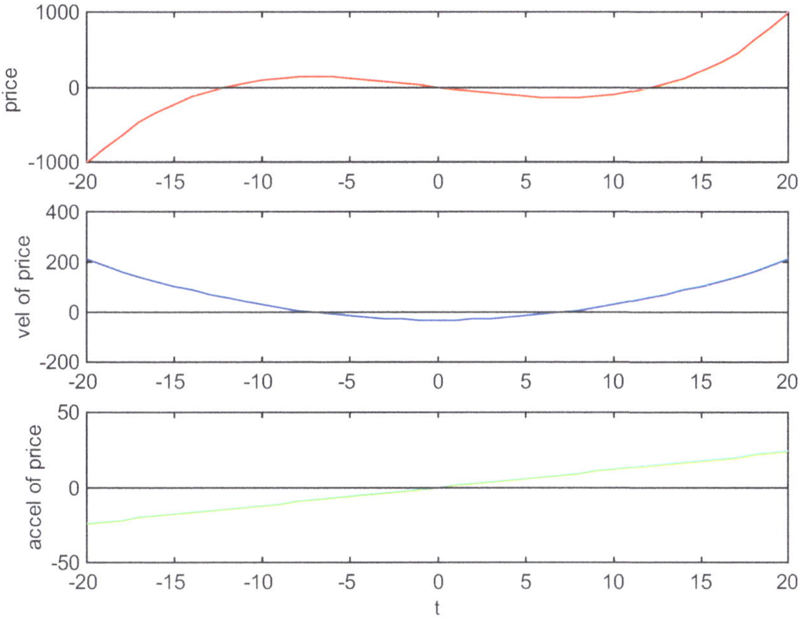

Fig. 2.13 Price data simulated by a cubic function. At the first turning point, velocity is zero, implying that the price will go down. However, acceleration, though negative, is pointing up, implying that it can change to positive. Acceleration changing from negative to positive, means that the price curve changes from concave down to concave up.

At t ≈ −7, velocity changes from +ve to −ve, meaning that the price data will be going south, and the trader should sell. However, it can be seen that the acceleration is increasing, implying the price data can change from a concave down to a concave up pretty soon. Thus, instead of selling, the trader can choose to hold. An example of real data can be found in Fig. 6.11 of Mak (2003).

Figure 2.14 shows a cubic function which falls to a local minimum, then traces to a local maximum and then continues downward. The slope of the price data are zero at the two turning points. When the market continues in the same original direction, the slope of the slope or the acceleration are close to zero and points down. This can be compared with the acceleration pattern of the sine wave when it experiences a major turning point turning up, when acceleration is not close to zero (Fig. 2.12).

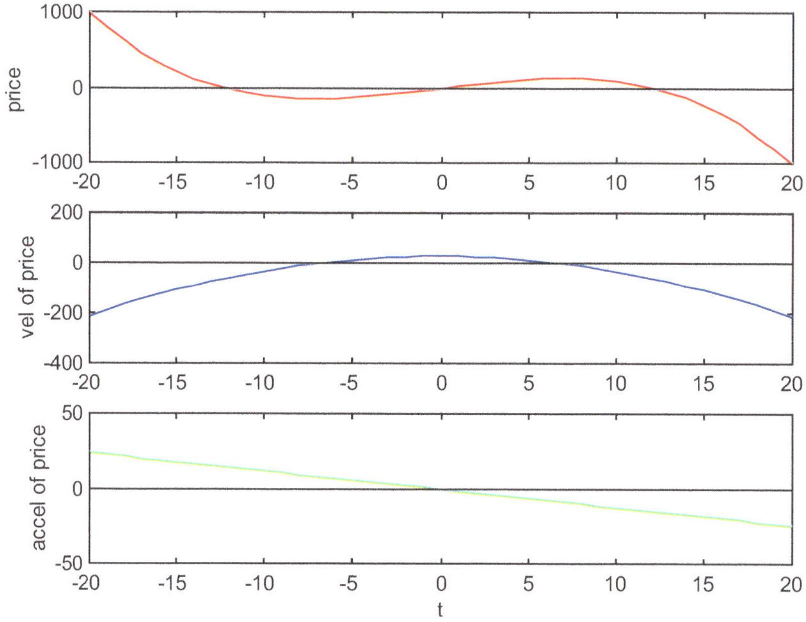

Fig. 2.14 Price data simulated by a cubic function. At the first turning point, velocity is zero, implying that the market price may turn up. However, acceleration, though positive, is pointing down, implying that it can turn negative, and the market can go further down shortly. Acceleration changing from positive to negative, means that the price curve changes from concave up to concave down.

At t ≈ −7, velocity changes from −ve to +ve, meaning that the price data will be going north, and the trader should buy. However, it can be seen that the acceleration is decreasing, implying the price data can change from a concave up to a concave down pretty soon. Thus, instead of buying, the trader can choose to hold if he sells short.

While the concept acceleration does make sense theoretically, this is actually not used in trading as it is difficult to simulate acceleration with a usable acceleration indicator. Instead, acceleration indicators are sometimes used as velocity indicators, and we will show later that there is actually a benefit of doing so.

2.6 Acceleration Indicators

Acceleration indicators (Mak 2003, 2006) simulating acceleration should ideally lead the price signal by π radians $= 180°$. However, the actual acceleration indicators created so far only lead the price signal by π radians at $\omega = 0$, and lead the price signal by less than π radians at other ω's. Thus, they are not used as acceleration indicators in trading, but are sometimes used as velocity indicators instead. Traders may not have realized that using acceleration indicators as velocity indicators actually has an advantage, as the ideal phase lead for velocity is $\pi/2$, which lies in the middle between 0 and π, the region where profit will be made.

Velocity indicators and acceleration indicators play a significant role in many traders' tactics, even though they may not have realized it. We will discuss these further in later chapters.

3 Simple Moving Average

It is very common for market data series to be smoothed, as smoothing reduces volatility, and allows traders to eliminate the bumpy movements. The two most common smoothing indicators are: Simple Moving Average (SMA) and Exponential Moving Average (EMA). As pointed out in Mak (2003), these smoothing indicators are actually low pass filters, which removes high frequency components and allows low frequency components to pass. As high frequency components are quite often considered to be noise, which is quite often difficult to trade with, and not very profitable, smoothing indicators perform the task of eliminating this noise before other indicators act on the smoothed data, so that buy sell indications can actually be identified. Smoothing indicators, unfortunately, are called trending indicators in the trading community, as traders claim the indicators can identify trends. That, of course, is a misnomer. As a matter of fact, velocity indicators, as described in the last chapter, are actually trending indicators. When velocity is positive, the trend is up. When velocity is negative, the trend is down. We will describe what smoothing indicators actually do in the following sections.

3.1 Simple Moving Average (SMA)

Simple moving average has been used quite often. A 10-day simple moving average shows the average price for the last 10 days, i.e., the prices of the last 10 days are added together and divided by 10. For the general case, an N-bar moving average is calculated by adding the prices over the last N bars and dividing by N. A bar represents a unit time interval being chosen by the trader, e.g., 1 day, 1 hour, 15 minutes, etc. SMA is called moving as the next bar's weighted price will be added to the average and the first bar's weighted price will be discarded. N is called the length of the simple moving average. A larger N will show a smoother average but a larger phase (or time or bar) lag.

An N-bar moving average can also be viewed as multiplying each of the last N bars by 1/N, and then adding these reduced prices together. Thus, for a 10-day

D. K. Mak, *Trading Tactics in the Financial Market*, Management for Professionals,
https://doi.org/10.1007/978-3-030-70622-7_3

moving average, the price of each of the last 10 days will be multiplied by 1/10, and these reduced prices will be added to form the moving average. 1/N is called the unit sample (impulse) response h(k), where k = 0, 1, 2, . . ., N−1. For a 10-day moving average, h(0) = h(1) = . . . = h(9) = 1/10. In signal processing, the unit sample response of a dynamic system (or technical indicator, in trading terminology) is its output when presented with a brief input signal, called an impulse. Here, each daily price is an impulse.

Figure 3.1 shows the S & P 500 daily index data taken from April 24, 2019 to August 12, 2019. A 10-day Simple Moving Average, plotted as a line, is used to smooth the data, showing that it lags behind the index.

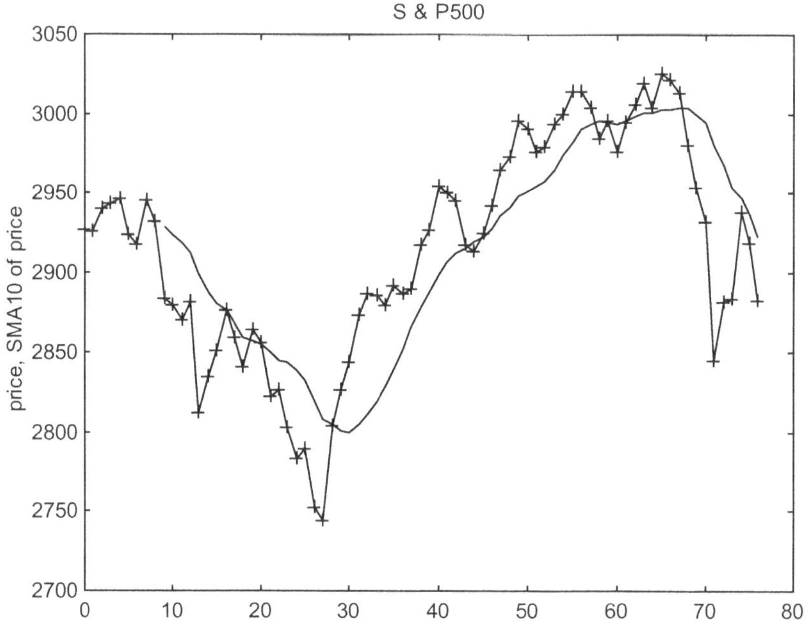

Fig. 3.1 The S & P 500 daily index from April 24, 2019 to August 12, 2019 are plotted (+), together with a 10-day Simple Moving Average (SMA) plotted as a line. Note that the SMA lags behind the index.

As emphasized in Mak (2003), it will be very informative for the traders to find out the frequency response of the unit sample response, H(ω), which is also called the Discrete Time Fourier Transform (DTFT) of the unit sample response. The frequency response will yield the amplitude as well as the phase (or time) lag of a signal at various frequencies. In signal processing, it is more common to find the frequency response in terms of the circular frequency ω, where ω = 2π × frequency. Frequency is equal to 1/period, where period is the duration of a cycle. If the price data goes through a 40 day cycle, frequency is equal to 1/(40 days). The circular frequency ω will be equal to 2π × (1/40) = π/20 radians. The equations of the frequency response of the SMA is given in Appendix B.

In Engineering, the amplitude response is important, and phase response is almost never calculated. However, in trading, phase is significant, as it tells the time delay of the output signal from the input signal after being operated on by the technical indicator.

3.1.1 Simple Moving Average, N = 10

The amplitude response of a simple moving average with N = 10 is shown in Fig. 3.2. It can be seen that the amplitude is zero at several frequencies.

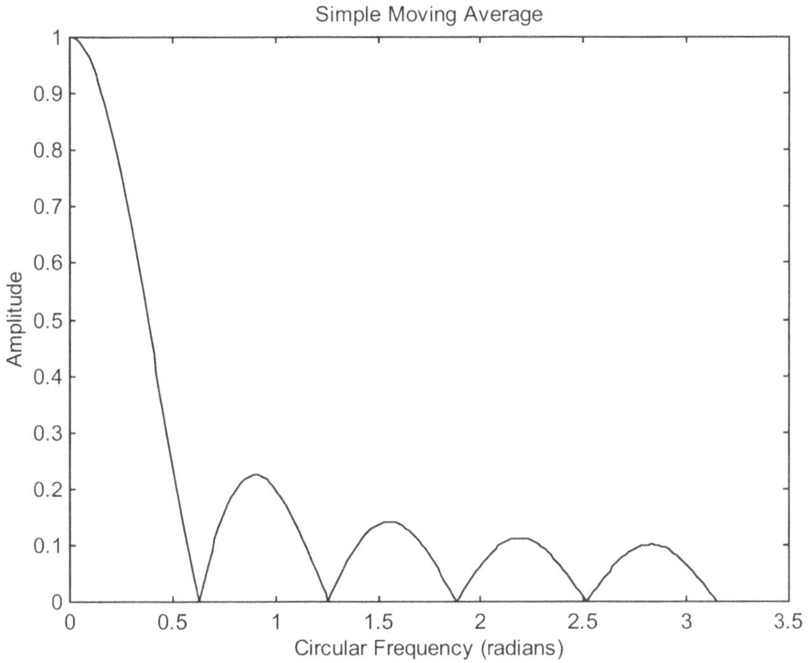

Fig. 3.2 The amplitude response of a simple moving average with N = 10.

From the Eq. (B.4) in Appendix B, one can see that the amplitude response of an N point moving average is zero when

$\omega = 2m\pi/N$, where $m = 1, 2, 3, 4, 5, \ldots.$

Thus, for a 10 point moving average, i,e., N = 10, its amplitude response is zero when

$\omega = \pi/5\ (\sim 0.628), 2\pi/5\ (\sim 1.257), 3\pi/5\ (\sim 1.885), 4\pi/5\ (\sim 2.513), \pi, \ldots.$ radians

as are shown in Fig. 3.2. That is, the simple moving average of the signal at those frequencies completely disappears from the radar.

Figure 3.3 shows one cycle of a sine wave of $\omega = \pi/5$. It can be seen that addition of those 10 points would yield a sum of 0. And that is why a simple moving average of the sine wave at that frequency would disappear.

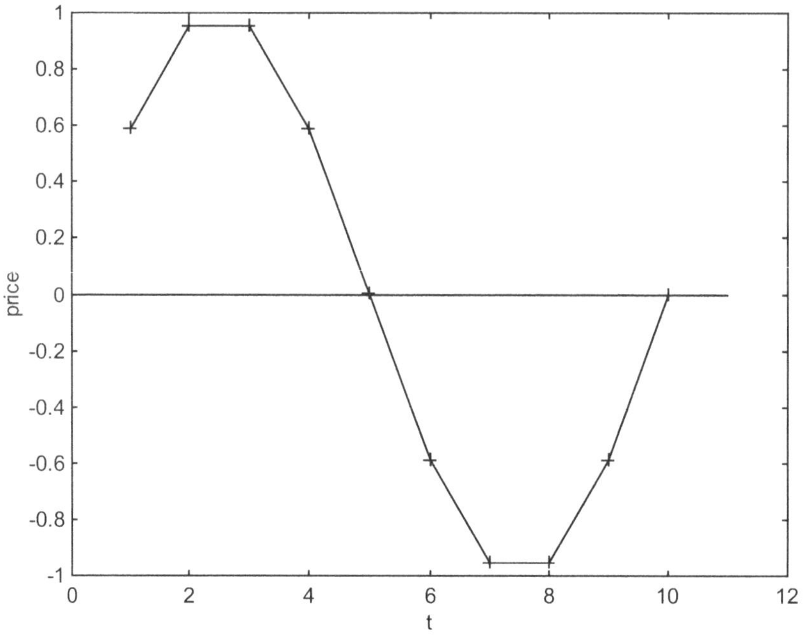

Fig. 3.3 One cycle of a sine wave of $\omega = \pi/5$. Addition of these 10 points (shown as +) would yield a sum of 0.

3.1.1.1 Wrapped and Unwrapped Phase

The phase of an indicator computed in trading programs is a wrapped phase, which is equal to the phase computed in DTFT using arctangent.

Figure 3.4 shows the wrapped phase of the phase response of a simple moving average with $N = 10$. Simple Moving Average, acting as a filter to the input signal, delays the signal by the wrapped phase, which is the angle of the frequency response of the unit sample response, $H(\omega)$. The wrapped phase is constrained to lie between the interval $-\pi$ to π, or 0 to 2π and does not necessarily represents the actual phase delay. The unwrapped phase, which is the actual phase delay, can be calculated from the wrapped phase by adding appropriate multiples of π, so that the frequency phase response is a continuous function of frequency. The unwrapped phase of the phase response of a simple moving average with $N = 10$ can be calculated from Eq. (B.7) in Appendix B, and is shown in Fig. 3.5.

The unwrapped phase of $H(\omega)$ of the SMA, for N, is given by (Mak 2003)

$$\phi(\omega) = -((N - 1)/2)\,\omega \qquad \text{(B.7)}$$

which is linear with respect to ω.

So, for $N = 10$, $\quad \phi(\omega) = -(9/2)\,\omega$

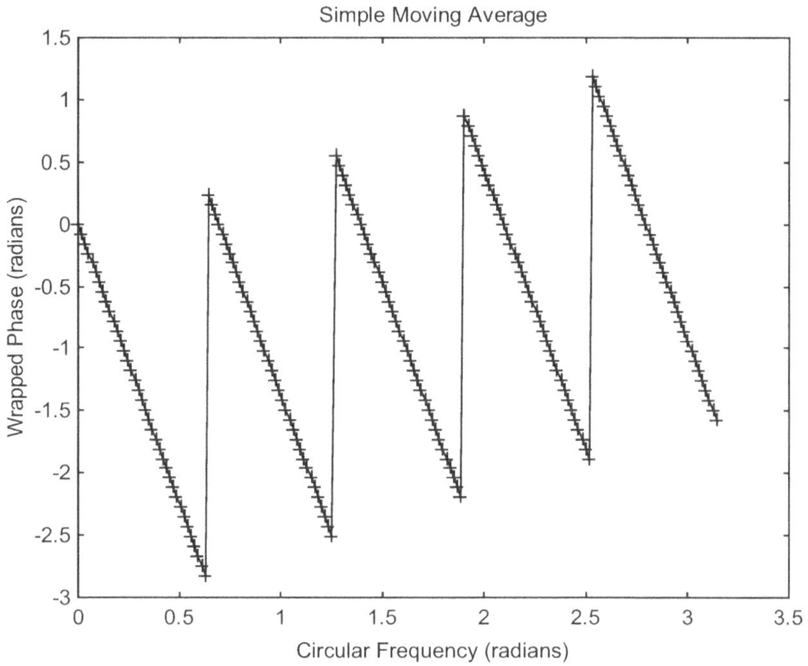

Fig. 3.4 The wrapped phase of the phase response of a simple moving average with N = 10.

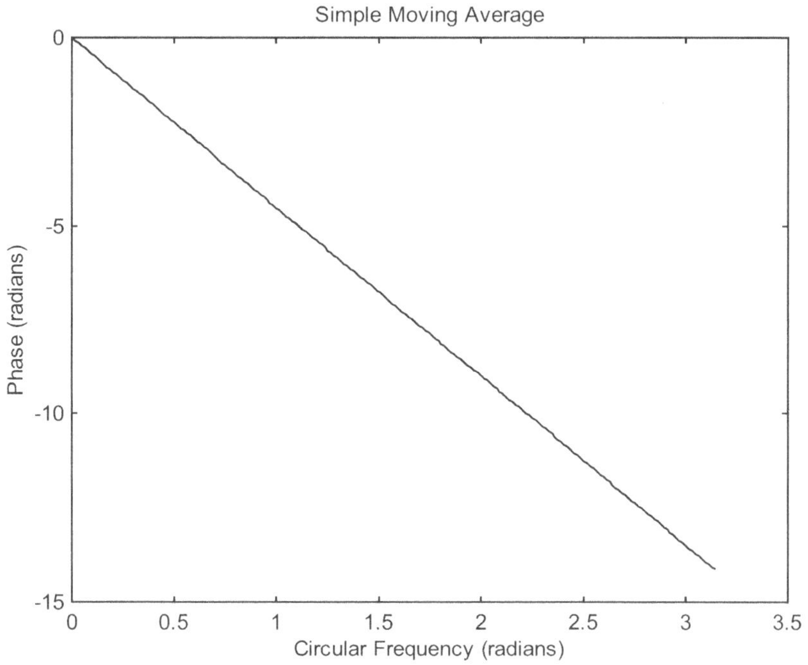

Fig. 3.5 The unwrapped phase of the phase response of a simple moving average with N = 10.

At those points where the amplitudes of SMA with N = 10 are 0, using Eq. (B.8), the wrapped phases $\phi(\omega)$ approaches

$$-(9/10)\ m\pi, \text{ where } m = 1, 2, 3, 4, 5, \ldots. \tag{3.1}$$

These wrapped phases and their corresponding unwrapped phases of SMA with N = 10 is shown in Table 3.1. The wrapped phase numbers correspond to the minimal points in Fig. 3.4. The amplitude, wrapped phase and unwrapped phase of the SMA can be computed from the program sma.

Table 3.1 Wrapped phases and unwrapped phases of SMA with N = 10, for Eq. (3.1) with m = 1, 2, 3, 4, 5. Amplitudes of SMA of the signals are 0.

m	Wrapped phase (radians)	Unwrapped phase (radians)
1	−2.83	$-(9/10)\ \pi\ (= -2.83)$
2	−2.52	$-(9/10)\ 2\pi\ (= -5.66 = -2.52 - \pi)$
3	−2.19	$-(9/10)\ 3\pi\ (= -8.48 = -2.19 - 2\pi)$
4	−1.89	$-(9/10)\ 4\pi\ (= -11.31 = -1.89 - 3\pi)$
5	−1.57	$-(9/10)\ 5\pi\ (= -14.14 = -1.57 - 4\pi)$

3.1.1.2 How Does the Wrapped and Unwrapped Phase Affect the Smoothed Output of a Signal?

We will show how the wrapped and unwrapped phase affect the smoothed output of a signal. Figures 3.6, 3.7, 3.8, 3.9, 3.10, 3.11, and 3.12 shows the 10 point Simple Moving Average (SMA) of price simulated as a sine wave with frequencies ω taken from Table 3.2. The SMA of price is phase shifted from the price by the wrapped phase. From Figs. 3.6, 3.7, and 3.8, the unwrapped phase is the same as the wrapped phase. Figure 3.9 is a more detailed version of Fig. 3.3. In Fig. 3.9, $\omega = \pi/5 \sim 0.628$ radians, the amplitude of the 10 point Simple Moving Average (SMA) equals 0, and the phase $\phi(\omega)$ approaches −2.83 radians, in consistent with Fig. 3.4, and Table 3.1. For an ω slightly larger than $\pi/5$, e.g., $\pi/4.95 \sim 0.6346$, amplitude = 0.0101, the wrapped phase, as shown in Fig. 3.4, is slightly larger than 0 (the unwrapped phase would be slightly larger than $-\pi$), it can be shown that the wrapped SMA does lead the signal slightly (figure not shown here).

Table 3.2 Wrapped phases, unwrapped phases and amplitudes of the frequency response of the SMA with N = 10 at various frequencies.

ω (radians)	Wrapped phase (radians)	Unwrapped phase (radians)	Amplitude (no unit)	Figure
$\pi/20.83 \sim 0.15$	−0.68	−0.68	0.9	3.6
$\pi/9 \sim 0.35$	$-\pi/2$	$-\pi/2$	0.57	3.7
$\pi/6.283 \sim 0.5$	−2.25	−2.25	0.24	3.8
$\pi/5 \sim 0.628$	−2.83	−2.83	0	3.9
$2\pi/9 \sim 0.698$	0	$-\pi$	0.09	3.10
$3\pi/9 \sim 1.047$	$-\pi/2$	$-3\pi/2$	0.17	3.11
$4\pi/9 \sim 1.396$	0	-2π	0.1	3.12

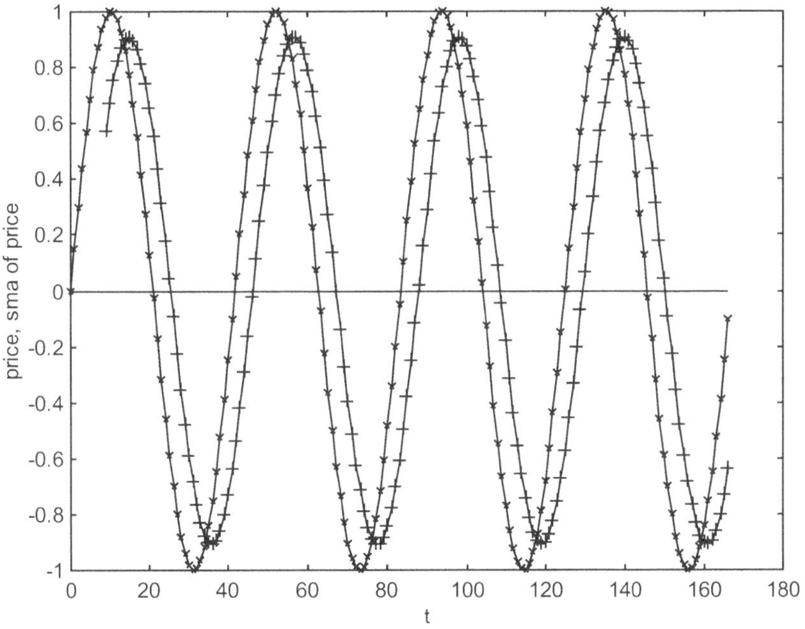

Fig. 3.6 Price simulated as a sine wave (marked as x) of amplitude = 1 and $\omega = \pi/20.83 \sim 0.15$ radian. Its 10 point Simple Moving Average (SMA) (marked as +) has a phase $\phi(\omega)$ of −0.68 radian from the sine wave. The amplitude of the Simple Moving Average is approximately 0.90. If a trader buys when the price crosses the SMA from below, and sells when the price crosses the SMA from above, he will make about 90% of the maximum possible profit. This figure can be drawn with the program smasig.

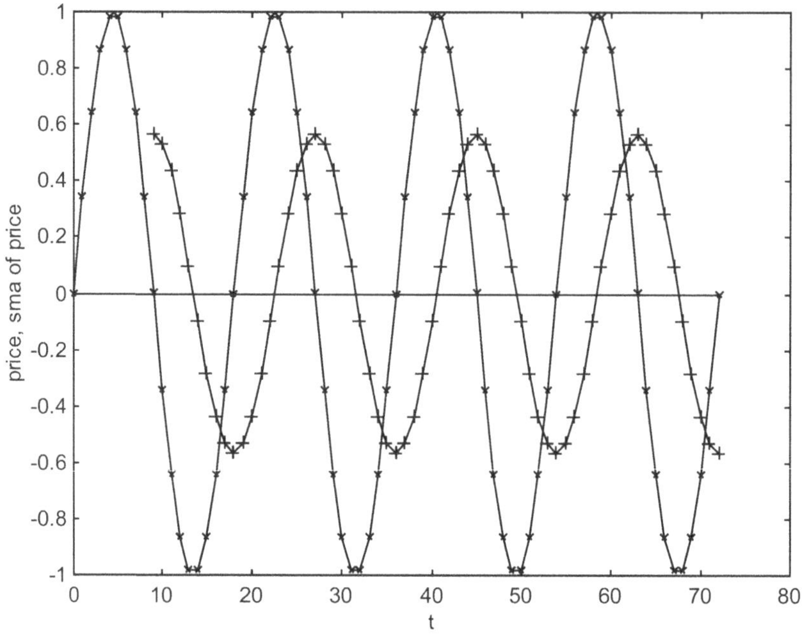

Fig. 3.7 Price simulated as a sine wave (marked as x) of amplitude = 1 and $\omega = \pi/9 \sim 0.35$ radian. Its 10 point Simple Moving Average (SMA) (marked as +) has a phase $\phi(\omega)$ of $-\pi/2$ radians from the sine wave. The amplitude of the Simple Moving Average is approximately 0.57.

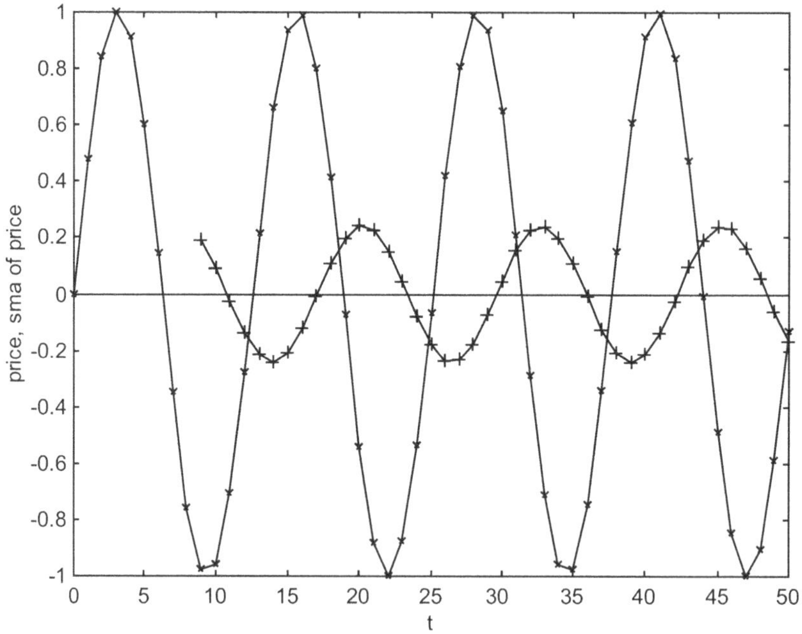

Fig. 3.8 Price simulated as a sine wave (marked as x) of amplitude = 1 and $\omega = \pi/6.283 \sim 0.5$ radian. Its 10 point Simple Moving Average (SMA) (marked as +) has a phase $\phi(\omega)$ of -2.25 radians from the sine wave. The amplitude of the Simple Moving Average is approximately 0.24.

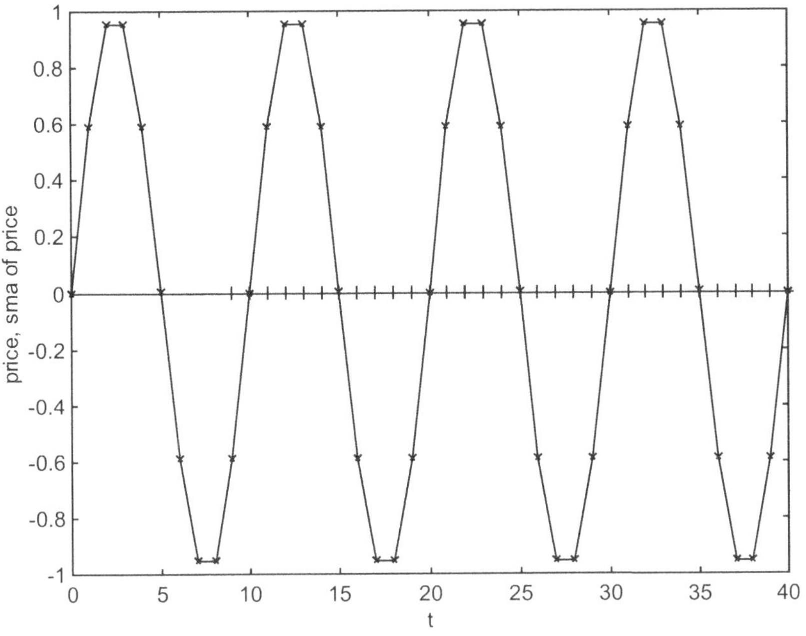

Fig. 3.9 Price simulated as a sine wave (marked as x) of amplitude = 1 and ω = π/5 ~ 0.63 radian. Its 10 point Simple Moving Average (SMA) (marked as +) approaches a phase ϕ(ω) of −2.83 radians from the sine wave. The amplitude of the Simple Moving Average equals 0.

For Figs. 3.10, 3.11, and 3.12, ω is larger than π/5 (~ 0.628), the unwrapped phase shift, which represents the real phase delay, is different from the wrapped phase shift. This simply means that the apparent SMA, as calculated in trading programs provided to traders, does not actually offer a real representation of the SMA of the price, and thus can cause errors in trading tactics using SMA as a technical indicator.

Nevertheless, we will see in the Fourier Analysis of real market data in Chapter 7, that the amplitudes of frequencies of ω less than 0.5 is much larger than those of frequencies of ω larger than 0.5, with amplitudes of frequencies of ω less than 0.11 most significant. Thus, trading tactics employing SMA with N = 10, may not be much affected. However, trading tactics using SMA with N much larger than 10, may contain errors. Thus, systematic errors do occur in Awesome Oscillator and Accelerator Oscillator, two popular trading indicators employing SMA with N larger than 10. We will further explain these problems in Chapter 5.

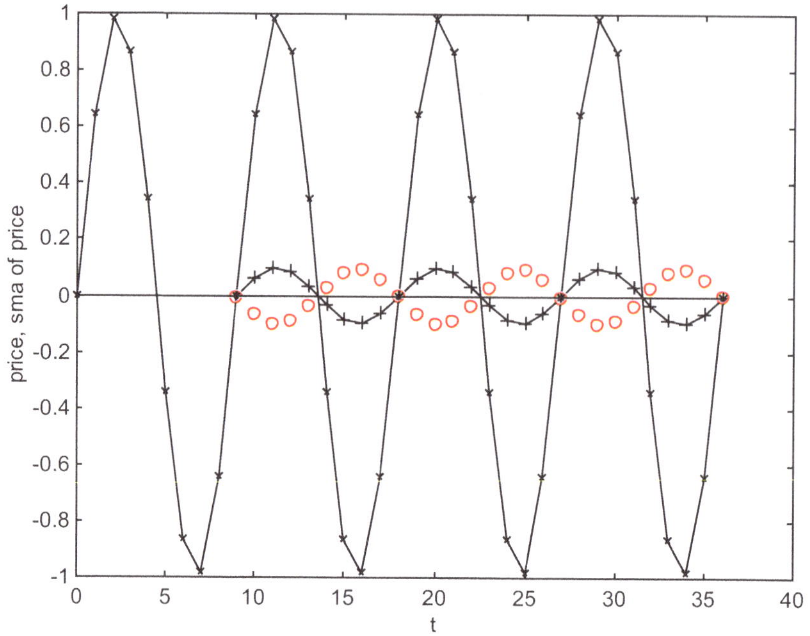

Fig. 3.10 Price simulated as a sine wave (marked as x) of amplitude = 1 and $\omega = 2\pi/9 \sim 0.698$ radian. Its 10 point Simple Moving Average (SMA) (marked as +) has a wrapped phase $\phi(\omega)$ of 0 radian from the sine wave. Its unwrapped phase is actually $-\pi$ radians and is marked by a red o. The amplitude of the Simple Moving Average is approximately 0.09. The program smasig2 is used to plot this figure.

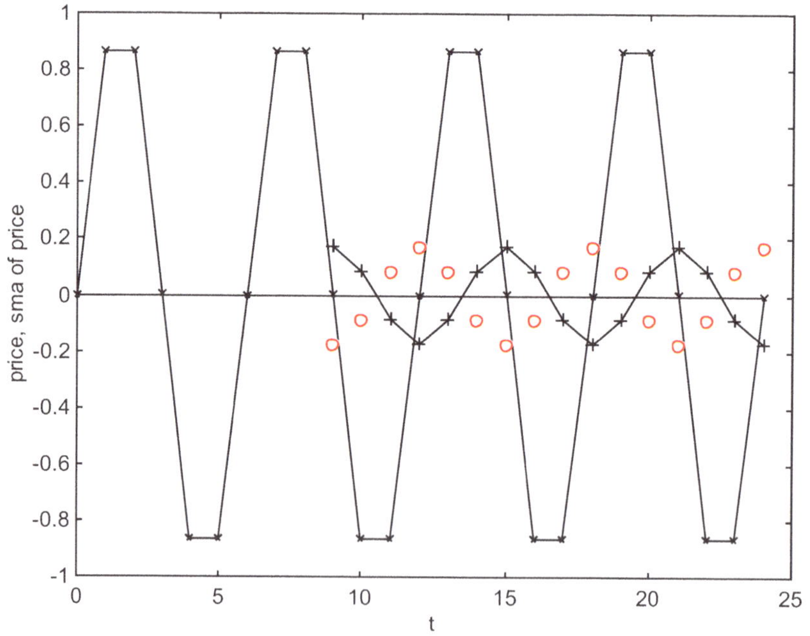

Fig. 3.11 Price simulated as a sine wave (marked as x) of amplitude = 1 and $\omega = 3\pi/9 \sim 1.05$ radians. Its 10 point Simple Moving Average (SMA) (marked as +) has a wrapped phase $\phi(\omega)$ of $-\pi/2$ radian from the sine wave. Its unwrapped phase is actually $-3\pi/2$ radians and is marked by a red o. The amplitude of the Simple Moving Average is approximately 0.17. The program smasig2 is used to plot this figure.

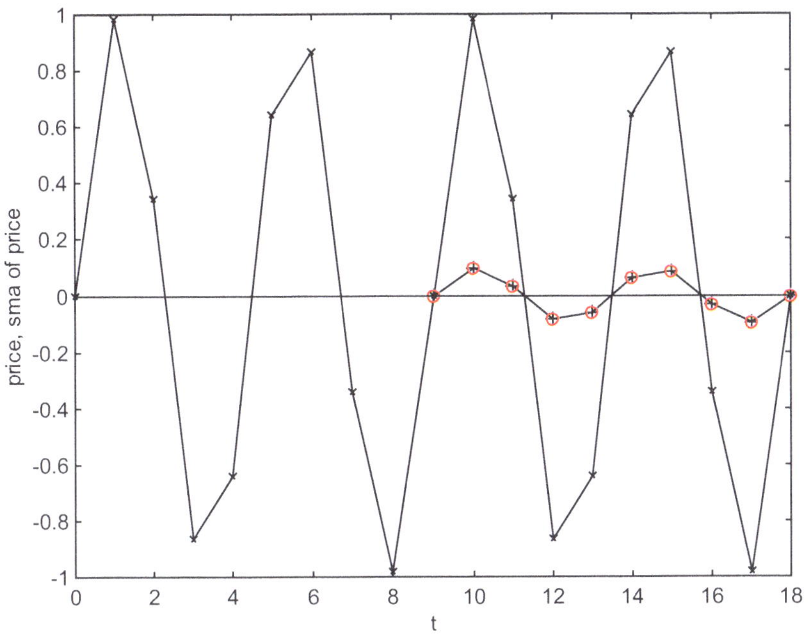

Fig. 3.12 Price simulated as a sine wave (marked as x) of amplitude = 1 and $\omega = 4\pi/9 \sim 1.4$ radians. Its 10 point Simple Moving Average (SMA) (marked as +) has a wrapped phase $\phi(\omega)$ of 0 radian from the sine wave. Its unwrapped phase is actually -2π, and is marked by a red o. As sine wave has a period of 2π, SMA with unwrapped phase here appears the same as SMA with wrapped phase. The amplitude of the Simple Moving Average is approximately 0.1. The program smasig2 is used to plot this figure.

3.1.2 Simple Moving Average, N = 20

The amplitude response of a simple moving average with N = 20 is shown in Fig. 3.13. Again it can be seen that the amplitude is zero at several frequencies.

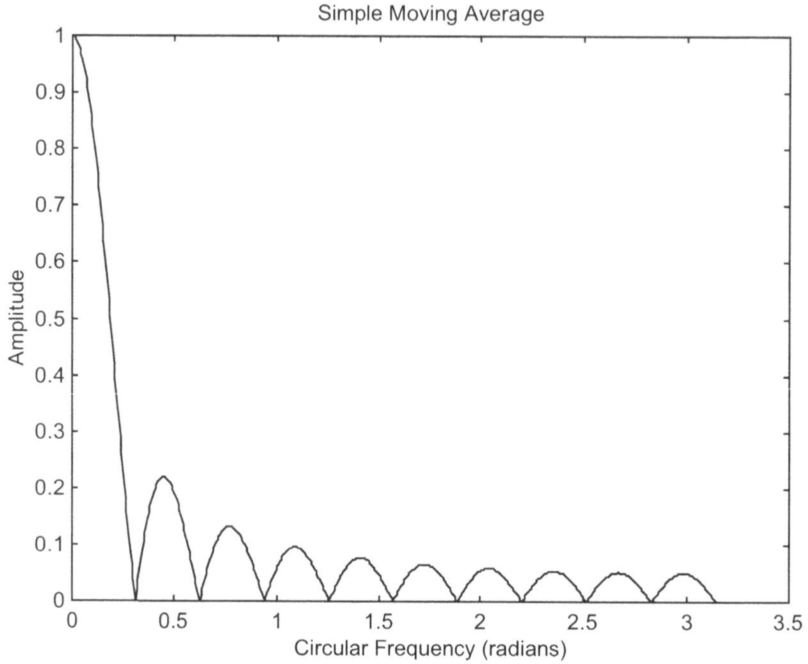

Fig. 3.13 The amplitude response of a simple moving average with N = 20.

From Eq. (B.4) in Appendix B, one can see that the amplitude response of an N point moving average is zero when

$\omega = 2m\pi/N$, where $m = 1, 2, 3, 4, 5, \ldots.$

Thus, amplitude response of SMA, N = 20 is zero when

$\omega = \pi/10(\sim 0.314), \pi/5, 3\pi/10, 4\pi/10, \pi/2, \ldots.$ radians

as are shown in Fig. 3.13.

The wrapped phase of the phase response of SMA with N = 20 is shown in Fig. 3.14, and its unwrapped phase in Fig. 3.15. For ω larger than π/10 (~0.314), the unwrapped phase shift, which represents the real phase delay, is different from the wrapped phase shift.

The unwrapped phase of H(ω) of the SMA, for N, is given by

$$\phi(\omega) = -((N - 1)/2)\,\omega \tag{B.7}$$

So, for N = 20, $\phi(\omega) = -(19/2)\,\omega$

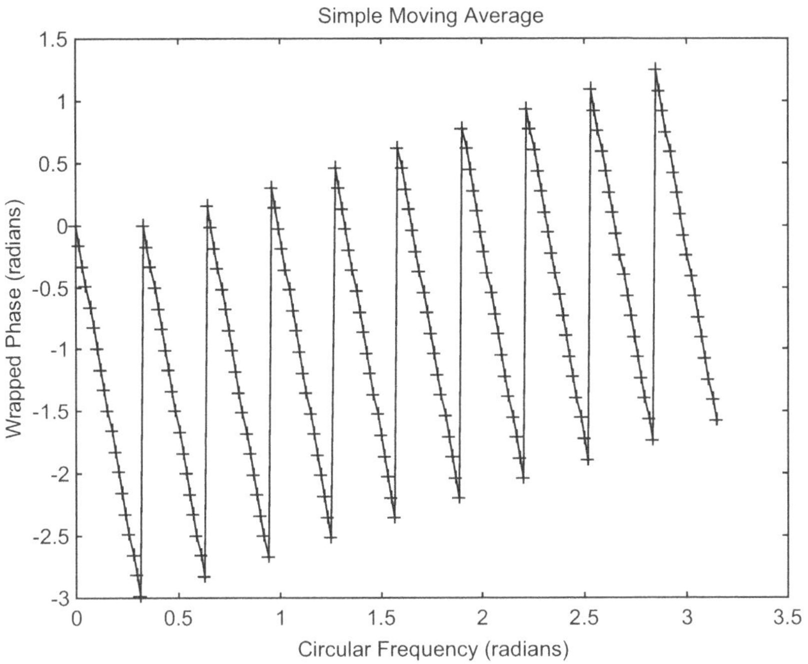

Fig. 3.14 The wrapped phase of the phase response of a simple moving average with N = 20.

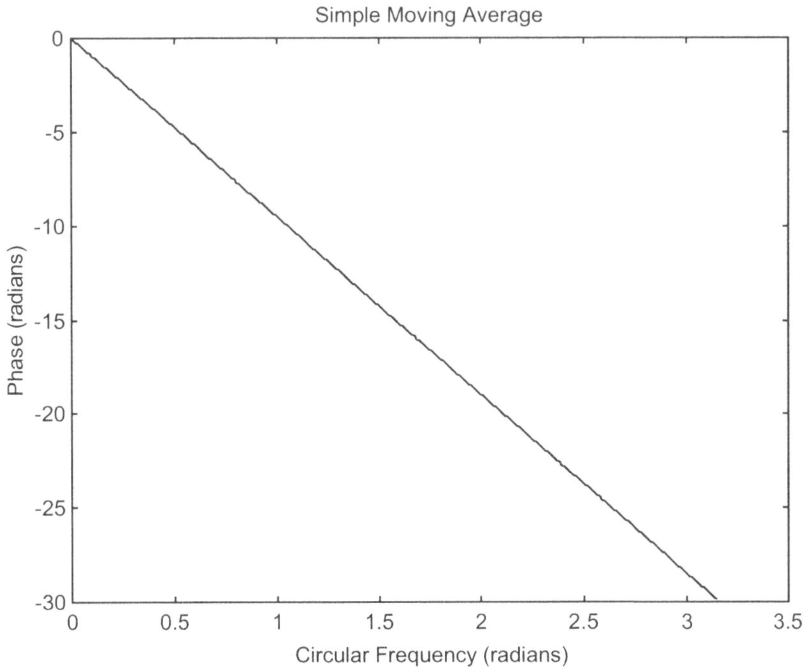

Fig. 3.15 The unwrapped phase of the phase response of a simple moving average with N = 20.

Examples of the unwrapped phase of SMA with N = 20, calculated from Eq. (B.7) are given in Table 3.3

Table 3.3 Examples of unwrapped phase and amplitudes of SMA with N = 20 at various frequencies.

ω (radians)	Unwrapped phase, ϕ(ω) (radians)	Amplitude
$\pi/19 = 0.165$	$-\pi/2$	0.61166
$2\pi/19 = 0.331$	$-\pi$	0.0565
$3\pi/19 = 0.496$	$-3\pi/2$	0.1972
$4\pi/19 = 0.661$	-2π	0.0563

3.1.3 Simple Moving Average, N = 100

The amplitude response of a simple moving average with N = 100 is shown in Fig. 3.16. Again it can be seen that the amplitude is zero at several frequencies. From Eq. (B.4) in Appendix B, its amplitude response is zero when

$$\omega = \pi/50(\sim 0.0628), 2\pi/50, 3\pi/50, 4\pi/50, \pi/10, 6\pi/50, 7\pi/50, 8\pi/10\ (\sim 0.503), \ldots.\ \text{radians}$$

as are shown in Fig. 3.16.

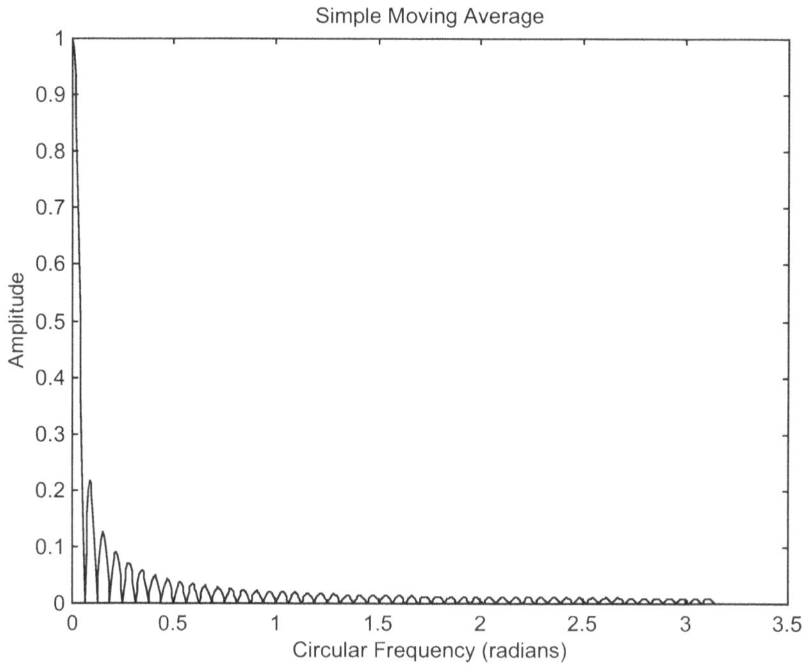

Fig. 3.16 The amplitude response of a simple moving average with N = 100.

The wrapped phase of the phase response of the simple moving average with N = 100 is shown in Fig. 3.17, and its unwrapped phase in Fig. 3.18. For ω larger than π/50 (~0.0628), the unwrapped phase shift, which represents the real phase delay, is different from the wrapped phase shift.

The unwrapped phase of H(ω) of the SMA, for N, is given by

$$\phi(\omega) = -((N - 1)/2)\,\omega \qquad \text{(B.7)}$$

So, for N = 100, $\phi(\omega) = -(99/2)\,\omega$

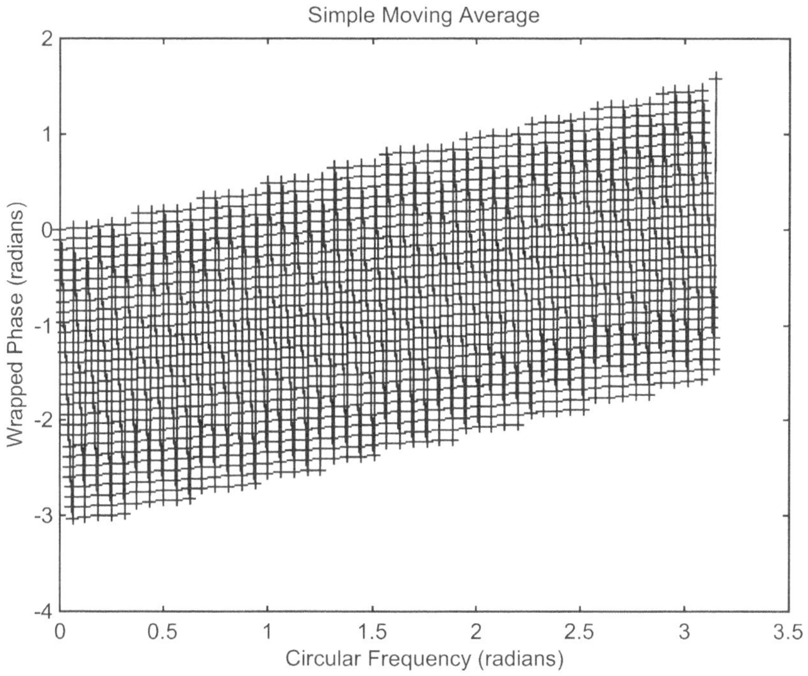

Fig. 3.17 The wrapped phase of the phase response of a simple moving average with N = 100.

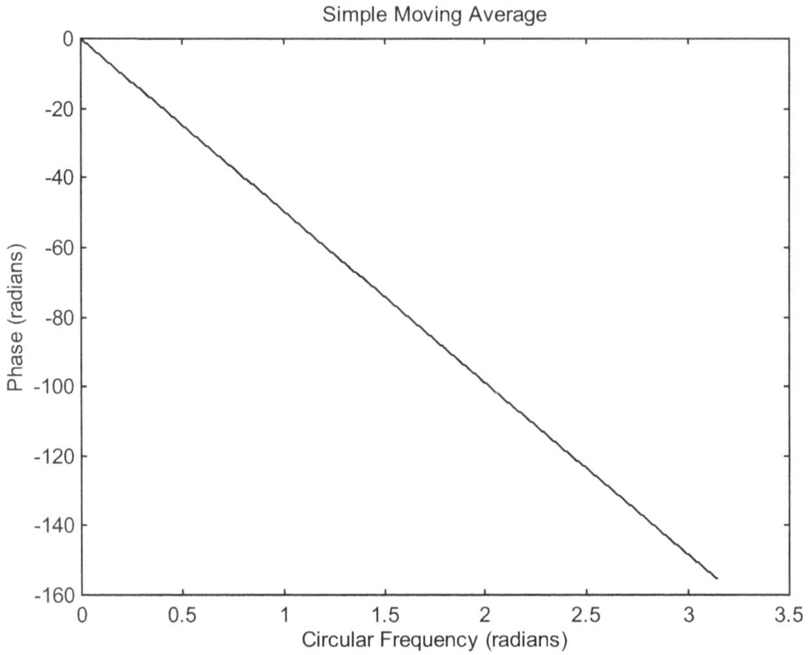

Fig. 3.18 The unwrapped phase of the phase response of a simple moving average with N = 100.

Examples of the unwrapped phase of SMA with N = 100, calculated from Eq. (B.7) are given in Table 3.4. Comparing the numbers in Table 3.4 with those in Table 3.3, it can be seen that the unwrapped phase decreases much faster for N = 100 than N = 20, as is also obvious from Eq. (B.7).

Table 3.4 Examples of unwrapped phase and amplitudes of SMA with N = 100 at various frequencies.

ω (radians)	Unwrapped phase, ϕ(ω) (radians)	Amplitude
$\pi/99 = 0.0317$	$-\pi/2$	0.6366
$2\pi/99 = 0.0635$	$-\pi$	≈ 0
$3\pi/99 = 0.0952$	$-3\pi/2$	0.2123
$4\pi/99 = 0.1269$	-2π	≈ 0

Trading tactics using SMA with N larger than 100 (Chan et al. 2014) are quite popular among traders. However, as said earlier, the Simple Moving Average has two disadvantages. Its amplitude can disappear at certain frequencies, and its phase delay can differ from the real phase delay. The problem is more amplified at large N, e.g., N = 100. As we will see in Chapter 7, frequencies, ω, of real market data are more relevant when ω is less than 0.5 radian. However, for N = 100, the amplitudes of its SMA are zero ten times for ω less than 0.5 radian, and its unwrapped phases differ from the wrapped phases for ω larger than π/50 (~ 0.0628 radian), and thus, not representing the real time delay. Thus, trading tactics employing SMA, and especially with N larger than e.g., 20 can generate a lot of erroneous signals.

3.2 Trading Tactics Using Simple Moving Average

A simple trading tactic that has been used by traders is to buy when the price crosses over the SMA of the price from below, and sells when price crosses over the SMA of the price from above. As (Price − SMA of Price) can be considered as a velocity indicator, the trading tactic is the same as buy when velocity changes from negative to positive, and sell when velocity changes from positive to negative. The mathematics of the frequency response of (Price − SMA of Price) can be found in section B.3 of Appendix B. The frequency response will be symbolized as (1 − SMA) (see Appendix B).

3.2.1 Price − Simple Moving Average of Price, N = 10

The amplitude of the frequency response of (1 − SMA, N = 10) is plotted in Fig. 3.19. Just like any velocity indicator, it is a high pass filter, filtering off the low frequency components. From Fig. 3.19, it can be seen that, for an input signal, a certain portion of ω less than 0.5 radians are retained in the output. This is useful as real market data contains significant percentage of low frequency components less than 0.5 radian.

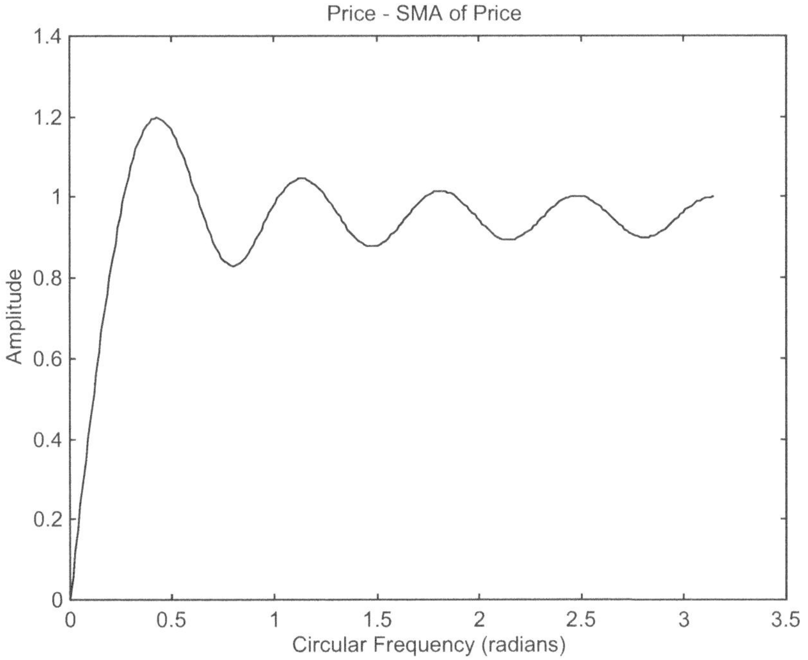

Fig. 3.19 The amplitude response of (1 − Simple Moving Average with N = 10).

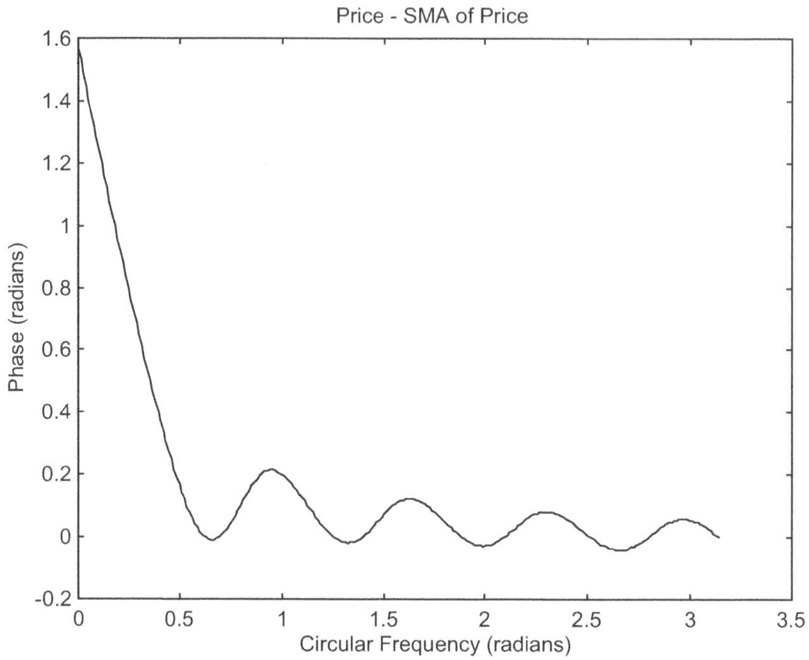

Fig. 3.20 The phase response of (1 − Simple Moving Average with N = 10).

The wrapped phase response of (1 − Simple Moving Average with N = 10) is plotted in Fig. 3.20. The unwrapped phase is the same as the wrapped phase. The phase is π/2 when ω approaches 0. The phase decreases to 0 when ω approaches 0.628 radians, where the amplitude is 0. As a matter of fact, when the amplitude of SMA is 0, the phase is 0 (Appendix B), i.e., when

$$\omega = \pi/5\ (\sim 0.628), 2\pi/5\ (\sim 1.257), 3\pi/5\ (\sim 1.885), 4\pi/5\ (\sim 2.513), \pi, \ldots. \quad \text{radians}$$

And it is also 0 when the phase of the SMA is 0 (Appendix B), i.e., when

$$\omega = 0.6981, 1.3963, 2.0944, 2.7925\ldots \quad \text{radians}$$

The phase is only slightly less than 0 when

$$0.628 < \omega < 0.6981$$
$$1.257 < \omega < 1.3963$$
$$1.885 < \omega < 2.0944$$
$$2.513 < \omega < 2.7925$$

As the phase lead of the above four zones lies between 0 and −π, the four zones can be considered as Loss Zones. However, for 0.628 < ω < π radians, the phase is always greater than −0.04 ≈ 0 radians. Thus, as an approximation, one can say that the Profit Zone, when the phase ϕ, lies between π and 0 in this case, is $0 < \omega < \pi$, and one would expect that this velocity indicator would yield a reasonably profitable indicator when $\omega < 0.628$. An example is given in Fig. 3.21 for price simulated as a sine wave of amplitude = 1 and $\omega = \pi/30 \sim 0.10$ radian. The velocity indicator, Price − Simple Moving Average (SMA), N = 10, of Price is also plotted. If traders buy when the velocity changes from negative to positive, and sell when the velocity changes from positive to negative, they will make about 91% of the maximum possible profit.

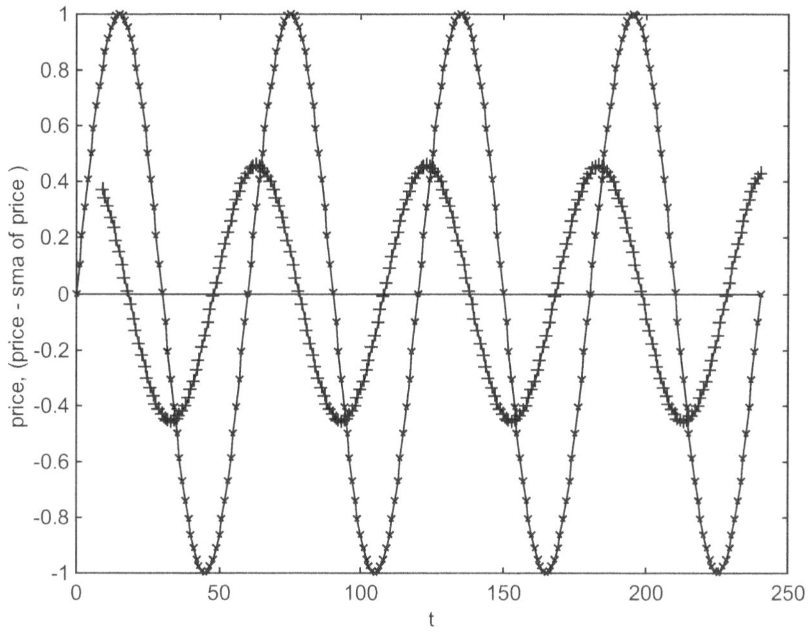

Fig. 3.21 Price simulated as a sine wave (marked as x) of amplitude = 1 and $\omega = \pi/30 \sim 0.10$ radians. The velocity indicator, Price − 10 point Simple Moving Average (SMA) of Price (marked as +) has a phase lead $\phi(\omega)$ of 1.24 radians from the sine wave. The amplitude of the (1 − Simple Moving Average, N = 10) is approximately 0.46. If traders buy when the velocity changes from negative to positive, and sell when the velocity changes from positive to negative, they will make 91.4% of the maximum possible profit (see also Table 3.5), where maximum possible profit = peak − valley = 2. The computer program pmsmasig has been used.

3.2.1.1 Computational and Theoretical Profit and Loss

The amount of profit traders made would depend on the frequency ω of the price signal, the initial phase angle, θ_0, of the price signal, as well as the phase lead, ϕ, of the velocity indicator. As the price data is not a continuous curve, the sampled price would correspond to the sampled velocity indicator when the velocity changes sign. As an example, Fig. 3.21 shows the price simulated as a sine wave of amplitude = 1 and $\omega = \pi/30 \sim 0.10$ radian. The velocity indicator, price – Simple Moving Average (SMA), N = 10, of price has a phase lead $\phi(\omega)$ of 1.24 radians from the sine wave. As one can see from the figure, the sampled velocity indicator is slightly less than 0 (at t = 48) before it changes to positive, and there is also a phase delay when it changes from positive to negative (at t = 78). The profit % can be computed from the price signal when the velocity indicator changes sign (using the program pmsmasig), and is given by (1/2) × (sell price – buy price) = (1/2) × (0.9135 – (−0.9135)) ≈ 0.914 = 91.4% as shown in Table 3.5. The factor of (1/2) is relevant as the maximum profit from valley to peak is 2.

Profit% can also be calculated by using Eqs. (2.1) – (2.7) in Chapter 2. This theoretical profit is calculated from the program buysellprice, using the phase, ϕ, which is computed from the program pmsma. The theoretical profit also yields 91.4% as shown in Table 3.5, and is in agreement with the computational result above.

Table 3.5 lists price data simulated as sine waves with frequencies from 0.1 to 0.5 radian, with initial phase angles, Theta0 (θ_0) of 0, $\pi/2$, π and $3\pi/2$ radians. The maximum possible gain traders can make equals (the peak of the price – the valley of the price), i.e., 2 × amplitude (with amplitude = 1). Profit % is the percentage of the maximum profit that can be made. The table shows that, for input price signal with $\omega < 0.5$, this trading tactic when the velocity indicator (Price – Simple Moving Average of Price with N = 10) changes sign, can make reasonably good profit.

Table 3.5 Price data simulated as sine waves with frequencies from 0.1 to 0.5 radian, with initial phase angles Theta0, θ_0, of 0, $\pi/2$, π and $3\pi/2$ radians.

	Theta 0 = 0 radian	Theta0 = $\pi/2$ radians	Theta0 = π radians	Theta0 = $3\pi/2$ radians	Theoretical ϕ taken from DTFT	
ω (radian)	profit (%)	profit (%)	profit (%)	profit (%)	ϕ (radians)	profit (%)
$\pi/30 \sim 0.1$	91.4	91.4	91.4	91.4	1.2404	91.4
$\pi/15 \sim 0.2$	74.3	66.9	74.3	66.9	0.9175	74.3, 66.9
$\pi/10 \sim 0.3$	30.9	30.9	30.9	30.9	0.6118	30.9
$\pi/8 \sim 0.4$	38.3	38.3	38.3	38.3	0.4020	38.3
$\pi/6 \sim 0.5$	0	0	0	0	0.1196	0

Profit % is the percentage of the maximum profit that can be made using the velocity indicator (Price – SMA of Price, with N = 10). The computer program pmsmasig is used to compute the profit % in columns 2–5. Theoretical profit % in column 7 is calculated from the program buysellprice, with ϕ(radians) taken from the program pmsma for the corresponding ω's.

When $\omega = \pi/30, \pi/15, \pi/10$ and $\pi/8$, $\phi > \omega$, the trade makes a profit. When $\omega = \pi/6$, $\phi < \omega$, the trade makes zero profit. The theoretical profit % agrees with the computational one very well.

However, real market signal consists of frequency ω higher than 0.5, where the phase of (1 − SMA with N = 10) can be equal to or close to 0. Because of sampling delay losses for phases close to 0, this trading tactic is not that profitable when real market data is used, as we will show later in Chapter 7.

3.2.1.2 Sure Profit Zone and Unsure Profit Zone

We have pointed out in Chapter 2, that the maximum phase shift of a buy/sell indication from a velocity indicator caused by sampling delay is ω for a certain ω. Thus, we can plot a straight line of Phase $\phi = \omega$ on a phase, ϕ, plot of a velocity indicator to show that there is a certain region of ω that the trade can surely make a profit, and some other part of the region when a trade may make a profit or a loss. As an example, we plot a straight line of $\phi = \omega$ on Fig. 3.20, thus producing Fig. 3.22. The intersection point of the straight line plot with the phase plot is approximately $\omega = 0.40$. We can describe $0 < \omega < 0.40$ as a Sure Profit Zone, as a trade with $0 < \phi < \pi/2$ and $\phi > \omega$ will surely make a profit. $0.40 < \omega < \pi$ is described as an Unsure Profit Zone. The trade will make a profit if μ, the phase shift caused by sampling delay, is less than the phase lead ϕ (> 0), of the velocity indicator. The trade will lose money if μ is larger than the phase lead of the velocity indicator. In the Sure Profit Zone, μ, whose maximum is ω, is always less than ϕ, and the trade will always make a profit. In the Unsure Profit Zone, μ may or may not be less than ϕ, and thus may or may not make a profit. This has been summarized in Table 2.3 in Chapter 2.

Table 2.3 Sure Profit Zone and Unsure Profit Zone.

Sure Profit Zone	$\phi > \omega$	Always makes a profit
Unsure Profit Zone	$\phi < \omega$	$\mu < \phi$ ($\mu > 0$) makes a profit $\mu \geq \phi$ ($\mu > 0$) makes a loss

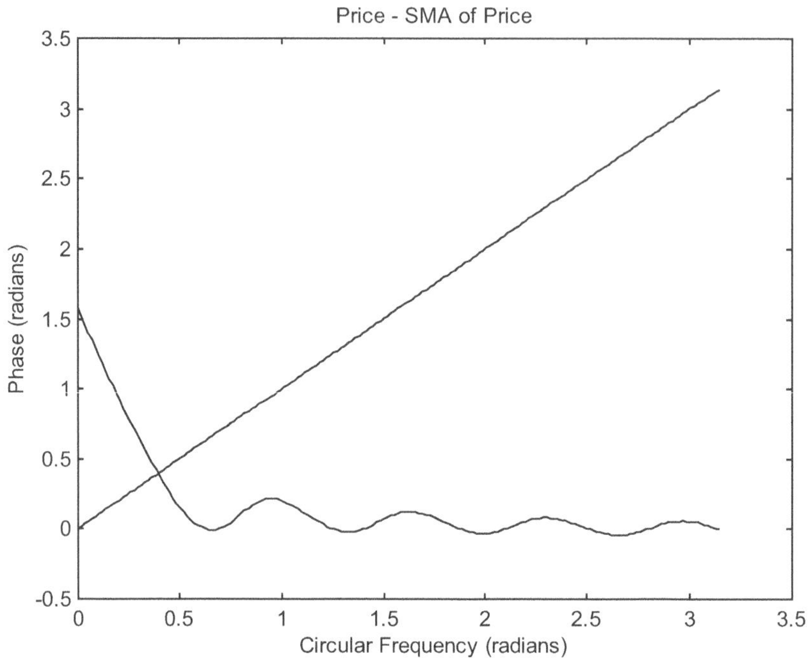

Fig. 3.22 The phase, ϕ, of (1 − Simple Moving Average with N = 10) plotted versus ω, as in Fig. 3.20. A straight line of Phase = ω is plotted, intersecting the phase plot at $\omega \approx 0.40$. The region $0 < \omega < 0.40$ is defined as the Sure Profit Zone, while the region $0.40 < \omega < \pi$ is defined as the Unsure Profit Zone.

3.2.2 Price − Simple Moving Average of Price, N = 20

The amplitude of the frequency response of (1 − SMA, N = 20) is plotted in Fig. 3.23. From Fig. 3.23, it can be seen that for an input signal, a certain portion of ω less than 0.5 radians are retained in the output.

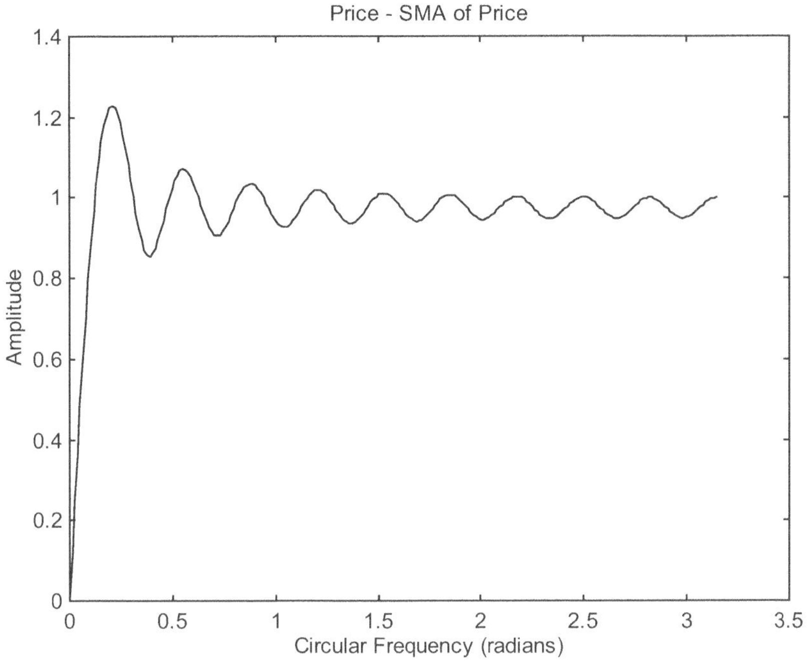

Fig. 3.23 The amplitude response of (1 − Simple Moving Average with N = 20).

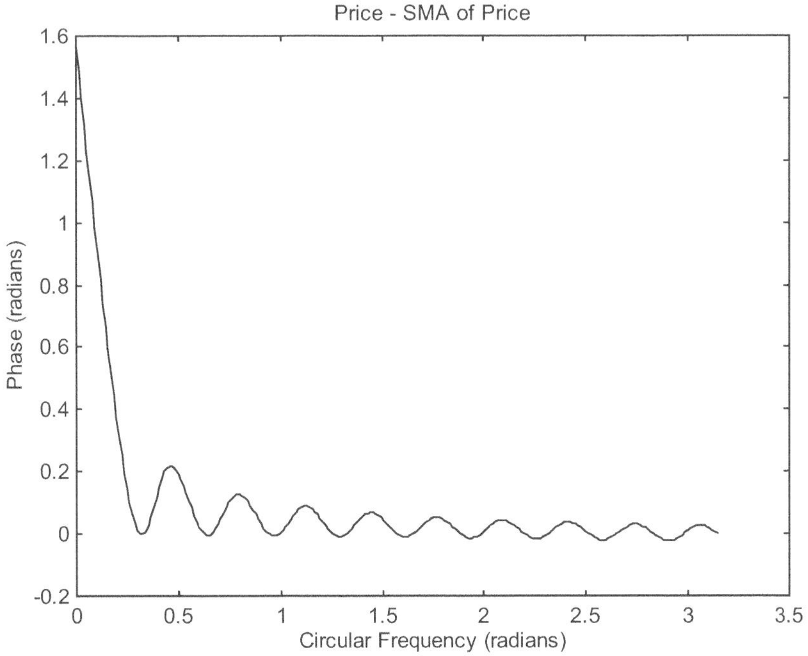

Fig. 3.24 The phase response of (1 − Simple Moving Average with N = 20).

The phase response of (1 − Simple Moving Average with N = 20) is plotted in Fig. 3.24. The unwrapped phase is the same as the wrapped phase. The phase is $\pi/2$ when ω approaches 0, and decreases to 0 when ω approaches 0.31 radians. For $\omega > 0.31$ radians, the phase is always greater than $-0.023 \approx 0$ radians. Thus, as an approximation, one can say that the Profit Zone, when the phase lies between π and 0 in this case, is $0 < \omega < \pi$. If a straight line of Phase $\phi = \omega$ is plotted on Fig. 3.24, it will intersect the phase plot at $\omega \approx 0.23$. The region $0 < \omega < 0.23$ is described as the Sure Profit Zone, while the region $0.23 < \omega < \pi$ is described as the Unsure Profit Zone. Because of the narrow Sure Profit Zone, one would not expect that this velocity indicator would yield a reasonably profitable indicator.

Table 3.6 lists price data simulated as sine waves with frequencies from 0.1 to 0.5 radian, with initial phase angles of 0, $\pi/2$, π and $3\pi/2$ radians. The table shows that this trading tactic when the velocity indicator (Price − SMA of Price, N = 20) changes sign, would not make reasonably good profit.

Table 3.6 Price data simulated as sine waves with frequencies from 0.1 to 0.5 radian, with initial phase angles of 0, $\pi/2$, π and $3\pi/2$ radians.

	Theta0 = 0 radian	Theta0 = $\pi/2$ radians	Theta0 = π radians	Theta0 = $3\pi/2$ radians	Theoretical ϕ taken from DTFT	
ω (radian)	profit (%)	profit (%)	profit (%)	profit (%)	ϕ (radians)	profit (%)
$\pi/30 \sim 0.1$	74.3	74.3	74.3	74.3	0.9011	74.3
$\pi/15 \sim 0.2$	20.8	10.5	20.8	10.5	0.3132	20.8, 10.5
$\pi/10 \sim 0.3$	−30.9	−30.9	−30.9	−30.9	0	−30.9
$\pi/8 \sim 0.4$	0	0	0	0	0.118	0
$\pi/6 \sim 0.5$	0	0	0	0	0.1537	0

Profit % is the percentage of the maximum profit that can be made using the velocity indicator (Price − SMA of Price, N = 20). The computer program pmsmasig is used to compute the profit % in columns 2–5. Theoretical profit % in column 7 is calculated from the program buysellprice, with ϕ(radians) taken from the program pmsma for the corresponding ω's.

It should be noted that when $\omega = \pi/10$, both the computational and theoretical calculations are not reliable, as the Simple Moving Average, N = 20 of the price signal is zero. Price − SMA20 is simply equal to the Price itself.

When $\omega = \pi/30$ and $\pi/15$, $\phi > \omega$, the trade makes a profit. When $\omega = \pi/8$ and $\pi/6$, $\phi < \omega$, the trade makes zero profit. This is in agreement with Table 2.3 that the trade can make a profit or a loss.

3.2.3 Price − Simple Moving Average of Price, N = 100

The amplitude of the frequency response of (1 − SMA, N = 100) is plotted in Fig. 3.25. From Fig. 3.25, it can be seen that, for an input signal, a certain portion of ω less than 0.5 radians are retained in the output.

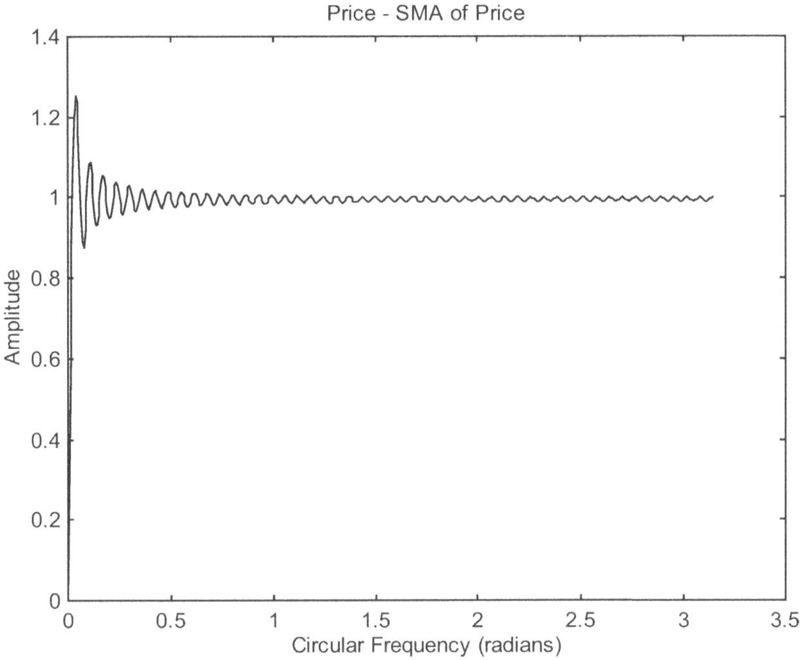

Fig. 3.25 The amplitude response of (1 − Simple Moving Average with N = 100).

The phase response of (1 − SMA, N = 100) is plotted in Fig. 3.26. The unwrapped phase is the same as the wrapped phase. The phase is $\pi/2$ when ω approaches 0, and decreases quickly to 0 when ω approaches 0.065 radians. For $\omega > 0.065$ radians, the phase is always greater than $-0.004 \approx 0$ radians. Thus, as an approximation, one can say that the Profit Zone, when the phase lies between π and 0 in this case, is $0 < \omega < \pi$. If a straight line of Phase $\phi = \omega$ is plotted on Fig. 3.26, it will intersect the phase plot at $\omega \approx 0.056$, 0.073 and 0.11. The region $0 < \omega < 0.056$ and $0.073 < \omega < 0.11$ are described as a Sure Profit Zones, and the regions $0.056 < \omega < 0.073$ and $0.11 < \omega < \pi$ are described as the Unsure Profit Zones. Because of the narrow Sure Profit Zones, one would not expect that this velocity indicator would yield a reasonably profitable indicator.

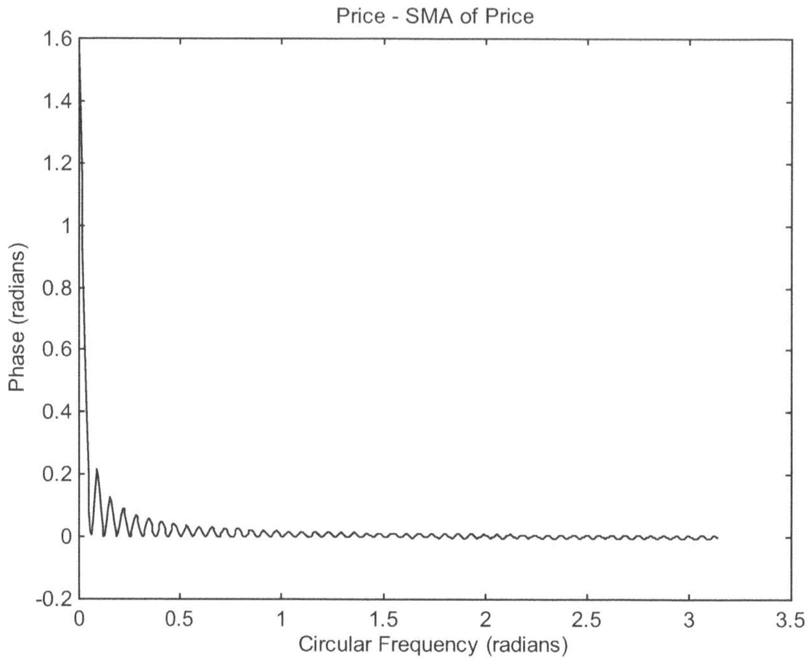

Fig. 3.26 The phase response of (1 − Simple Moving Average with N = 100).

Table 3.7 lists price data simulated as sine waves with frequencies from 0.1 to 0.5 radian, with initial phase angles of 0, π/2, π and 3π/2 radians. The table shows that this trading tactic when the velocity indicator, (Price − SMA of Price, N = 100) changes sign, cannot make good profit. As a matter of fact, there is a high chance that traders would lose some money.

Table 3.7 Price data simulated as sine waves with frequencies from 0.1 to 0.5 radian, with initial phase angles of 0, π/2, π and 3π/2 radians.

	Theta0 = 0 radian	Theta0 = π/2 radians	Theta0 = π radians	Theta0 = 3π/2 radians	Theoretical ϕ taken from DTFT	
ω (radian)	profit (%)	profit (%)	profit (%)	profit (%)	ϕ (radians)	profit (%)
π/30 ~ 0.1	10.5	10.5	10.5	10.5	0.1363	10.5
π/15 ~ 0.2	0	−10	0	−10	0.0703	0, −10
π/10 ~ 0.3	−15, −31	−15	−15	−31	0	−31
π/8 ~ 0.4	0	0	0	0	0.0208	0
π/6 ~ 0.5	0	0	0	0	0.0242	0

Profit % is the percentage of the maximum profit that can be made using the velocity indicator (Price − SMA of Price, N = 100). The computer program pmsmasig is used to compute the profit % in columns 2–5. Theoretical profit % in column 7 is calculated from the program buysellprice, with ϕ(radians) taken from the program pmsma for the corresponding ω's.

It should be noted that when $\omega = \pi/10$, both the computational and theoretical calculations are not reliable, as the Simple Moving Average, N = 100 of the price signal is zero. Price – SMA100 is simply equal to the Price itself.

When $\omega = \pi/30$, $\phi > \omega$, the trade makes a profit. When $\omega = \pi/15$, $\phi < \omega$, the trade makes zero profit or makes a loss, depending on the sampling delay. When $\omega = \pi/10$, $\pi/8$, and $\pi/6$, $\phi < \omega$, the trades do not make any profit. This is in agreement with Table 2.3 that the trade can make a profit or a loss.

3.2.4 Comparison of *Price – Simple Moving Average of Price, N = 10, 20 and 100*

As mentioned earlier, to a good approximation, we can consider the Profit Zone of (Price – SMA of Price) to be $0 < \omega < \pi$.

Price – SMA of Price with N = 10, popular among traders, apparently looks like a profitable trading tactic. However, as pointed out in the above sections, the high frequency components in real market data can generate whipsaws, and can easily turn an originally profitable trade into a loss.

Some traders like to use larger N, e.g., N = 20, 100 or more (Chan et al. 2014). Nevertheless, the larger the N, the less is the Sure Profit Zone, as we can see in Table 3.8, and there is less chance a trade will make money. Also, within the Unsure Profit Zone, the larger the area enclosed by the straight line Phase $\phi = \omega$, the phase plot and $\omega = \pi$ (as in Fig. 3.22), the higher the probability that a trade will lose money. It can be seen from the phase plots that the area gets larger and larger as N increases. Thus, the larger the N, the less the probability that a trade will make money.

Table 3.8 Sure and Unsure Profit Zones for SMA for N = 10, 20 and 100.

SMA, N	Sure Profit Zone (radians)	Unsure Profit Zone (radians)
10	$0 < \omega < 0.40$	$0.40 < \omega < \pi$
20	$0 < \omega < 0.23$	$0.23 < \omega < \pi$
100	$0 < \omega < 0.056$ $0.073 < \omega < 0.11$	$0.056 < \omega < 0.073$ $0.11 < \omega < \pi$

As we do not think that Price – SMA of Price, N = 100, would make good profit, this tactic would not be used in trading real market data in Chapter 7.

In the next chapter, we will discuss the smoothing indicator, exponential moving average, and the trading tactic, Price – Exponential Moving Average of Price. We will show later that this tactic is more reliable and more profitable than Price – Simple Moving Average of Price.

Exponential Moving Average

4

Exponential Moving Average (EMA) is another smoothing indicator. Like the Simple Moving Average, it is a low pass filter, which removes high frequency components and allows low frequency components to pass.

4.1 Exponential Moving Average (EMA)

An exponential moving average is a better indicator than a simple moving average as it puts greater weight to most recent data more than older data. The equation for the EMA is given by

$$\text{NEW EMA} = \alpha \times (\text{NEW PRICE}) + (1 - \alpha) \times (\text{OLD EMA}) \tag{4.1}$$

where $\alpha = 2/(M + 1)$

M is quite often called the length of the EMA. It is sometimes described by some traders as the number of data points (e.g. days) in the EMA. This is incorrect as the number of data points used in the calculation is usually much higher than M. For the EMA, a larger M will provide a smoother average but a larger phase lag. Figure 4.1 shows the S & P 500 daily index data taken from April 24, 2019 to August 12, 2019. An Exponential Moving Average of length 6, plotted as a line, is used to smooth the data, showing that it lags behind the index. Characteristics of the EMA are described in Appendix C.

D. K. Mak, *Trading Tactics in the Financial Market*, Management for Professionals,
https://doi.org/10.1007/978-3-030-70622-7_4

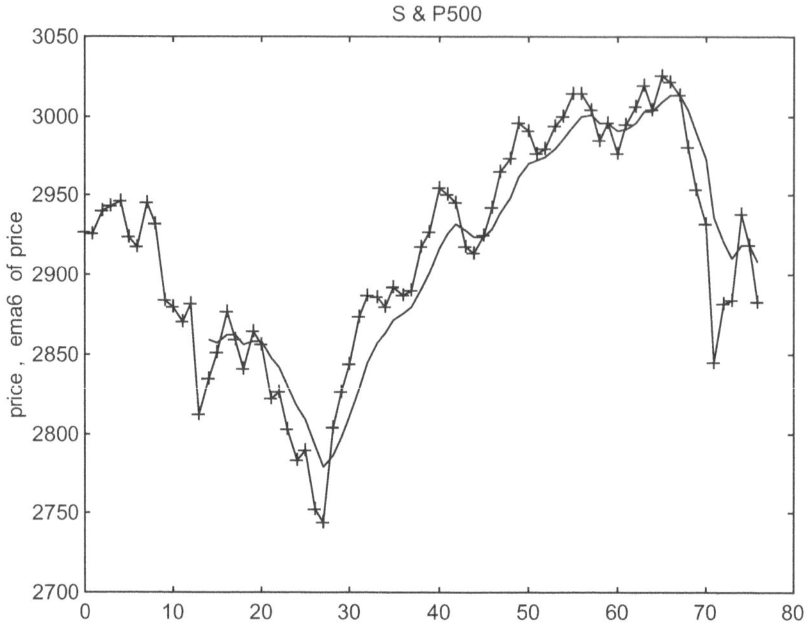

Fig. 4.1 The S & P 500 daily index from April 24, 2019 to August 12, 2019 are plotted (+), together with an Exponential Moving Average (EMA) of length 6, plotted as a line. Note that the EMA lags behind the index.

An exponential moving average (EMA) gives greater weight to the latest data and thus responds to changes faster. It does not drop old data suddenly the way an SMA does. Old data simply fade away.

Equation (4.1) for the output response of an EMA can be re-written as

$$y(n) = \alpha x(n) + (1 - \alpha) y(n - 1) \tag{4.2}$$

where y(n) is the output data, x(n) is the input data, and is equal to price here.

Equation (4.2) makes use of an output response that has already been processed. Iterating the previously processed y value in Eq. (4.2), we can write y(n) as

$$y(n) = \sum_{k=0}^{\infty} \alpha(1 - \alpha)^k x(n - k) \tag{4.3}$$

Thus, the unit sample (impulse) response h(k) can be written as

$$h(k) = \alpha(1 - \alpha)^k \tag{4.4}$$

where $k = 0, 1, 2, \ldots, \ldots\infty$

Note that when $k = 0$, $h(k) = \alpha = 2/(M + 1)$.

Thus, it can be seen that exponential moving average (EMA), which is also known as exponentially weighted moving average (EWMA), is an infinite impulse response filter that applies weighting factor which decreases exponentially.

For M = 3, 6, 9, 12, 26, h(k) are plotted in Fig. 4.2.

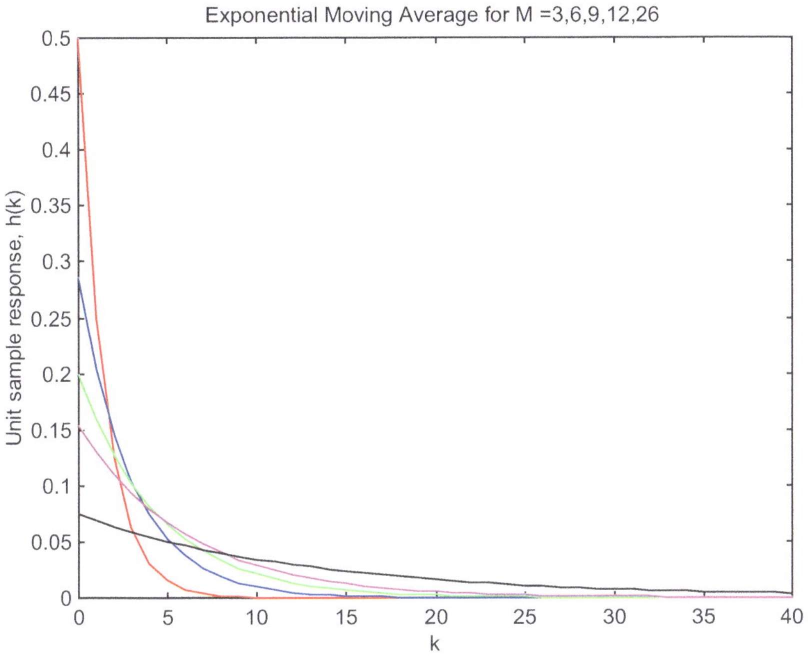

Fig. 4.2 Unit sample response, h(k), of an exponential moving average are plotted for M = 3 (red), 6 (blue), 9 (green), 12 (magenta), 26 (black). The figure can be plotted with the program hema.

The equations of H(ω), the frequency response of the EMA is given in Appendix C.

The amplitude and phase of H(ω) of the EMA, for M = 3 and 6 are plotted in Figs. 4.3 and 4.4.

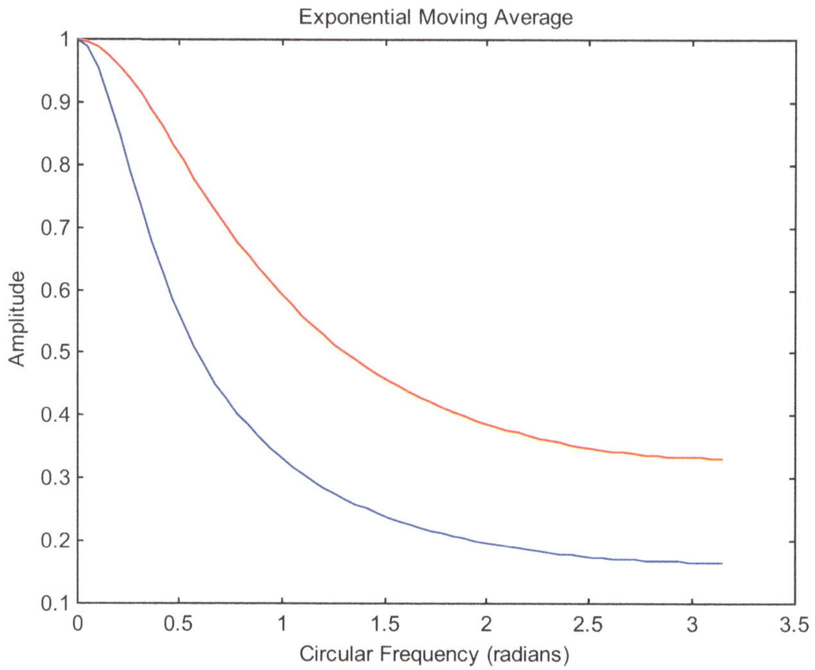

Fig 4.3 Amplitudes of H(ω) of the EMA, for M = 3 (red) and 6 (blue).

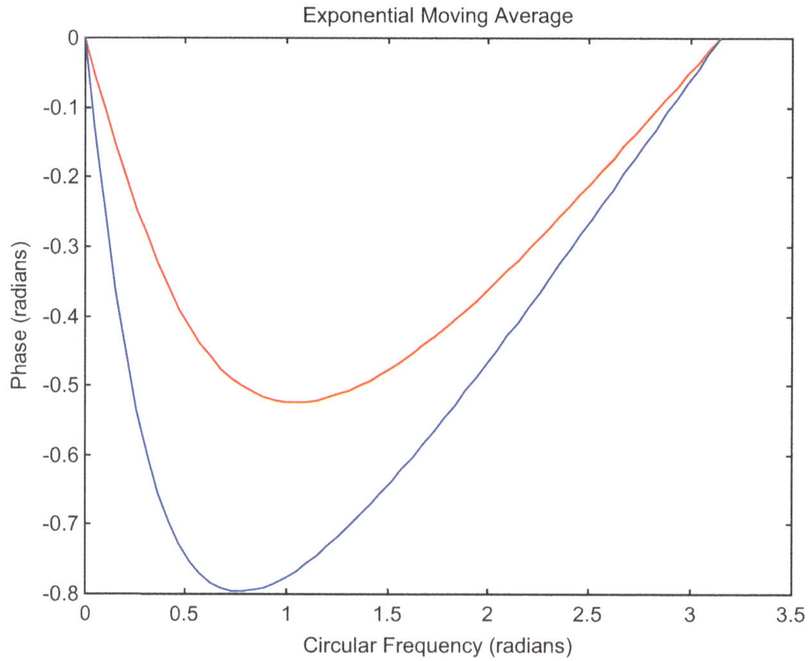

Fig 4.4 Phases of H(ω) of the EMA, for M = 3 (red) and 6 (blue).

Note that the amplitudes of EMA do not go to zero, as in SMA. Also, the phases of EMA do not necessarily decrease as the circular frequency ω gets larger, as in SMA. These are the advantages of EMA over SMA, rendering trading tactics using EMA more reliable than those using SMA.

4.2 Trading Tactics Using Exponential Moving Average

A simple trading tactic that has been used by traders is to buy when the price crosses over the EMA of the price from below, and sells when price crosses over the EMA of the price from above. As (Price − EMA of Price) can be considered as a velocity indicator, the trading tactics is the same as buy when velocity changes from negative to positive, and sell when velocity changes from positive to negative.

4.2.1 Price − Exponential Moving Average of Price, M = 3

The frequency response of (Price − EMA of Price) is shown in Appendix C, and will be denoted as (1 − EMA). The amplitude response of (1 − EMA, M = 3) is plotted in Fig. 4.5. Just like any velocity indicator, it is a high pass filter, filtering off the low frequency components. From Fig. 4.5, it can be seen that a certain portion of ω less than 0.5 radians are retained. This is useful as real market data contains significant percentage of low frequency components less than 0.5 radians.

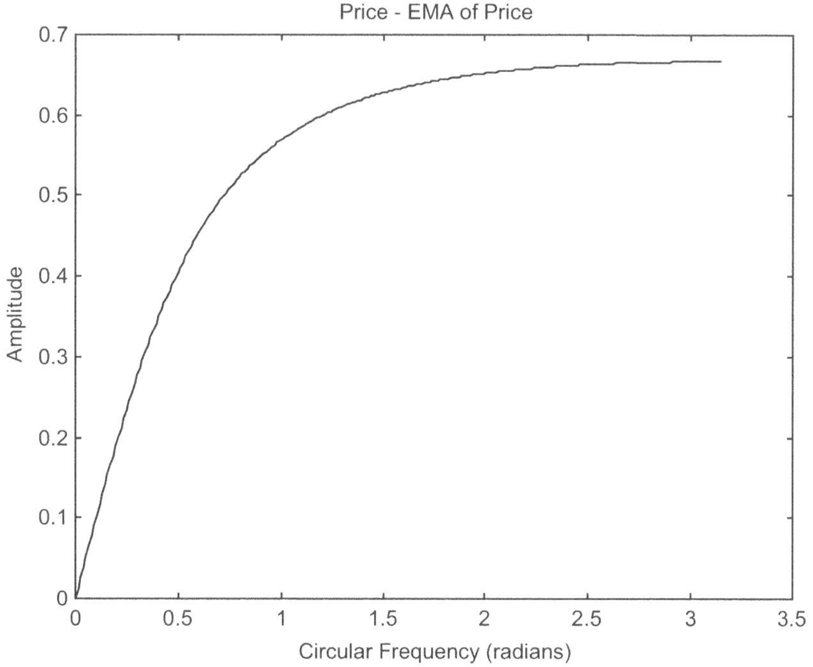

Fig. 4.5 The amplitude response of (1 − exponential moving average with M = 3).

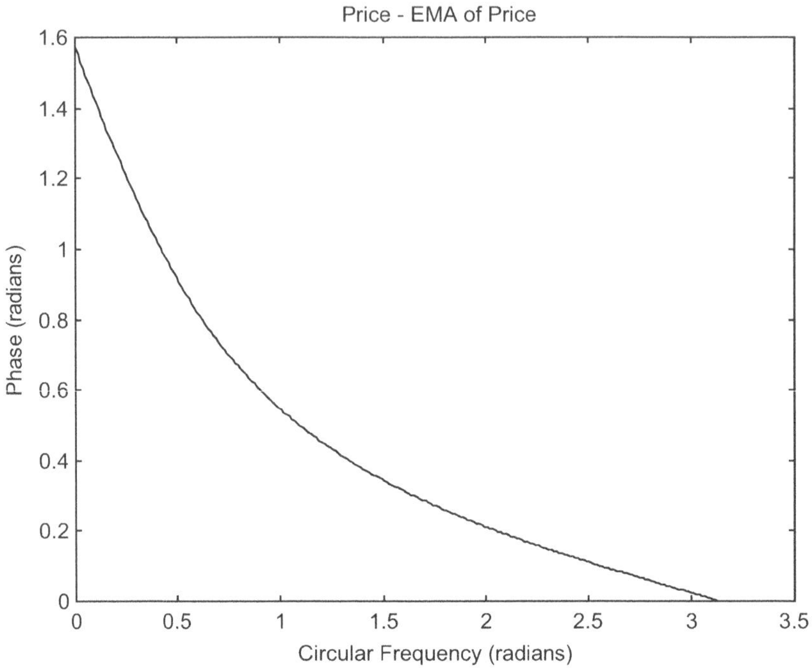

Fig. 4.6 The phase response of (1 − exponential moving average with M = 3).

The phase response of (1 − exponential moving average with M = 3) is plotted in Fig. 4.6. The phase is $\pi/2$ when ω approaches 0, and decreases to 0 when ω approaches π radians. As all phase lies between $\pi/2$ and 0, the Profit Zone would be $0 < \omega < \pi$. A straight line of Phase $\phi = \omega$ can be plotted on Fig. 4.6. The intersection point of the straight line plot with the phase plot is approximately $\omega = 0.72$. We can describe $0 < \omega < 0.72$ as a Sure Profit Zone, as a trade with $0 < \phi < \pi/2$ and $\phi > \omega$ will surely make a profit. $0.72 < \omega < \pi$ is described as an Unsure Profit Zone. The trade will make a profit if μ, the phase shift caused by sampling delay, is less than the phase lead ϕ (> 0), of the velocity indicator. The trade will lose money if μ is larger than the phase lead of the velocity indicator. In the Sure Profit Zone, μ, whose maximum is ω, is always less than ϕ, and the trade will always make a profit. In the Unsure Profit Zone, μ may or may not be less than ϕ, and thus may or may not make a profit.

As the Sure Profit Zone is reasonably large, one would expect that this velocity indicator would yield a reasonably profitable indicator. An example is given in Fig. 4.7 for price simulated as a sine wave of amplitude = 1 and $\omega = \pi/30 \approx 0.10$ radian. The velocity indicator, Price − Exponential Moving Average of Price with M = 3 is also plotted. If traders buy when the velocity changes from negative to positive, and sell when the velocity changes from positive to negative, they will make about 98% of the maximum possible profit.

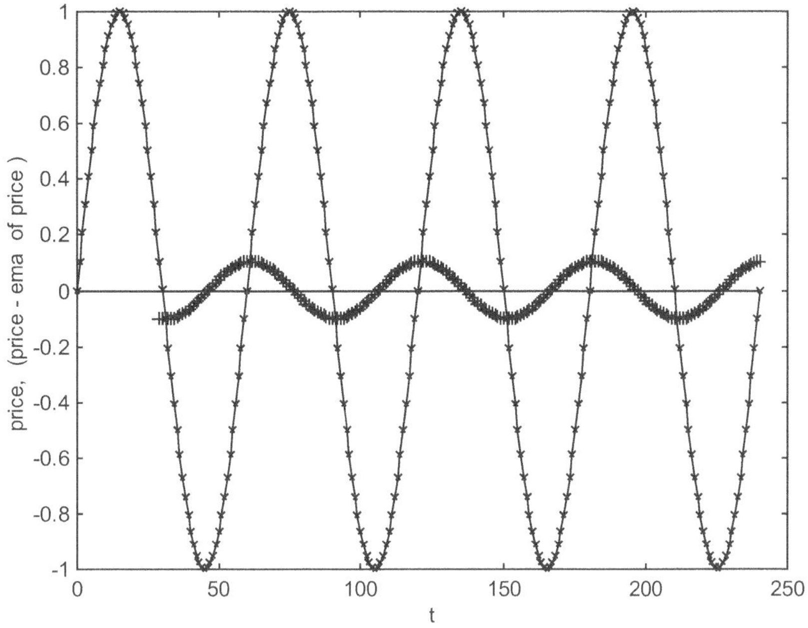

Fig. 4.7 Price simulated as a sine wave (marked as x) of amplitude = 1 and $\omega = \pi/30 \sim 0.10$ radians. The velocity indicator, Price − EMA of Price with M = 3 (marked as +) has a phase lead $\phi(\omega)$ of 1.4 radians from the sine wave. The amplitude of the (1 − EMA with M = 3) is approximately 0.1. If traders buy when the velocity changes from negative to positive, and sell when the velocity changes from positive to negative, they will make about 98% of the maximum possible profit.

Table 4.1 lists price data simulated as sine waves with frequencies from 0.1 to 0.5 radian, at initial phase angles of 0, $\pi/2$, π and $3\pi/2$ radians. The maximum possible gain traders can make equals (the peak of the price − the valley of the price), i.e., 2 × amplitude (with amplitude = 1). Profit % is the percentage of the maximum profit that can be made. The table shows that this trading tactic when the velocity indicator (Price − EMA of Price with M = 3) changes sign, can make reasonably good profit.

Table 4.1 Price data simulated as sine waves with frequencies from 0.1 to 0.5 radian, with initial phase angles Theta0, θ_0, of 0, $\pi/2$, π and $3\pi/2$ radians.

	Theta0 = 0 radian	Theta0 = $\pi/2$ radians	Theta0 = π radians	Theta0 = $3\pi/2$ radians	Theoretical ϕ taken from DTFT	
ω (radian)	profit (%)	profit (%)	profit (%)	profit (%)	ϕ (radians)	profit (%)
$\pi/30 \sim 0.1$	97.8	97.8	97.8	97.8	1.4148	97.8
$\pi/15 \sim 0.2$	95.1	91.4	95.1	91.4	1.2654	95.1, 91.4
$\pi/10 \sim 0.3$	80.9	80.9	80.9	80.9	1.1272	80.9
$\pi/8 \sim 0.4$	70.7	70.7	70.7	70.7	1.0328	70.7
$\pi/6 \sim 0.5$	50.0	50.0	50.0	50.0	0.8937	50.0

Profit % is the percentage of the maximum profit that can be made using the velocity indicator (Price − EMA of Price, with M = 3). The computer program pmemasig is used to compute the profit % in columns 2–5. Theoretical profit % in column 7 is calculated from the program buysellprice, with ϕ (radians) taken from the program pmema for the corresponding ω's.

In Table 4.1, for each ω, $\phi > \omega$, thus, all trades make a profit.

4.2.2 Price − Exponential Moving Average of Price, M = 6

The amplitude response of (1 − EMA, M = 6) is plotted in Fig. 4.8. From Fig. 4.8, it can be seen that a certain portion of ω less than 0.5 radian are retained.

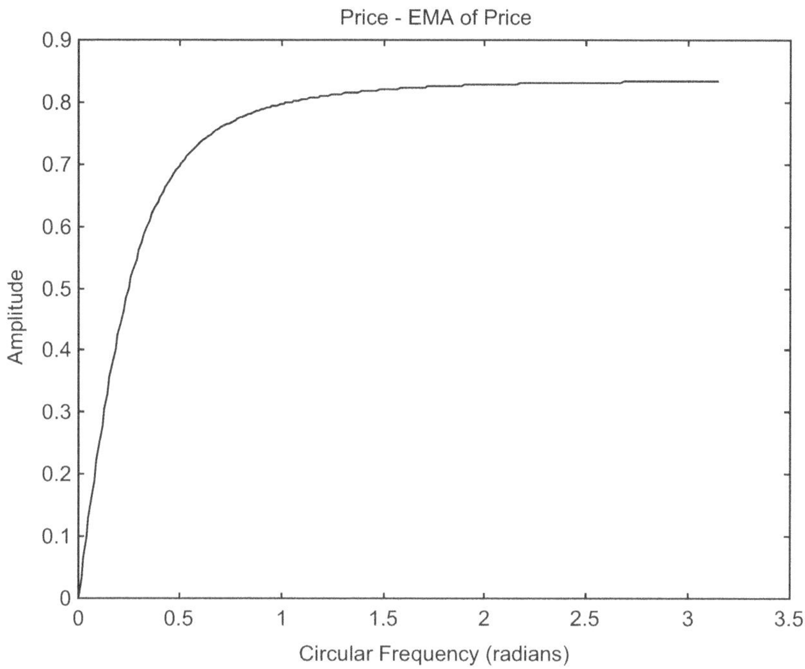

Fig. 4.8 The amplitude response of (1 − exponential moving average with M = 6).

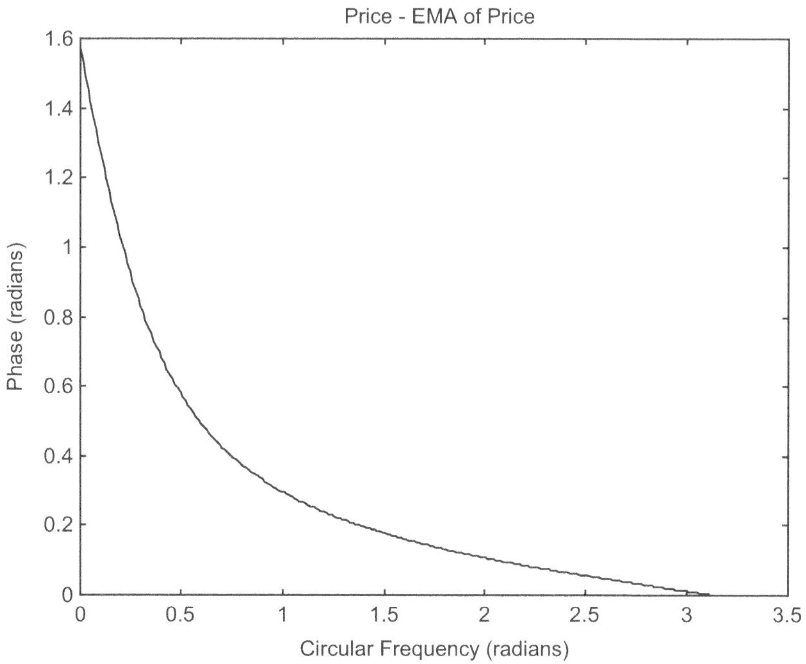

Fig. 4.9 The phase response of (1 − exponential moving average with M = 6).

The phase response of (1 − exponential moving average with M = 6) is plotted in Fig. 4.9. The phase is $\pi/2$ when ω approaches 0, and decreases to 0 when ω approaches π radians. As all phase lies between $\pi/2$ and 0, the Profit Zone would be $0 < \omega < \pi$. A straight line of Phase $\phi = \omega$ can be plotted on Fig. 4.9. The intersection point of the straight line plot with the phase plot is approximately $\omega = 0.54$. We can describe $0 < \omega < 0.54$ as a Sure Profit Zone, as a trade with $0 < \phi < \pi/2$ and $\phi > \omega$ (i.e., $\omega < \phi < \pi/2$) will surely make a profit. $0.54 < \omega < \pi$ is described as an Unsure Profit Zone. The trade will make a profit if μ, the phase shift caused by sampling delay, is less than the phase lead ϕ (>0), of the velocity indicator. The trade will lose money if μ is larger than the phase lead of the velocity indicator. In the Sure Profit Zone, μ, whose maximum is ω, is always less than ϕ, and the trade will always make a profit. In the Unsure Profit Zone, μ may or may not be less than ϕ, and thus may or may not make a profit.

One would expect that this velocity indicator would yield a reasonably profitable indicator, even though it may not be as profitable as the velocity indicator (1 − exponential moving average with M = 3), as the area below the phase curve is less than the corresponding area for M = 3.

Table 4.2 lists price data simulated as sine waves with frequencies from 0.1 to 0.5 radian, at initial phase angles of 0, $\pi/2$, π and $3\pi/2$ radians. The shows that this trading tactic, when the velocity indicator (price − exponential moving average of price with M = 6) changes sign, can make reasonably good profit.

Table 4.2 Price data simulated as sine waves with frequencies from 0.1 to 0.5 radian, with initial phase angles Theta0, θ_0, of 0, $\pi/2$, π and $3\pi/2$ radians.

ω (radian)	Theta0 = 0 radian profit (%)	Theta0 = $\pi/2$ radians profit (%)	Theta0 = π radians profit (%)	Theta0 = $3\pi/2$ radians profit (%)	Theoretical ϕ taken from DTFT ϕ (radians)	profit (%)
$\pi/30 \sim 0.1$	95.1	95.1	95.1	95.1	1.2661	95.1
$\pi/15 \sim 0.2$	74.3	80.9	74.3	80.9	1.0082	74.3, 80.9
$\pi/10 \sim 0.3$	58.8	58.8	58.8	58.8	0.8109	58.8
$\pi/8 \sim 0.4$	38.3	38.3	38.3	38.3	0.6974	38.3
$\pi/6 \sim 0.5$	50.0	50.0	50.0	50.0	0.5564	50.0

Profit % is the percentage of the maximum profit that can be made using the velocity indicator (Price − EMA of Price, with M = 6). The computer program pmemasig is used to compute the profit % in columns 2–5. Theoretical profit % in column 7 is calculated from the program buysellprice, with ϕ (radians) taken from the program pmema for the corresponding ω's.

In Table 4.2, for each ω, $\phi > \omega$, thus, all trades make a profit.

4.2.3 EMA of Price, M = 3 − EMA of Price, M = 6

In the trading tactic Price − EMA of Price, as the first parameter Price is not smoothed, its high frequencies can produce some whipsaws. We will see whether having it smoothed can provide a more profitable trading tactic. We will try using (EMA, M = 3 − EMA, M = 6). The amplitude response of (EMA, M = 3 − EMA, M = 6) is plotted in Fig. 4.10. From Fig. 4.10, it can be seen that a certain portion of ω less than 0.5 radians are retained.

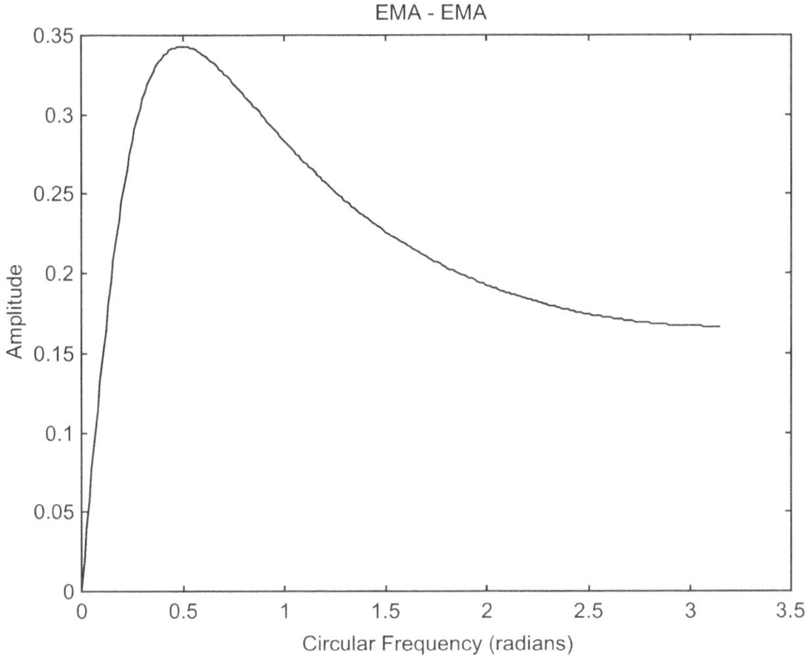

Fig. 4.10 The amplitude response of (EMA with M = 3 − EMA with M = 6).

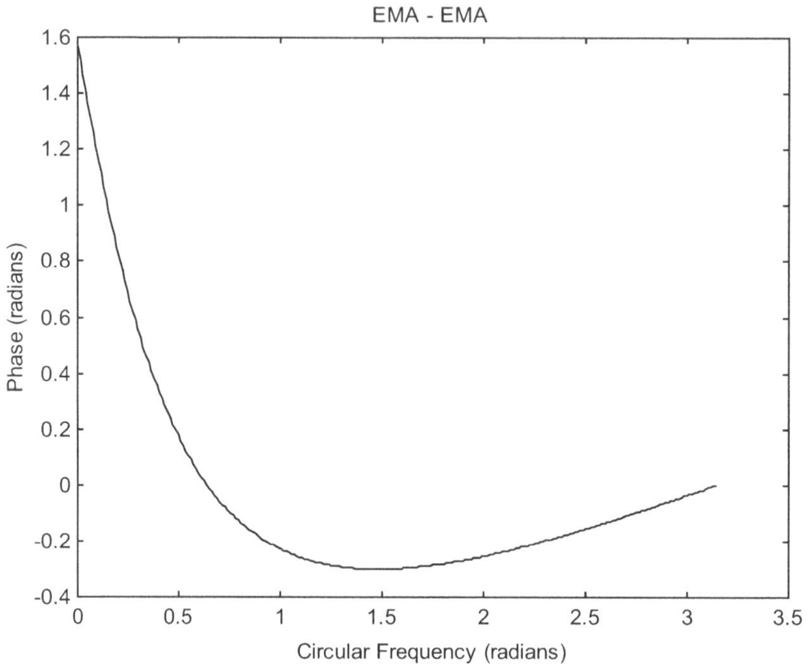

Fig. 4.11 The phase response of (EMA with M = 3 − EMA with M = 6).

The phase response of (EMA with M = 3 − EMA with M = 6) is plotted in Fig. 4.11. The phase is $\pi/2$ when ω approaches 0, and decreases to 0 when ω approaches 0.64 radian. The phase then becomes negative and increases back to 0 when ω approaches π radians. If a straight line of Phase $\phi = \omega$ is plotted on Fig. 4.11, it will intersect the phase plot at $\omega \approx 0.38$. The region $0 < \omega < 0.38$ is described as a Sure Profit Zone, while the region $0.38 < \omega < 0.64$ is described as the Unsure Profit Zone. $0.64 < \omega < \pi$ is described as the Loss Zone, as $\phi < 0$ and a trade will always lose money. Because of the narrow Sure Profit Zone and the long Loss Zone, one would not expect that this velocity indicator would yield a reasonably profitable indicator.

Table 4.3 lists price data simulated as sine waves with frequencies from 0.1 to 0.5 radian, at initial phase angles of 0, $\pi/2$, π and $3\pi/2$ radians. From $\pi/30$ to $\pi/10$, $\phi > \omega$, the trade is in the Sure Profit Zone, and it will always make a profit. For $\pi/8$ and $\pi/6$, $0 < \phi < \omega$, the trade lies in the Unsure Profit Zone, and may or may not make a profit.

Table 4.3 Price data simulated as sine waves with frequencies from 0.1 to 0.5 radian, with initial phase angles Theta0, θ_0, of 0, $\pi/2$, π and $3\pi/2$ radians.

ω (radian)	Theta0 = 0 radian profit (%)	Theta0 = π/2 radians profit (%)	Theta0 = π radians profit (%)	Theta0 = 3π/2 radians profit (%)	Theoretical ϕ taken from DTFT ϕ (radians)	profit (%)
π/30 ~ 0.1	91.4	91.4	91.4	91.4	1.1626	91.4
π/15 ~ 0.2	58.8	66.9	58.8	66.9	0.8074	58.8, 66.9
π/10 ~ 0.3	30.9	30.9	30.9	30.9	0.5244	30.9
π/8 ~ 0.4	0	0	0	0	0.3558	0
π/6 ~ 0.5	0	0	0	0	0.1412	0

Profit % is the percentage of the maximum profit that can be made using the velocity indicator (EMA of Price, M = 3 – EMA of Price, M = 6). The computer program macdsig (with M1 = 3, and M2 = 6) is used to compute the profit % in columns 2–5. Theoretical profit % in column 7 is calculated from the program buysellprice, with ϕ (radians) taken from the program emamema for the corresponding ω's.

4.2.4 EMAACCEL

We can create an acceleration indicator using EMA's, and call it EMAACCEL. This would be similar to the Moving Average Convergence Divergence Histogram (MACDH) which is a popular indicator used by traders, and which will be described in Chapter 6. It has been said that MACDH, even though it is an acceleration indicator, has been used by aggressive trader as a velocity indicator (Chan et al. 2014). We will show later that MACDH does perform quite well when used as a velocity indicator. Here, for EMAACCEL we would be using M's, lengths of the EMA, much lower than the M's used by MACDH, to see whether we can make any improvement on MACDH. EMAACCEL is defined as

EMAACCEL = (ema3 – ema6) – ema9 (ema3 – ema6)
where ema3 = EMA, M = 3 of price
ema6 = EMA, M = 6 of price
ema9 (ema3 – ema6) = EMA, M=9 of (ema3 – ema6)

As (ema3 – ema6) and ema9 (ema3 – ema6) are both velocity indicators, EMAACCEL will be an acceleration indicator. The amplitude response of EMAACCEL is plotted in Fig. 4.12. From Fig. 4.12, it can be seen that a certain portion of ω less than 0.5 radians are retained. The phase response of EMAACCEL is plotted in Fig. 4.13. The phase is π when ω approaches 0, and decreases to 0 when ω approaches 0.96 radian. The phase then becomes negative and decreases to

-0.1935 radian at $\omega = 1.73$ radians. It then increases back to 0 when ω approaches π radians. If a straight line of Phase $\phi = \omega$ is plotted on Fig. 4.13, it will intersect the phase plot at $\omega \approx 0.53$. The region $0 < \omega < 0.53$ is described as a Sure Profit Zone, while the region $0.53 < \omega < 0.96$ is described as the Unsure Profit Zone. $0.96 < \omega < \pi$ is described as the Loss Zone, as $\phi < 0$ and a trade will always lose money. Because of the long Loss Zone, it is not at all clear whether this acceleration indicator, when used as a velocity indicator, would yield a reasonably profitable indicator.

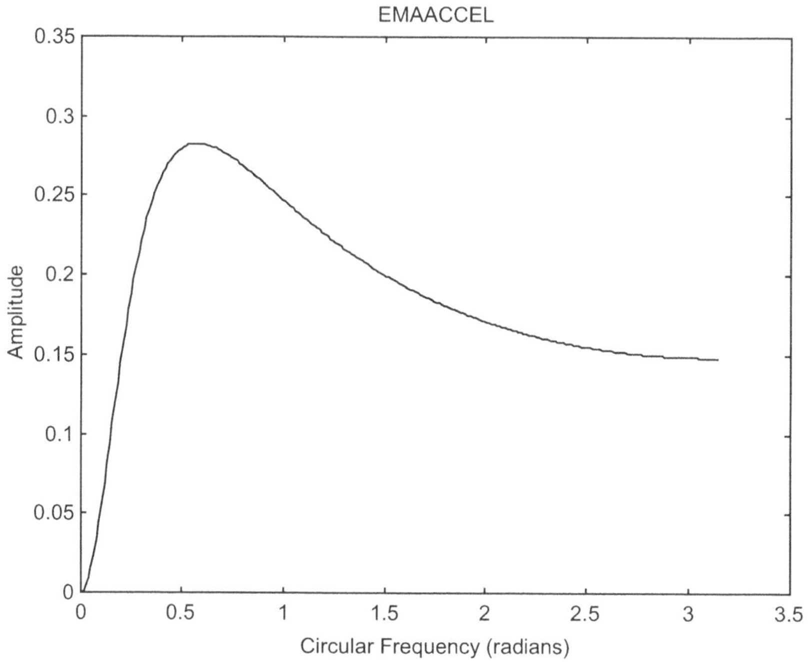

Fig. 4.12 The amplitude response of EMAACCEL.

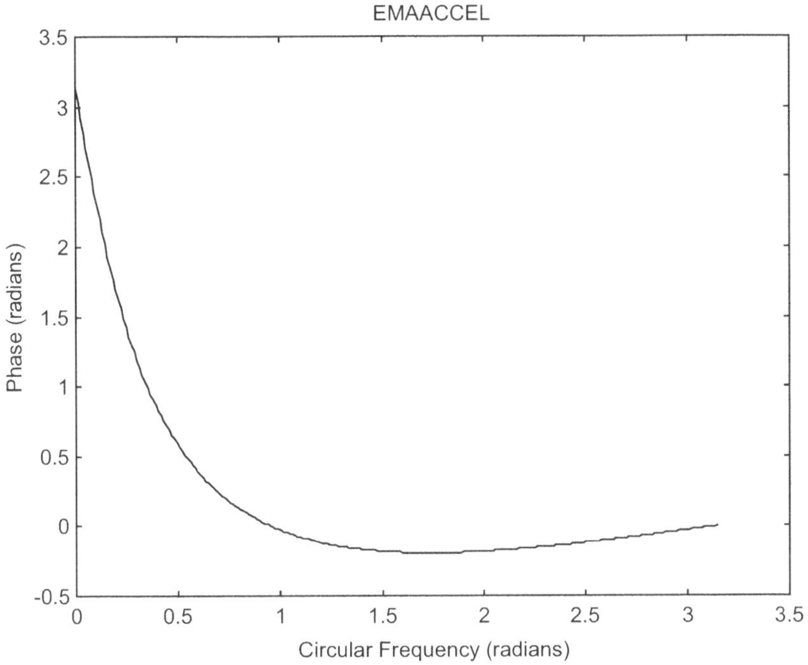

Fig. 4.13 The phase response of EMAACCEL.

Table 4.4 lists price data simulated as sine waves with frequencies from 0.1 to 0.5 radian, at initial phase angles of 0, π/2, π and 3π/2 radians. For all ω listed, ϕ > ω, the trade is thus in the Sure Profit Zone, and it will always make a profit.

Table 4.4 Price data simulated as sine waves with frequencies from 0.1 to 0.5 radian, with initial phase angles Theta0, θ_0, of 0, π/2, π and 3π/2 radians.

	Theta0 = 0 radian	Theta0 = π/2 radians	Theta0 = π radians	Theta0 = 3π/2 radians	Theoretical ϕ taken from DTFT	
ω (radian)	profit (%)	profit (%)	profit (%)	profit (%)	ϕ (radians)	profit (%)
π/30 ~ 0.1	80.9	80.9	80.9	80.9	2.2926	80.9
π/15 ~ 0.2	99.5	100	99.5	100	1.6206	99.5, 100
π/10 ~ 0.3	80.9	80.9	80.9	80.9	1.1361	80.9
π/8 ~ 0.4	70.7	70.7	70.7	70.7	0.8652	70.7
π/6 ~ 0.5	50.0	50.0	50.0	50.0	0.5343	50.0

Profit % is the percentage of the maximum profit that can be made using EMAACCEL as a velocity indicator. The computer program emaaccelsig is used to compute the profit % in columns 2–5. Theoretical profit % in column 7 is calculated from the program buysellprice, with ϕ (radians) taken from the program emaaccel for the corresponding ω's.

We will use EMAACCEL on real market data in Chapter 7, and see how it would perform.

Awesome Oscillator and Accelerator Oscillator 5

In this chapter, we will analyze two popular trading tactics that use Simple Moving Averages.

5.1 Awesome Oscillator (AO)

Awesme Oscillator (AO) has been developd by Bill Williams to measure market momentum (or actually, velocity). The indicator is based on his recommendations from his books "Trading Chaos" (Williams 1995), and "New Trading Dimensions" (Williams 1998). It calculates the difference of a 5 period ($N = 5$) and a 34 period ($N = 34$) Simple Moving Average of the price. Thus, AO is a velocity indicator. The price used to calculate the Simple Moving Averages is not closing price, but rather each bar's midpoints. Here, we will take an approximation, and perform the calculations using closing prices, as the end results would not be that much different.

The AO can be compared to the MACD (which will be discused in Chapter 6) introduced by Gerald Appel in the late 1970's. While the MACD employs Exponential Moving Averages (EMA), the AO employs Simple Moving Aveerages (SMA).

The amplitudes of the frequency response $H(\omega)$ of the Simple Moving Averages ($N = 5$ and 34) are plotted in Fig. 5.1. The phases of the frequency response $H(\omega)$ of the Simple Moving Averages ($N = 5$ and 34) are plotted in Fig. 5.2.

D. K. Mak, *Trading Tactics in the Financial Market*, Management for Professionals,
https://doi.org/10.1007/978-3-030-70622-7_5

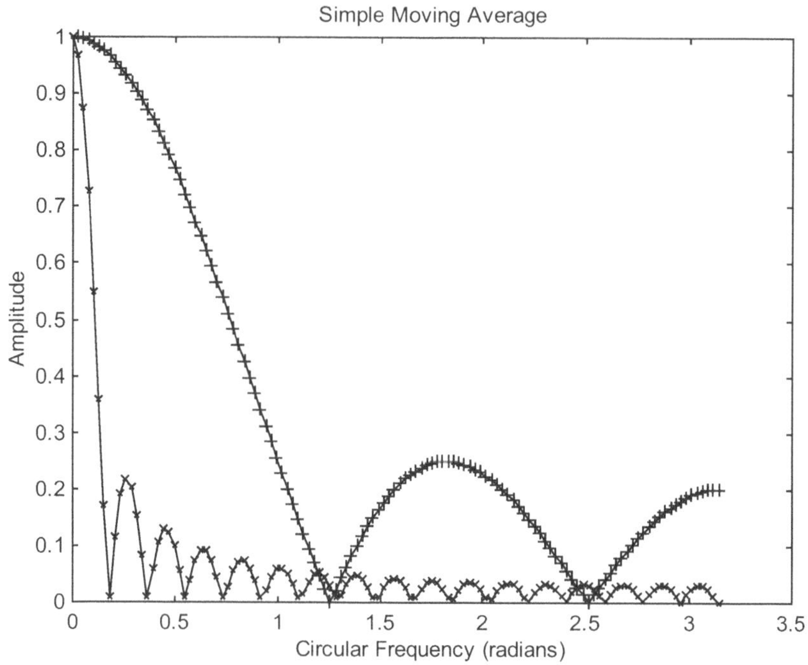

Fig. 5.1 The amplitudes of the frequency response H(ω) of the Simple Moving Averages N = 5 (+) and N = 34 (x).

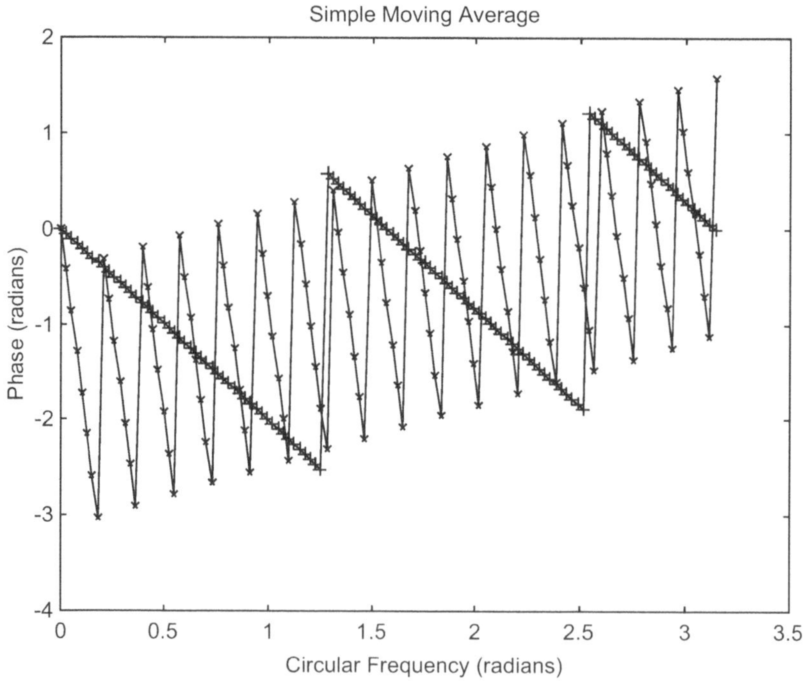

Fig. 5.2 The phases of the frequency response H(ω) of the Simple Moving Averages N = 5 (+) and N = 34 (x).

The amplitude of the frequency response H(ω) of the Awesome Oscillator is plotted in Fig. 5.3, using the program awesome. The Awesome Oscillator attains a maximum amplitude of 1.15 at $\omega = 0.13$ radians. It retains a significant portion of frequencies less than 0.5 radian. This would be useful, as the amplitudes of frequencies ω of real market data less than 0.5 radian are much larger than those of frequencies ω larger than 0.5 radian.

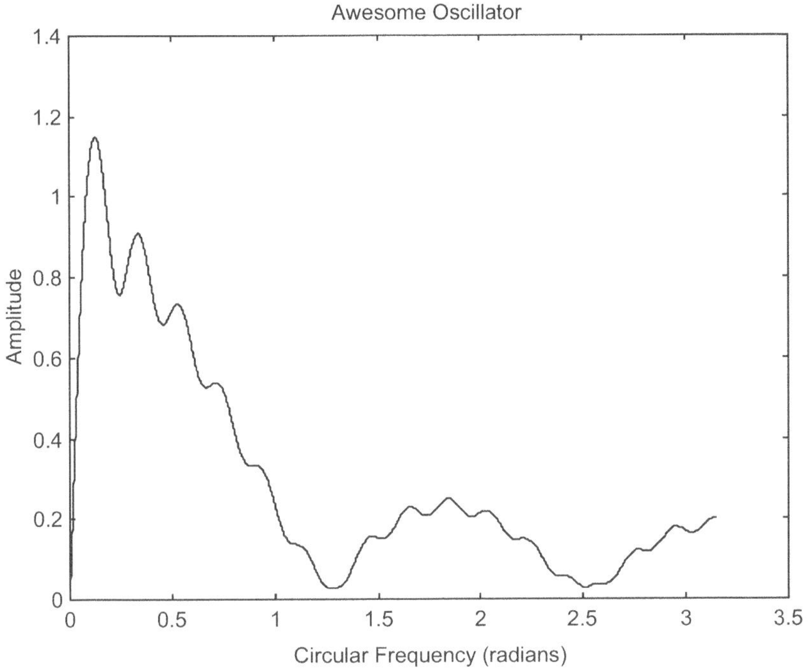

Fig. 5.3 The amplitudes of the frequency response H(ω) of the Awesome Oscillator.

The phase of the frequency response H(ω) of the Awesome Oscillator (AO) is plotted in Fig. 5.4. The phase lies between $-\pi$ and π. When the phase is constrained between $-\pi$ and π, it is called wrapped phase (see Chapter 3).

The wrapped phase of the AO lies between

$\pi/2 < \phi < 0$	for $0 \leq \omega < 0.13$ radian,
$0 < \phi < -\pi$	for $0.13 < \omega < 1.19$ radians
$\pi < \phi < 0$	for $1.19 \leq \omega < 1.62$ radian,
$0 < \phi < -\pi$	for $1.62 < \omega < 2.5$ radians
$\pi < \phi < 0$	for $2.5 \leq \omega < \pi$ radian

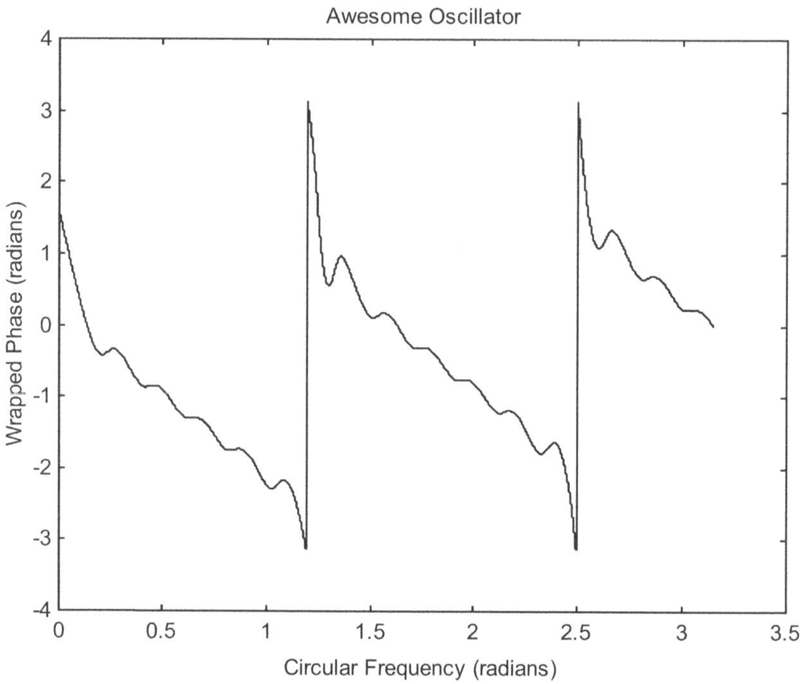

Fig. 5.4 The wrapped phase of the frequency response H(ω) of the Awesome Oscillator.

It is quite often necessary to unwrap the phase by adding appropriate multiples of 2π in order to get the correct phase delay. The unwrapped phase of the frequency response H(ω) of the Awesome Oscillator is plotted in Fig. 5.5.

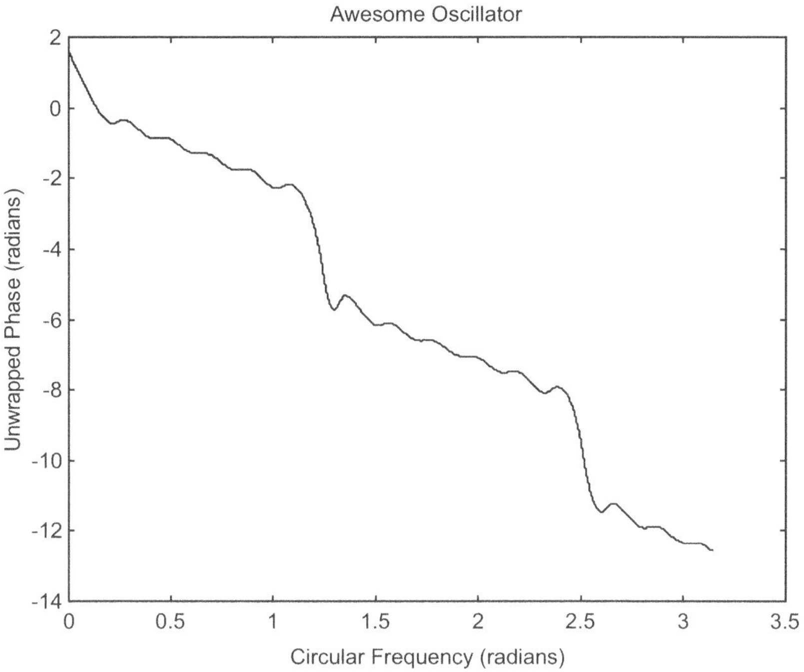

Fig. 5.5 The unwrapped phase of the frequency response H(ω) of the Awesome Oscillator.

The unwrapped phase of the AO is the same as the wrapped phase between $\omega = 0$ and 1.19 radians. The unwrapped phase is $\pi/2$ when ω approaches 0, and decreases to 0 when ω approaches 0.13 radian. If a straight line of Phase $\phi = \omega$ is plotted on Fig. 5.5, it will intersect the phase plot at $\omega \approx 0.12$ radian. The region $0 < \omega < 0.12$ is described as a Sure Profit Zone, while the region $0.12 < \omega < 0.13$ is described as the Unsure Profit Zone. $0.13 < \omega < \pi$ is described as the Loss Zone, as $\phi < 0$ and a trade will always lose money. Because of the short Profit Zone ($0 < \omega < 0.13$), and the long Loss Zone, Awesome Oscillator is definitely not a profitable indicator. Furthermore, for $\omega > 1.19$ radians, the wrapped phase is different from the unwrapped phrase, which represents the real time delay, thus causing a systematic error in the AO.

Table 5.1 lists price data simulated as sine waves with frequencies from 0.1 to 0.5 radian, at initial phase angles of 0, $\pi/2$, π and $3\pi/2$ radians. The maximum possible gain traders can make equals (the peak of the price − the valley of the price), i.e., 2 × amplitude of the sine wave (with amplitude = 1). Profit % is the percentage of the maximum profit that can be made. The table shows that the trading tactic using the Awesome Oscillator as a velocity indicator, cannot make good profit. As a matter of fact, it can lose a lot of money.

Table 5.1 Price data simulated as sine waves with frequencies from 0.1 to 0.5 radian, with initial phase angles Theta0, θ_0, of 0, $\pi/2$, π and $3\pi/2$ radians.

	Theta0 = 0 radian	Theta0 = $\pi/2$ radians	Theta0 = π radians	Theta0 = $3\pi/2$ radians	Theoretical ϕ taken from DTFT	
ω (radian)	profit (%)	profit (%)	profit (%)	profit (%)	ϕ (radians)	profit (%)
$\pi/30 \sim 0.1$	20.8	20.8	20.8	20.8	0.3099	20.8
$\pi/15 \sim 0.2$	−58.8	−50	−58.8	−50	−0.4331	−58.8, −50
$\pi/10 \sim 0.3$	−58.8	−58.8	−58.8	−58.8	−0.4593	−58.8
$\pi/8 \sim 0.4$	−92.4	−92.4	−92.4	−92.4	−0.8252	−92.4
$\pi/6 \sim 0.5$	−86.6	−86.6	−86.6	−86.6	−0.9723	−86.6

Profit % is the percentage of the maximum profit that can be made using the velocity indicator Awesome Oscillator. The computer program awesig is used to compute the profit % in columns 2–5. Theoretical profit % in column 7 is calculated from the program buysellprice, with ϕ (radians) taken from the program awesome for the corresponding ω's.

As said earlier, the phase of AO lies between $\pi/2$ and 0 only for $0 \leq \omega \leq 0.13$ radian. Thus, it will only be profitable for signals of ω less than 0.13 radian, and will not be profitable for signals of ω greater than 0.13 radian. This is reflected in Table 5.1.

5.2 Accelerator Oscillator (AC)

Accelerator Oscillator (AC) was introduced by Bill Williams (who also developed the Awesome Oscillator) in his book "Trading Chaos" (Williams 1995) to help traders gauge the change in momentum (or actually, acceleration). The AC can be compared to the MACDH (which will be discussed in Chapter 6) introduced by Thomas Aspray in 1986. While the MACDH employs Exponential Moving Averages (EMA), the AC employs Simple Moving Averages (SMA). The AC measures the difference between the Awesome Oscillator (AO) and its 5 period Simple Moving Average. We will call the 5 period Simple Moving Average of the Awesome Oscillator SMA(5) ∗ Awesome Oscillator.

Thus,

$$AC = AO - SMA(5) * AO$$

As the Awesome Oscillator is a velocity indicator, the Accelerator Oscillator is therefore an acceleration indicator. Figure 5.6 plots the amplitudes of the frequency response $H(\omega)$ of the Awesome Oscillator and the SMA(5) ∗ Awesome Oscillator. And Fig. 5.7 plots the phases of the frequency response $H(\omega)$ of the Awesome Oscillator and the SMA(5) ∗ Awesome Oscillator.

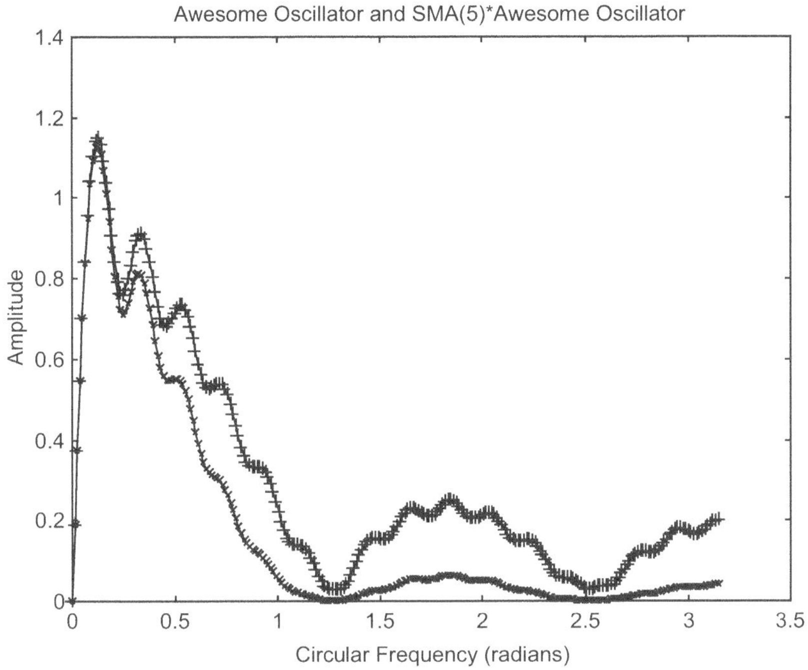

Fig. 5.6 The amplitudes of the frequency responses H(ω) of the Awesome Oscillator (+) and the SMA(5) ∗ Awesome Oscillator (x).

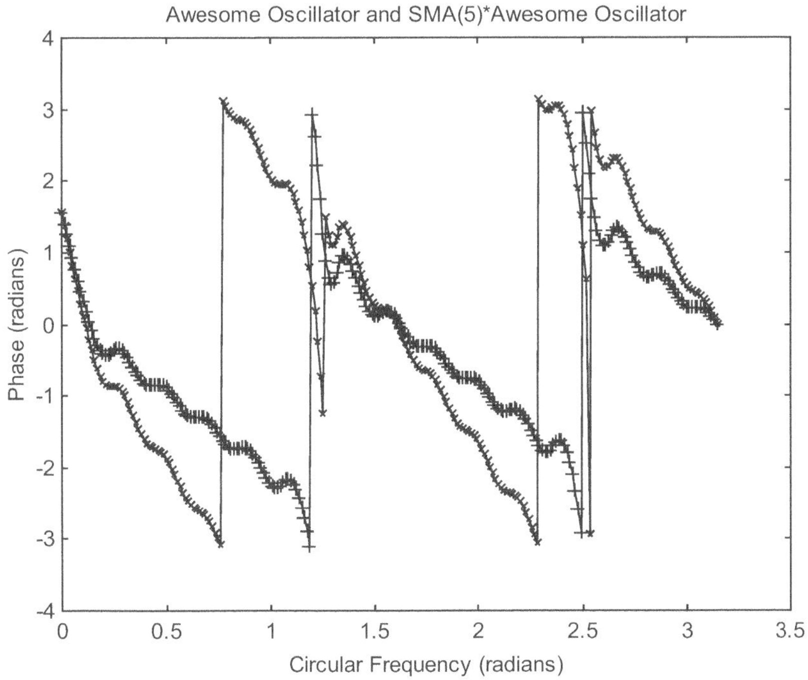

Fig. 5.7 The phases of the frequency responses H(ω) of the Awesome Oscillator (+) and the SMA(5) ∗ Awesome Oscillator (x).

Figure 5.8 plots the amplitude of the frequency response H(ω) of the Accelerator Oscillator. The Accelerator Oscillator attains a maximum amplitude of 0.67 at ω = 0.55 radians.

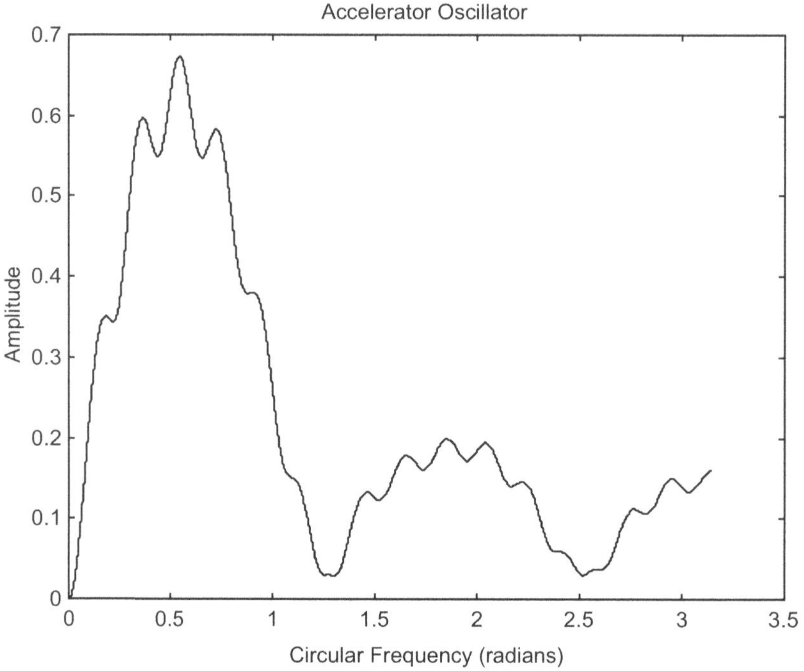

Fig. 5.8 The amplitude of the frequency response H(ω) of the Accelerator Oscillator.

Figure 5.9 plots the wrapped phase of the frequency response H(ω) of the Accelerator Oscillator. And Fig. 5.10 plots the unwrapped phases of the frequency response H(ω) of the Accelerator Oscillator. The unwrapped phase is the same as the wrapped phase between ω = 0 and 1.19 radians.

The phase of the AC equals π when ω approaches 0. This is a typical property of an acceleration indicator. The wrapped phase of the AC lies between

$\pi < \phi < 0$ for $0 \leq \omega < 0.47$
$0 < \phi < -\pi$ for $0.47 < \omega < 1.19$
$\pi < \phi < 0$ for $1.19 \leq \omega < 1.62$
$0 < \phi < -\pi$ for $1.62 < \omega < 2.5$
$\pi < \phi < 0$ for $2.5 \leq \omega < \pi$

It is equal to $\pi/2$ radian at $\omega \approx 0.14$ ($= \pi/22.4$) radian. As described earlier, $\pi/2$ radian is the most profitable phase shift for a velocity indicator. AC, even though it is an acceleration indicator, can be used as a velocity indicator. AC will be profitable for $0 \leq \omega \leq 0.47$ radians when $\pi < \phi < 0$. Its phase characteristics provides a much wider range of profitability than that of the AO, whose phase lies between $\pi/2$ and 0 only for $0 \leq \omega \leq 0.13$ radians.

If a straight line of Phase $\phi = \omega$ is plotted on Fig. 5.10, it will intersect the phase plot at $\omega \approx 0.36$. The region $0 < \omega < 0.36$ is described as a Sure Profit Zone, while the region $0.36 < \omega < 0.47$ is described as the Unsure Profit Zone. $0.47 < \omega < \pi$ is described as the Loss Zone, as $\phi < 0$ and a trade will always lose money. Accelerator Oscillator may be a profitable indicator. However, for $\omega > 1.19$ radians, the wrapped phase is different from the unwrapped phrase, which represents the real time delay, thus causing a systematic error in the AC.

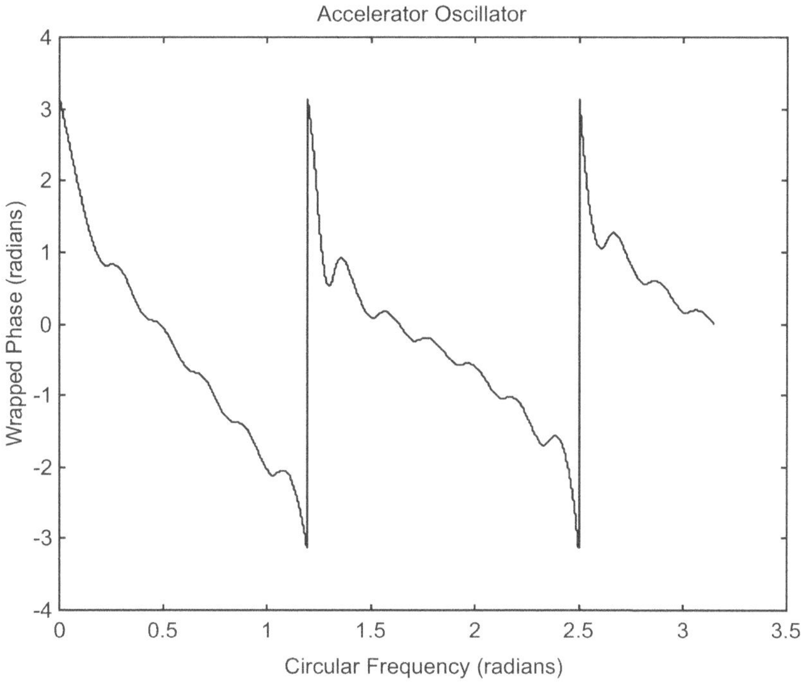

Fig. 5.9 The wrapped phase of the frequency response H(ω) of the Accelerator Oscillator.

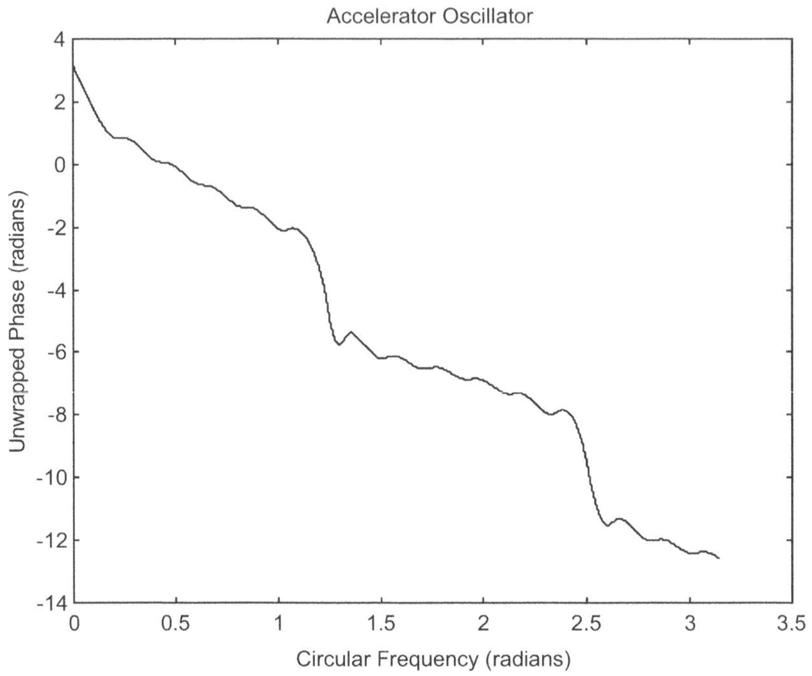

Fig. 5.10 The unwrapped phases of the frequency response H(ω) of the Accelerator Oscillator.

Table 5.2 lists price data simulated as sine waves with frequencies from 0.1 to 0.5 radian, at initial phase angles of 0, π/2, π and 3π/2 radians. The maximum possible gain traders can make equals (the peak of the price – the valley of the price), i.e., 2 × amplitude of the sine wave (with amplitude = 1). Profit % is the percentage of the maximum profit that can be made. The table shows that the trading tactic, using the Accelerator Oscillator as a velocity indicator, may make a reasonably good profit.

Table 5.2 Price data simulated as sine waves with frequencies from 0.1 to 0.5 radian, with initial phase angles Theta0, θ_0, of 0, $\pi/2$, π and $3\pi/2$ radians.

	Theta0 = 0 radian	Theta0 = $\pi/2$ radians	Theta0 = π radians	Theta0 = $3\pi/2$ radians	Theoretical ϕ taken from DTFT	
ω (radian)	profit (%)	profit (%)	profit (%)	profit (%)	ϕ (radians)	profit (%)
$\pi/30 \sim 0.1$	99.5	99.5	99.5	99.5	1.7237	99.5
$\pi/15 \sim 0.2$	58.8	66.9	58.8	66.9	0.8245	58.8, 66.9
$\pi/10 \sim 0.3$	58.8	58.8	58.8	58.8	0.6435	58.8
$\pi/8 \sim 0.4$	0	0	0	0	0.1628	0
$\pi/6 \sim 0.5$	−50.0	−50.0	−50.0	−50.0	−0.1715	−50.0

Profit % is the percentage of the maximum profit that can be made using the Accelerator Oscillator as a velocity indicator. The computer program accelsig is used to compute the profit % in columns 2–5. Theoretical profit % in column 7 is calculated from the program buysellprice, with ϕ (radians) taken from the program accelosc for the corresponding ω's.

Table 5.2 reflects what is described above. The region $0 < \omega < 0.36$ is described as a Sure Profit Zone, while the region $0.36 < \omega < 0.47$ is described as the Unsure Profit Zone. $0.47 < \omega < \pi$ is described as the Loss Zone, as $\phi < 0$ and a trade will always lose money.

The mathematical characteristics of Accelerator Oscillator (AC), and also Awesome Oscillator (AO), have never been described, and traders may not have understood their properties. AC and AO are sometimes used somewhat differently from what is described above. However, no matter how they are being employed, their inherent properties remain the same. Thus, it is important to understand how they behave at various frequencies of the signal.

Moving Average Convergence-Divergence and Its Histogram

6

The Moving Average Convergence-Divergence (MACD) and its Histogram (MACDH), which use exponential moving averages for smoothing the price data, are two indicators that have been used by traders for the last 40 years.

6.1 Moving Average Convergence-Divergence (MACD)

The Moving Average Convergence-Divergence (MACD) indicator is a popular indicator used by traders (Elder 1993, 2002; Pring 1991; Appel 1991). The indicator was developed by Gerald Appel, an analyst and money manager in New York (Elder 1993, 2002) in the late 1970s.

The MACD indicator, often called the MACD line, is composed of two exponential moving averages, a fast EMA and a slow EMA. The line is called MACD (moving average convergence-divergence) because the fast EMA is continually converging toward and diverging from the slow EMA. Fast EMA has a smaller length, M, than that of slow EMA. The slow EMA ($M_2 = 26$) is subtracted from the fast EMA ($M_1 = 12$). Their difference, i.e., MACD = fast EMA − slow EMA, is plotted.

The trading rule used is based on the crossover between the fast EMA and the slow EMA. When the fast EMA crosses above the slow EMA, i.e., MACD changes from negative to positive, a buy indication is generated. When the fast EMA crosses below the slow EMA, i.e., MACD changes from positive to negative, a sell indication is implemented.

As the MACD line is actually the difference between two exponential moving averages of the price signal, it was pointed out by Chan et al. (2014) that it is actually a velocity indicator. As said earlier, it is very beneficial to take a look at the frequency response of a velocity indicator by applying Fourier Transform. The Fourier Transform of an exponential moving average is a low pass filter. The Fourier Transform of the difference of two exponential moving averages is simply the

D. K. Mak, *Trading Tactics in the Financial Market*, Management for Professionals,
https://doi.org/10.1007/978-3-030-70622-7_6

difference in their respective Fourier Transform (Brigham 1974, p. 31). Let $H_1(\omega)$ and $H_2(\omega)$ be the Fourier Transform of the fast EMA and the slow EMA respectively. The Fourier Transform of the MACD line, $H_4(\omega)$ is simply given by:

$$H_4(\omega) = H_1(\omega) - H_2(\omega) \tag{6.1}$$

As both $H_1(\omega)$ and $H_2(\omega)$ are low pass filters, their difference, $H_4(\omega)$ can be considered to be a band-pass filter (Mak 2006), which passes frequencies within a certain range, and rejects or attenuates frequencies outside that range. It can be shown that at $\omega = 0$, the phase of $H_4(\omega) = \pi/2$ (Appendix C), i.e., MACD leads the signal by $\pi/2$, which is the characteristics of velocity as discussed earlier. This also somewhat justifies that the MACD is a velocity indicator.

The amplitude of fast EMA ($M_1 = 12$) and slow EMA ($M_2 = 26$), and MACD are plotted in Fig. 6.1. The amplitude of MACD attains a maximum of 0.37 at $\omega = 0.12$ radian.

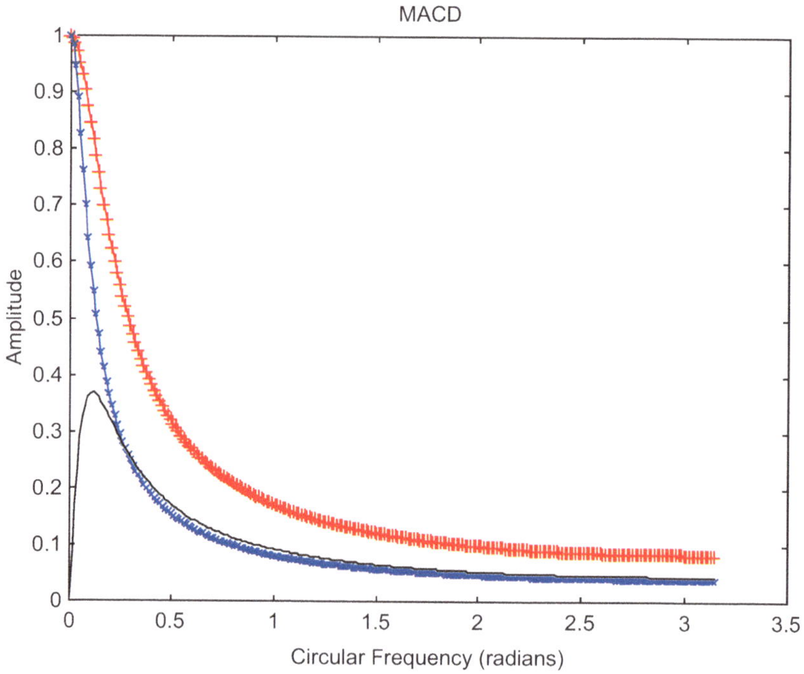

Fig. 6.1 The amplitude of fast EMA ($M_1 = 12$) (red), slow EMA ($M_2 = 26$) (blue), and MACD (black) are plotted versus circular frequency, ω.

The phase of fast EMA ($M_1 = 12$) and slow EMA ($M_2 = 26$), and MACD are plotted in Fig. 6.2.

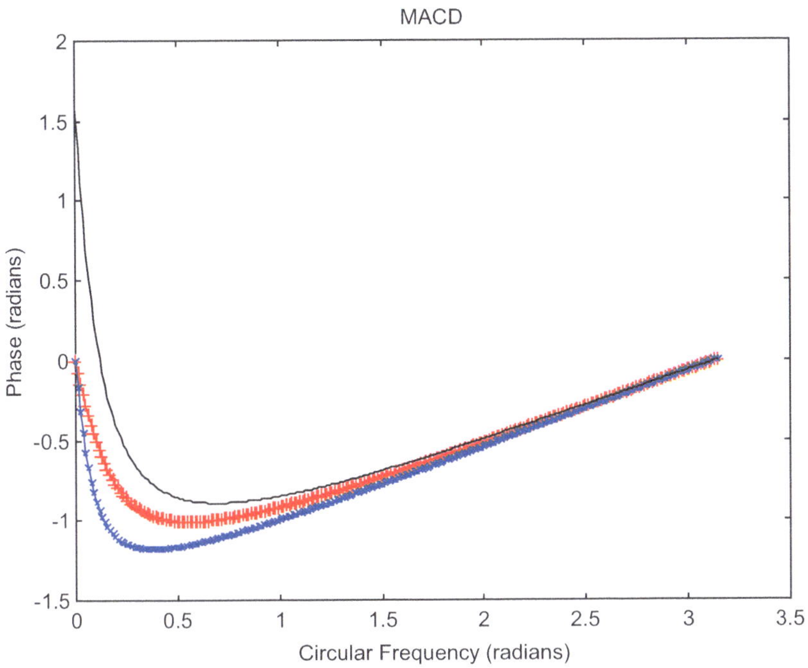

Fig. 6.2 The phase of fast EMA ($M_1 = 12$) (red), slow EMA ($M_2 = 26$) (blue), and MACD (black) are plotted versus circular frequency, ω.

The phase of MACD starts off as $\pi/2$ at $\omega = 0$. It decreases to 0 at $\omega = \pi/26.18 \approx 0.12$ radian, and further decreases to a maximum phase lag of -0.8914 ($= -\pi/3.5 > -\pi/2$) radian at $\omega = 0.6938$ radian, and then slowly increases back to 0 at $\omega = \pi$ radians. That is, the phase remains negative for $0.12 < \omega < \pi$ radians. This would mean that if a trader uses MACD as a velocity indicator, he will only make a profit when the circular frequency of the signal ω is less than 0.12 radian. $0 < \omega < 0.12$ is therefore described as the Profit Zone. He would lose money when $0.12 < \omega < \pi$ radians, which is described as the Loss Zone. If a straight line of Phase $\phi = \omega$ is plotted on Fig. 6.2, it will intersect the phase plot of MACD at $\omega \approx 0.11$. The region $0 < \omega < 0.11$ is described as a Sure Profit Zone, while the region $0.11 < \omega < 0.12$ is described as the Unsure Profit Zone. Because of the narrow Profit Zone as well as the Sure Profit Zone, one would not expect that this velocity indicator would yield a reasonably profitable indicator.

Table 6.1 lists price data simulated as sine waves with frequencies from 0.1 to 0.5 radian, at initial phase angles of 0, $\pi/2$, π and $3\pi/2$ radians. The maximum possible gain traders can make equals (the peak of the price – the valley of the price), i.e., 2 × amplitude (with amplitude = 1). Profit % is the percentage of the maximum profit that can be made. The table shows that the trading tactic employing the sign changes of the velocity indicator MACD, cannot make good profit.

Table 6.1 Price data simulated as sine waves with frequencies from 0.1 to 0.5 radian, with initial phase angles Theta0, θ_0, of 0, $\pi/2$, π and $3\pi/2$ radians.

	Theta0 = 0 radian	Theta0 = $\pi/2$ radians	Theta0 = π radians	Theta0 = $3\pi/2$ radians	Theoretical ϕ taken from DTFT	
ω (radian)	profit (%)	profit (%)	profit (%)	profit (%)	ϕ (radians)	profit (%)
$\pi/30 \sim 0.1$	10.5	10.5	10.5	10.5	0.1241	10.5
$\pi/15 \sim 0.2$	−58.8	−50.0	−58.8	−50.0	−0.4449	−58.8, −50.0
$\pi/10 \sim 0.3$	−80.9	−80.9	−80.9	−80.9	−0.6911	−80.9
$\pi/8 \sim 0.4$	−81.5	−81.5	−81.5	−81.5	−0.7867	−92.4
$\pi/6 \sim 0.5$	−86.6	−86.6	−86.6	−86.6	−0.8649	−86.6

Profit % is the percentage of the maximum profit that can be made using the velocity indicator MACD. The computer program macdsig is used to compute the profit % in columns 2–5. Theoretical profit % in column 7 is calculated from the program buysellprice, with ϕ(radians) taken from the program macd for the corresponding ω's.

At $\omega = \pi/8$ radian, the theoretical result is not equal to the computational result. This is caused by the latter using only limited past data while the former uses infinite past data. The limited past data results in the sell price not equal to −buy price, as is assumed in the theoretical calculation. In this particular case, the buy price is 0.924, while the sell price is −0.707, thus yielding a profit % of −81.5.

6.2 Moving Average Convergence-Divergence Histogram (MACDH)

MACDH was introduced by Thomas Aspray in 1986 (Penn 2010). It has received high praise from several traders, as it has been claimed to offer a deeper insight between the power of bulls and bears than the original MACD (Elder 1993; Murphy 1996). The indicator consists of two lines: the MACD line and the Signal line. The MACD line is composed of two exponential moving averages, a fast EMA and a slow EMA. Fast EMA has a smaller length, M, than that of slow EMA. The slow EMA ($M_2 = 26$) is subtracted from the fast EMA ($M_1 = 12$). Their difference is plotted. This is called the (fast) MACD line. An EMA ($M_3 = 9$) of the (fast) MACD line is calculated and plotted on the same chart. This is called the slow Signal line.

The trading rule is based on the crossover between the MACD and Signal lines. When the fast MACD line crosses above the slow Signal line, a buy indication is generated. When the fast line crosses below the slow line, a sell indication is implemented.

As has been said, the MACD-Histogram offers a better insight into the balance of power between the bulls and bears than the MACD (Elder 1993, 2002). Not only does it show whether the bulls or bears are in control, it also shows whether they are growing stronger or weaker. Now, is this claim correct? It is, in a certain sense, correct, as MACDH emulates acceleration.

First, we can take a look at how the MACD-Histogram is defined. It is defined as the difference between the MACD line and the Signal line:

$$\text{MACD} - \text{Histogram} = \text{MACD line} - \text{Signal line} \tag{6.2}$$

The MACD-Histogram is usually plotted as a histogram to distinguish it from the MACD line, but it can just as well be plotted as a line. As discussed earlier, the Signal line is the exponential moving average of the MACD line. That means, the MACD line is smoothed to form the Signal Line. As both the MACD line and Signal Line can be considered as velocity indicators, their difference, the MACD-Histogram, can be considered to be an acceleration indicator (Chan et al. 2014).

Let the Fourier Transform of the exponential moving average applied on the MACD (to form the Signal Line) be denoted by $H_3(\omega)$. Then the Fourier Transform of the Signal line will be given by $H_3(\omega)\ H_4(\omega)$. The Fourier Transform of the MACD-Histogram, $H_5(\omega)$, according to Eq. (6.2) will be given by

$$H_5(\omega) = H_4(\omega) - H_3(\omega)\ H_4(\omega) \tag{6.3a}$$

$$= (1 - H_3(\omega))H_4(\omega) \tag{6.3b}$$

As $H_3(\omega)$ is a low pass filter, and $H_4(\omega)$ is a band-pass filter, $H_3(\omega)\ H_4(\omega)$ is a band-pass filter. Eq (6.3a) would mean that $H_5(\omega)$ is a band-pass filter, which is formed from the difference between two band-pass filters. Eq (6.3a) can be rewritten in the form of Eq. (6.3b). As $(1 - H_3(\omega))$ is a high pass filter, $H_5(\omega)$ is a band-pass filter as it can also be considered as a combination between a high pass filter and a band-pass filter.

Taking the lengths of the fast EMA, slow EMA and the EMA of the MACD line to be 12, 26 and 9, the amplitudes and phases of the MACD line, Signal line and MACD-Histogram are plotted in Figs. 6.3 and 6.4. Figure 6.3 shows that the MACD-Histogram is a band-pass filter, having a peak at a frequency slightly larger than that of the MACD line (which is also a band-pass filter). It filters off more of the low frequency component of a signal than the MACD line. MACDH attains a maximum amplitude of 0.19 at $\omega = 0.22$ radians.

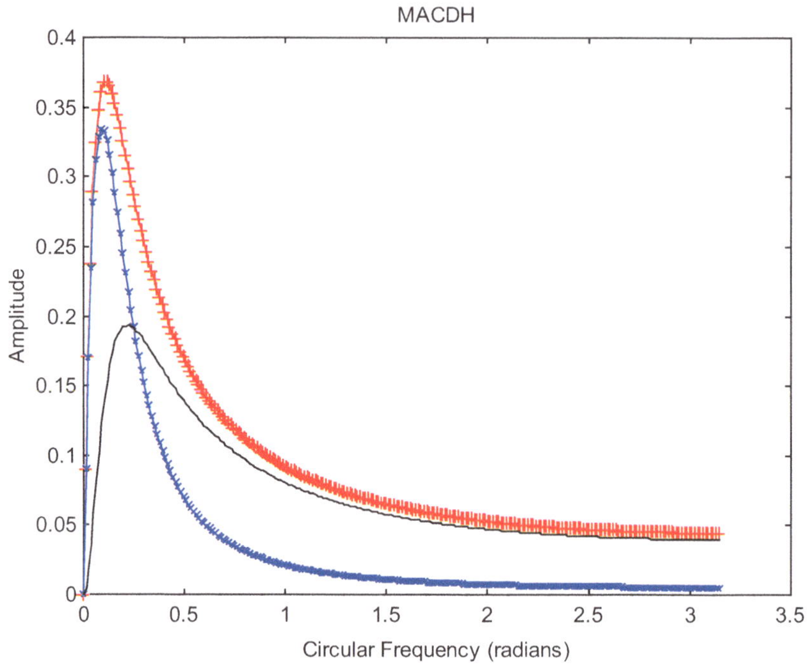

Fig. 6.3 The amplitudes of the MACD line (red), Signal line (blue) and MACD-Histogram (black). The lengths of the fast EMA, slow EMA and the EMA of the MACD line are 12, 26 and 9 (Mak 2006).

Figure 6.4 shows that MACDH has less phase lag than the MACD line. The phase of the Signal line is the sum of the phase of $H_3(\omega)$ and the phase of $H_4(\omega)$. At $\omega = 0$, since the phase of $H_3(\omega) = 0$ and the phase of $H_4(\omega) = \pi/2$, the phase of $H_3(\omega)$ $H_4(\omega) = \pi/2$. At $\omega = 0$, the amplitude of $H_5(\omega)$ is 0, which implies that the real and imaginary part of $H_5(\omega)$ is 0, and the phase is in an indeterminate form. To calculate that phase, it would be easier to use Eq. (6.3b) than Eq. (6.3a), as the phase of $H_5(\omega)$ is simply given by the sum of the phase of $(1 - H_3(\omega))$ and the phase of $H_4(\omega)$. Using again the De l'Hopital's Rule, the phase of the high pass filter, $(1 - H_3(\omega))$ at $\omega = 0$ is found to be $\pi/2$. As the phase of $H_4(\omega)$ at $\omega = 0$ is $\pi/2$, the phase of $H_5(\omega)$ is π, i.e., MACDH leads the signal by π, which is the characteristics of acceleration as discussed earlier. This somewhat justifies that MACDH is an acceleration indicator. However, MACDH is quite often used as a velocity indicator for "aggressive" trading (Chan et al. 2014).

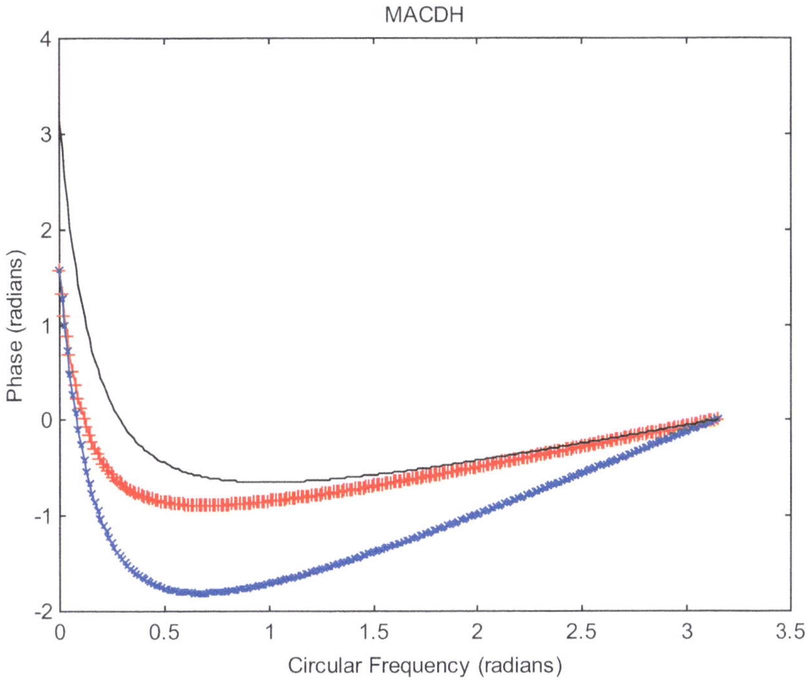

Fig. 6.4 The phases of the MACD line (red), Signal line (blue) and MACD-Histogram (black). The lengths of the fast EMA, slow EMA and the EMA of the MACD line are 12, 26 and 9 (Mak 2006).

The phase of MACDH starts off as π at $\omega = 0$. It decreases to $\pi/2$ radian at $\omega = 0.0809$ radian ($=\pi/38.8$), and then to 0 at $\omega = 0.29$ radian, and further decreases to a maximum phase lag of -0.6485 ($= -\pi/4.8 > -\pi/2$) radians at $\omega = 0.9948$ radian, and then slowly increases to 0 at $\omega = \pi$ radians. That is, the phase remains negative for $0.29 < \omega < \pi$ radians. This would mean that if a trader uses MACDH as a velocity indicator, he will only make a profit when the circular frequency of the signal ω is less than 0.29 radian and would lose money when $0.29 < \omega < \pi$ radians. Thus, the Profit Zone for MACDH is $0 < \omega < 0.29$ radian. And the Loss Zone is $0.29 < \omega < \pi$ radians.

If a straight line of Phase $\phi = \omega$ is plotted on Fig. 6.4, it will intersect the phase plot of MACDH at $\omega \approx 0.24$. The region $0 < \omega < 0.24$ is described as the Sure Profit Zone, while the region $0.24 < \omega < 0.29$ is described as the Unsure Profit Zone. Because of the narrow Profit Zone and Sure Profit Zone, one would not expect that this velocity indicator would yield a reasonably profitable indicator. However, as we will see later in Chapter 7, MACDH does make a very profitable velocity indicator. This is because, unlike other velocity indicators, which are mostly high pass filters, it is a band-pass filter, filtering off the high frequency signals, and eliminating all the whipsaws that will sell off a trade. Thus, it will be a very useful velocity indicator for traders when the market is in general trending with only some moments of volatility.

Table 6.2 lists price data simulated as sine waves with frequencies from 0.1 to 0.5 radian, at initial phase angles of 0, π/2, π and 3π/2 radians. The maximum possible gain traders can make equals (the peak of the price − the valley of the price), i.e., 2 × amplitude (with amplitude = 1). Profit % is the percentage of the maximum profit that can be made. The table shows that the trading tactic employing the acceleration indicator MACDH as a velocity indicator, may not make good profit.

Table 6.2 Price data simulated as sine waves with frequencies from 0.1 to 0.5 radian, with initial phase angles Theta0, θ_0, of 0, π/2, π and 3π/2 radians.

ω (radian)	Theta0 = 0 radian profit (%)	Theta0 = π/2 radians profit (%)	Theta0 = π radians profit (%)	Theta0 = 3π/2 radians profit (%)	Theoretical ϕ taken from DTFT ϕ (radians)	profit (%)
π/30 ~ 0.1	91.4	91.4	91.4	91.4	1.2541	91.4
π/15 ~ 0.2	20.8	30.9	20.8	30.9	0.3683	20.8, 30.9
π/10 ~ 0.3	−30.9	−30.9	−30.9	−30.9	−0.0794	−30.9
π/8 ~ 0.4	−38.3	−38.3	−38.3	−38.3	−0.2773	−38.3
π/6 ~ 0.5	−50.0	−68.3	−50.0	−68.3	−0.4718	−50.0

Profit % is the percentage of the maximum profit that can be made using MACDH as a velocity indicator. The computer program macdhsig is used to compute the profit % in columns 2–5. Theoretical profit % in column 7 is calculated from the program buysellprice, with ϕ(radians) taken from the program macdh for the corresponding ω's

At ω = π/6 radian, the theoretical result is not equal to the computational result when θ_0 = π/2 and 3π/2 radians. This is caused by the latter using only limited past data while the former uses infinite past data. The limited past data results in the sell price not equal to −buy price, as is assumed in the theoretical calculation.

6.3 MACDH1, MACDH with Price Replacing the Fast EMA

A trading tactic not uncommon with traders is buy when the market price rises above an EMA, and sell when the price crosses below the EMA. Price minus EMA can be considered to be a velocity indicator. Price minus EMA has an advantage that its phase is always greater than 0, i.e, 0 < ω < π radians is the Profit Zone (see Chapter 4). As we will show later in Chapter 7 that MACDH would be a reasonably profitable velocity indicator, we would like to see whether we can improve it to make it more profitable. We will replace the fast EMA in MACD with price (i.e., $M_1 = 1$), and leaving $M_2 = 26$, and $M_3 = 9$. Figures 6.5 and 6.6 plot the amplitudes and phases of the MACD1 line, Signal line and MACDH1 respectively. From the amplitudes, one can see that the MACD1 and MACDH1 are high pass filters, allowing high frequency signals to go through. However, the advantages gained are that the phase of MACD1 lies between $\pi/2$ and 0 and the phase of MACDH1 lies between π and 0 for $0 < \omega < \pi$ radians. Thus, MACDH1 will be profitable no matter what frequencies the price signal consists of. $0 < \omega < \pi$ will be the Profit Zone for MACDH1.

A straight line of Phase $\phi = \omega$ can be plotted on Fig. 6.6. The intersection point of the straight line plot with the phase plot of MACDH1 is approximately $\omega = 0.53$. We can describe $0 < \omega < 0.53$ as a Sure Profit Zone, and $0.53 < \omega < \pi$ as an Unsure Profit Zone.

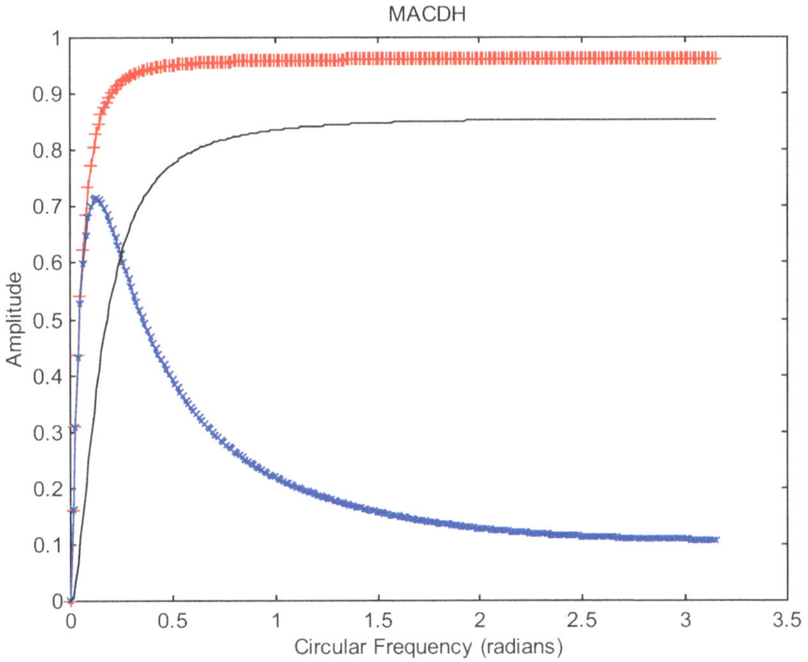

Fig. 6.5 The amplitudes of the MACD1 line (red), Signal line (blue) and MACDH1 (black). The lengths of the fast EMA, slow EMA and the EMA of the MACD1 line are 1, 26 and 9.

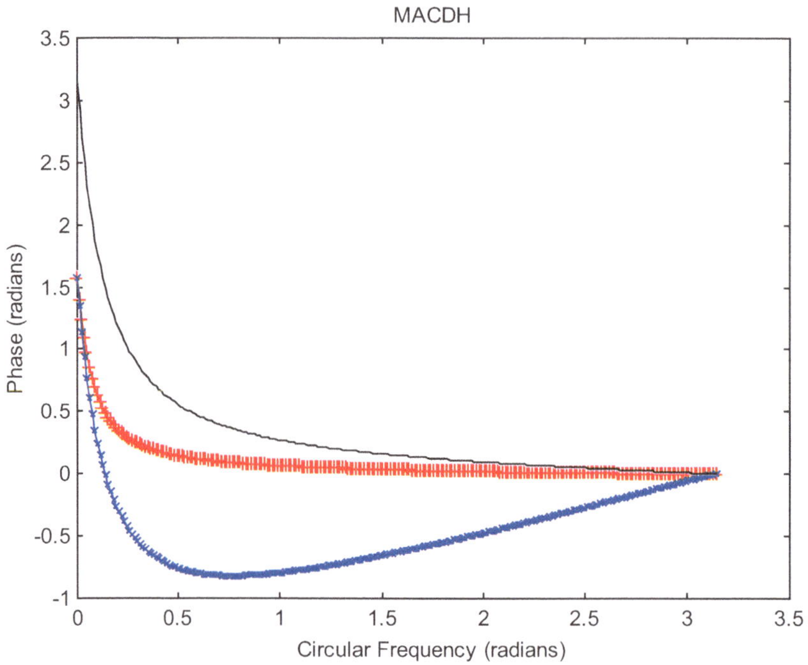

Fig. 6.6 The phases of the MACD1 line (red), Signal line (blue) and MACDH1 (black). The lengths of the fast EMA, slow EMA and the EMA of the MACD1 line are 1, 26 and 9.

Table 6.3 lists price data simulated as sine waves with frequencies from 0.1 to 0.5 radian, at initial phase angles of 0, $\pi/2$, π and $3\pi/2$ radians. The maximum possible gain traders can make equals (the peak of the price − the valley of the price), i.e., $2 \times$ amplitude (with amplitude = 1). Profit % is the percentage of the maximum profit that can be made. The table shows that the trading tactic employing the acceleration indicator MACDH1 as a velocity indicator, may make good profit.

Table 6.3 Price data simulated as sine waves with frequencies from 0.1 to 0.5 radian, with initial phase angles Theta0, θ_0, of 0, $\pi/2$, π and $3\pi/2$ radians.

	Theta0 = 0 radian	Theta0 = $\pi/2$ radians	Theta0 = π radians	Theta0 = $3\pi/2$ radians	Theoretical ϕ taken from DTFT	
ω (radian)	profit (%)	profit (%)	profit (%)	profit (%)	ϕ (radians)	profit (%)
$\pi/30 \sim 0.1$	99.5	99.5	99.5	99.5	1.7632	99.5
$\pi/15 \sim 0.2$	86.6	91.4	86.6	91.4	1.1640	86.6, 91.4
$\pi/10 \sim 0.3$	58.8	58.8	58.8	58.8	0.8500	58.8
$\pi/8 \sim 0.4$	38.3	38.3	38.3	38.3	0.7004	38.3
$\pi/6 \sim 0.5$	50.0	25.0	50.0	25.0	0.5357	50.0

Profit % is the percentage of the maximum profit that can be made using MACDH1 as a velocity indicator. The computer program macdh1sig is used to compute the profit % in columns 2–5. Theoretical profit % in column 7 is calculated from the program buysellprice, with ϕ(radians) taken from the program macdh1 for the corresponding ω's.

At $\omega = \pi/6$ radian, the computational result is not equal to the theoretical result when $\theta_0 = \pi/2$ and $3\pi/2$ radians. This is caused by the former using only limited past data while the latter uses infinite past data. The limited past data results in the sell price not equal to −buy price, as is assumed in the theoretical calculation.

The mathematical characteristics of MACD and MACDH are seldom mentioned, and traders may not have understood their properties. MACD and MACDH are sometimes used somewhat differently from what is described above (Elder 1993, 2002; Pring 1991; Mak 2003, 2006). However, no matter how they are being employed, their inherent properties remain the same. Thus, it is important to understand how they behave at various frequencies of the signal.

Trading Tactics in the Real Market 7

Many trading rules have already been developed by traders. However, many of them are velocity related without their realizing them. Some of the most common trading rules are;

1. Fast Simple Moving Average (SMA) crossover of a slow SMA (Pring 1991)
   N is the length of the SMA. An N-bar SMA is calculated by adding the prices over the last N bars and dividing by N. A fast SMA would have a smaller N than that of a slow SMA, which would be smoother. The trader will buy when a fast SMA crosses over and is higher than a slow SMA. He will sell when the former crosses over and is lower than the latter.

   As pointed out by Chan et al. (2014), (Fast SMA − Slow SMA) can be considered to be a velocity indicator. When velocity is greater than 0, the trader can buy. When velocity is less than 0, the trader can sell.

2. Price crossover of an SMA
   Price can be considered as an SMA with N = 1, and thus this rule can be considered as a particular case of Rule (1).

3. Fast Exponential Moving Average(EMA) crossover of a slow EMA
   M is the length of the EMA. A fast EMA would have a smaller M than that of a slow EMA, which would be smoother. The trader will buy when a fast EMA crosses over and is higher than a slow EMA. He will sell when the former crosses over and is lower than the latter.

   Again, as pointed out by Chan et al. (2014), (Fast EMA − Slow EMA) can be considered to be a velocity indicator. When velocity is greater than 0, the trader can buy. When velocity is less than 0, the trader can sell.

4. Price crossover of an EMA
   Price can be considered as an EMA with M = 1, and thus this rule can be considered as a particular case of Rule (3).

D. K. Mak, *Trading Tactics in the Financial Market*, Management for Professionals,
https://doi.org/10.1007/978-3-030-70622-7_7

5. Awesome Oscillator(AO)
   This is a particular case of Rule (1), with the length of the fast SMA being 5 and that of the slow SMA being 34.

6. Moving Average Convergence Divergence (MACD)
   This is a particular case of Rule (3), with the length of the fast EMA being 12 and that of the slow EMA being 26.

7. Accelerator Oscillator (AC)
   AC is defined as the subtraction of the 5 period SMA of AO from an AO. It is thus an acceleration indicator, but has been used as a velocity indicator. When AC is greater than 0, the trader can buy. When AC is less than 0, the trader can sell.

8. Moving Average Convergence Divergence Histogram (MACDH)
   This is actually an MACD crossover of a smoothed MACD. It is defined as the subtraction of a smoothed (EMA, $M = 9$) MACD from an MACD, and is thus an acceleration indicator. However, it is not uncommonly used as a velocity indicator by aggressive traders (Chan et al. 2014). When MACDH is greater than 0, the trader can buy. When MACDH is less than 0, the trader can sell.

9. EMA3 – EMA6
   This is similar to MACD, but with $M_1 = 3$, and $M_2 = 6$. The idea is to see whether there can be any increase in profitability from that of MACD, which we will show later, is not a very profitable velocity indicator.

10. EMAACCEL
    This is similar to MACDH, but with $M_1 = 3$, $M_2 = 6$, and $M_3 = 9$. The idea is to see whether profitability can be improved from that of MACDH, which we will show later, is a very profitable indicator.

11. Moving Average Convergence Divergence Histogram1 (MACDH1)
    This is actually an MACD1 crossover of a smoothed MACD1, where the original Fast EMA is replaced with market price. The Fast EMA is replaced with the market price, so that the phase characteristics can be improved over the original MACDH. Again, this is an acceleration indicator, but can be used as a velocity indicator. When MACDH1 is greater than 0, the trader can buy. When MACDH1 is less than 0, the trader can sell.

The trading rule for all the above indicators is: when velocity (or acceleration) changes from negative to positive, traders will buy, and when velocity (or acceleration) changes from positive to negative, traders will sell. The above indicators, when used as velocity indicators, can be divided into Profit Zone and Loss Zone. The Profit Zone can further be divided into Sure Profit Zone and Unsure Profit Zone. We will summarize the characteristics of the indicators listed above in Table 7.1.

Table 7.1 Mathematical characteristics of various velocity indicators.

Velocity indicator	Phase at $\omega = 0$ radians	Profit zone ω, radian: Sure profit zone ω, radian	Profit zone ω, radian: Unsure profit zone ω, radian	Loss zone, ω, radian	Filter
Price – SMA10[a]	$\pi/2$	$0 \leq \omega < 0.40$	$0.40 \leq \omega \leq \pi$		High Pass
Price – SMA20[a]	$\pi/2$	$0 \leq \omega < 0.23$	$0.23 \leq \omega \leq \pi$		High Pass
Awesome Oscillator	$\pi/2$	$0 \leq \omega < 0.12$	$0.12 \leq \omega \leq 0.13$	$0.13 < \omega < \pi$	High Pass
Accelerator Oscillator	π	$0 \leq \omega < 0.36$	$0.36 \leq \omega \leq 0.47$	$0.47 < \omega < \pi$	High Pass
Price – EMA3	$\pi/2$	$0 \leq \omega < 0.72$	$0.72 < \omega < \pi$		High Pass
Price – EMA6	$\pi/2$	$0 \leq \omega < 0.54$	$0.54 < \omega < \pi$		High Pass
EMA3 – EMA6	$\pi/2$	$0 \leq \omega < 0.38$	$0.38 < \omega < 0.64$	$0.64 < \omega < \pi$	High Pass
EMAACCEL	π	$0 \leq \omega < 0.53$	$0.53 < \omega < 0.96$	$0.96 < \omega < \pi$	High Pass
MACD	$\pi/2$	$0 \leq \omega < 0.11$	$0.11 < \omega < 0.12$	$0.12 < \omega < \pi$	Band Pass
MACDH	π	$0 \leq \omega < 0.24$	$0.24 < \omega < 0.29$	$0.29 < \omega < \pi$	Band Pass
MACDH1	π	$0 \leq \omega < 0.53$	$0.53 < \omega < \pi$		High Pass

[a]The Profit Zones for Price – SMA10 and Price – SMA20 are only approximations, as the former can be negative up to –0.018 radian for $0.63 < \omega < \pi$, and the latter can be negative up to –0.023 radian for $0.31 < \omega < \pi$. As the negative numbers are small, and approximately equal to 0, it can be considered a good approximation that the two indicators do not have a Loss Zone.

We can attempt to draw certain conjectures from Table 7.1.

1. For the velocity indicators, the phase at $\omega = 0$ equals to $\pi/2$. For the acceleration indicators, the phase at $\omega = 0$ equals to π. As amplitudes of frequencies of real market signals less than 0.5 radians usually are much larger than those of frequencies greater than 0.5 radian (as we will show later), and $\pi/2$ being the

optimal phase shift for velocity indicators, using acceleration indicators as velocity indicators does having certain advantages, as there is a higher chance that the filtered price signal has a phase shift closer to $\pi/2$.
2. The larger the Profit Zone, and the less the Loss Zone, the more profitable the trading tactic should be. Thus, it would be best if the Profit Zone covers the range of circular frequency $0 \leq \omega \leq \pi$.
3. The larger the Sure Profit Zone, the more profitable the trading tactic should be.

Thus, by looking at Table 7.1, we can probably conclude that Price − EMA3, and Price − EMA6 are profitable trading tactics, as they have the two largest Sure Profit Zones among all the indicators. By contrast, Awesome Oscillator and MACD are not very profitable trading tactics as they have the two least Sure Profit Zones. As we will see later in the real market data analysis, these seem to be correct.

One surprising result, which we will soon see, is MACDH. It is an acceleration indicator but used as a velocity indicator only by some aggressive traders, who may not have realized its potentials. MACDH does not look like a profitable trading tactic, as its Sure Profit Zone is $0 \leq \omega < 0.24$, which is not very wide. However, it is a band pass filter, filtering off most of the high frequency signals, and thus avoiding the positions to be closed by whipsaws. It is particularly profitable when the market is in general trending, and it involves less trade executions.

Real market data would have a spectrum of many frequencies. If we employ an indicator as a velocity indicator, we would prefer it to have a large Sure Profit Zone, but preferably be able to eliminate the noisy high frequency signals that will terminate a trade. That way, the velocity indicator would have a higher probability of catching profits.

Let us take a look at how some of these trading tactics apply to real market data. The market price data are taken from Yahoo Finance. All trading tactics described in Table 7.1 are applied to the following markets. Only some examples will be shown.

7.1 S & P 500 Index

The S & P 500 index data are taken from April 24, 2019 to August 12, 2019 ($n = 0$ to $n = 76$, i.e., 77 data points)). Profit % for each trading tactic can be computed using the program tradesp500, by choosing different 'tactic' parameter in the program. Some of the examples are shown below.

7.1.1 MACDH

The top figure of Fig. 7.1 shows the S&P500 index. The middle figure shows the data being filtered by MACDH. In the bottom figure, x shows when the index is bought, and + shows when it is sold. The vertical position of + also shows the total profit of all the trades, while the vertical position of the green circle shows the profit of each trade. As it happened, only one trade is executed, making a profit of 152 points. As the minimum index is 2744, and the maximum index is 3026, the profit % is 152/(3026 − 2744) × 100% = 54%.

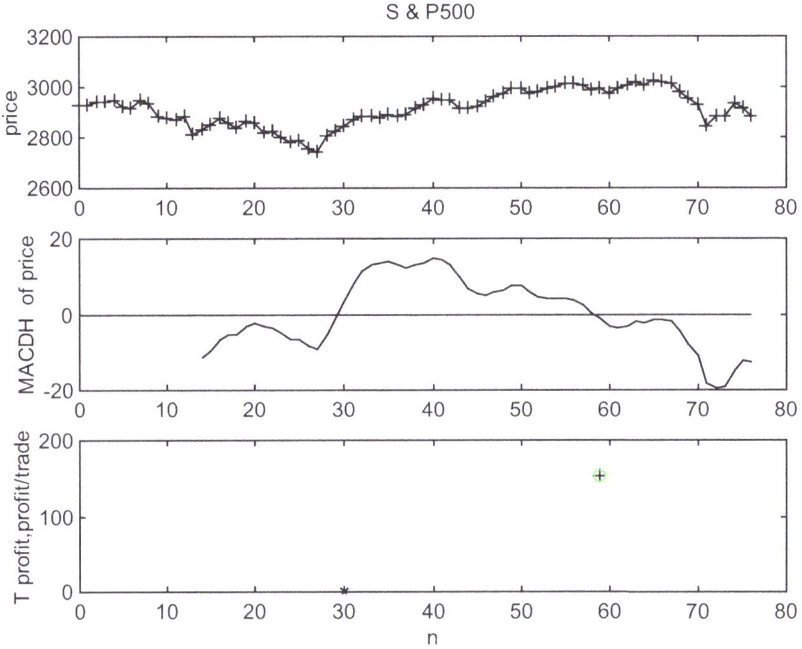

Fig. 7.1 The top figure shows the S&P500 index. The middle figure shows the data being filtered by MACDH. In the bottom figure, x shows when the index is bought, and + shows when it is sold. The vertical position of + also shows the total profit of all the trades, while the vertical position of the green circle shows the profit of each trade.

7.1.2 MACD

Had MACD been used on the same S&P500 data, the result would have been disastrous. The top figure of Fig. 7.2 shows the S&P500 index. The middle figure shows the data being filtered by MACD. In the bottom figure, x shows when the index is bought, and + shows when it is sold. The vertical position of + also shows the total profit of all the trades, while the vertical position of the green circle shows the profit of each trade. Only one trade is executed, with a loss of 15% of the (maximum index − minimum index). MACD is a band pass filter, filtering off the high frequencies. However, unlike MACDH, it has a much larger phase lag (equivalent to much less phase lead) for lower frequencies (see Fig. 6.4), thus contributing to a loss. A buy indication is triggered at nbuy = 36, and a sell indication at nsell = 71. This can be compared to nbuy = 30 and nsell = 59 for MACDH. Thus, for MACD, both buy and sell indications are delayed, causing a lost.

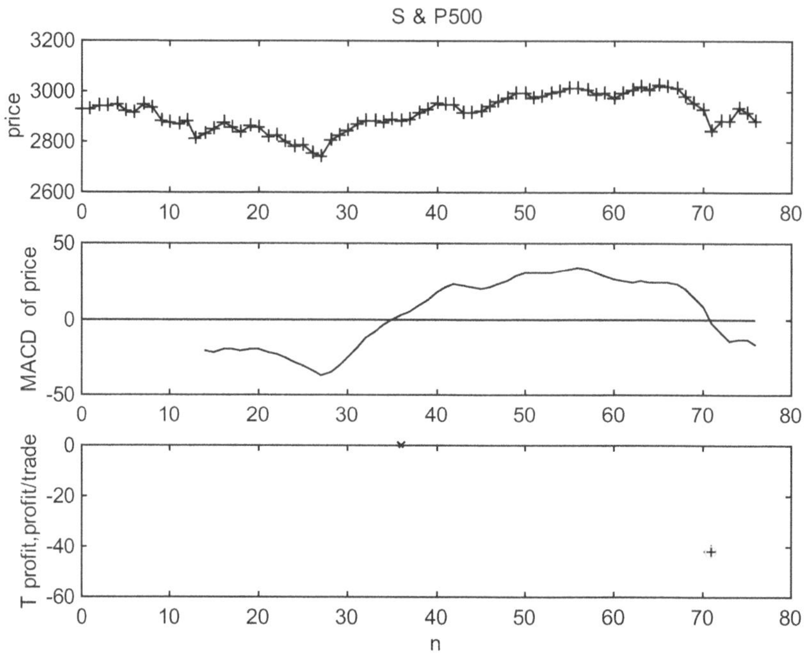

Fig. 7.2 The top figure shows the S&P500 index. The middle figure shows the data being filtered by MACD. In the bottom figure, x shows when the index is bought, and + shows when it is sold. The vertical position of + also shows the total profit of all the trades, while the vertical position of the green circle shows the profit of each trade.

7.1.3 Price − EMA3

Both MACDH and MACD are band pass filters, and they eliminate most of the high frequencies, thus producing a very smooth filtered data. However, Price − EMA3 is a high pass filter, and it retains all the high frequencies. The advantage of a high pass filter is that it can respond to fast changes. The disadvantage is that it will involve a large number of trades.

The top figure of Fig. 7.3 shows the S&P500 index. The middle figure shows the data being filtered by Price − EMA3. In the bottom figure, x shows when the index is bought, and + shows when it is sold. The vertical position of + also shows the total profit of all the trades, while the vertical position of the green circle shows the profit of each trade. Thus, the vertical position of the first x is 0. Subsequent position of the x is equal to the vertical position of the previous +. High frequency trades can be seen when the + is located close to the x. Some of the high frequency trades are profitable, and some are not. This would have been expected from Table 7.1, as the high frequencies are in the Unsure Profit Zone, where a trade can make a profit or a loss. Eight trades are executed, making a total profit of 42%.

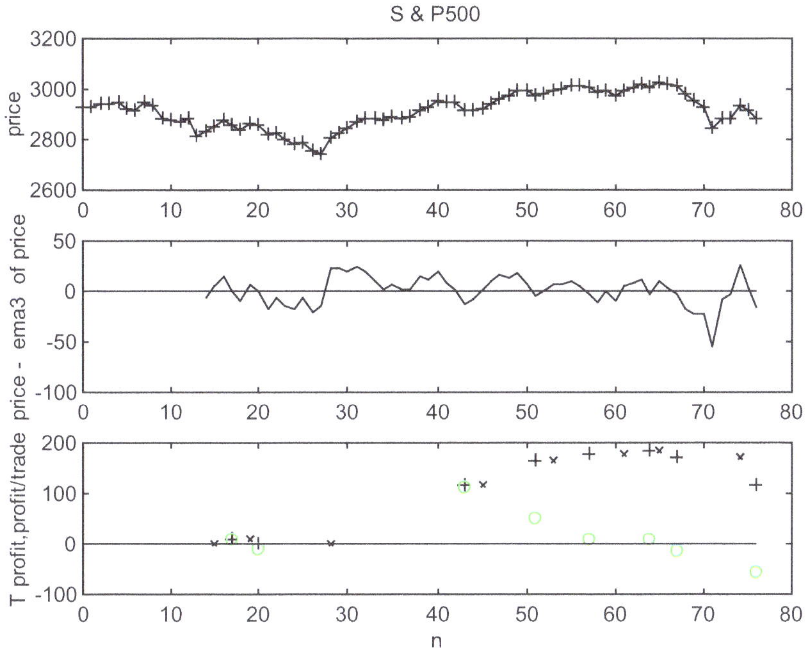

Fig. 7.3 The top figure shows the S&P500 index. The middle figure shows the data being filtered by Price – EMA3. In the bottom figure, x shows when the index is bought, and + shows when it is sold. The vertical position of + also shows the total profit of all the trades, while the vertical position of the green circle shows the profit of each trade.

7.1.4 Fast Fourier Transform and Inverse Fast Fourier Transform of S&P500 Index

As the phase lags of the indicators would depend on the frequency contents of the past data, we definitely would be interested to find out the frequency spectrum of the data. The circular frequencies of the S&P500 data can be calculated using the subroutine fft (Fast Fourier Transform) in the MATLAB program. Its magnitude is plotted in Fig. 7.4. The first point, corresponding to $\omega = 0$, is not plotted as it represents a constant in the signal, and its magnitude is much larger than those of the rest of the frequencies. As mentioned in Chapter 2, this constant does not affect the calculation of the velocity and acceleration indicators. The magnitude of the fft is mirrored at the center of the plot as the data is real and not complex. The interval of the circular frequency is calculated as $2\pi/77 = 0.0816$ radian, as there are 77 data points. It can be seen from Fig. 7.4 that frequencies of signals of larger amplitudes are less than $10 \times 0.0816 \approx 0.8$ radians. However, higher frequencies do exist, and can generate whipsaws, which usually result in trading losses.

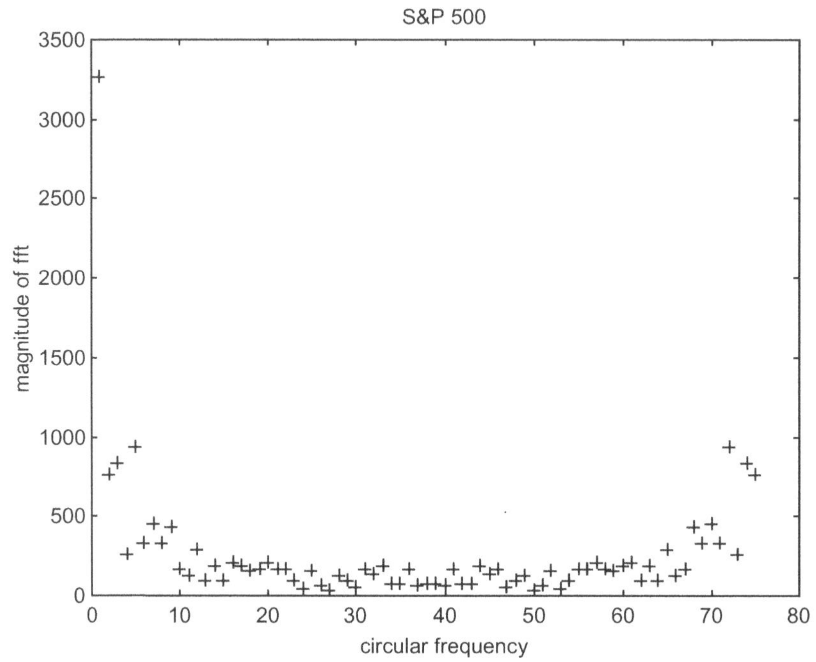

Fig. 7.4 Magnitude of the circular frequencies ω of the S&P500 index calculated from Fast Fourier Transform (fft). The first point, corresponding to circular frequency $\omega = 0$, is not plotted as it represents a constant in the signal, and its magnitude is much larger than those of the rest of the frequencies. The magnitude of the fft is mirrored at the center of the plot. This figure can be plotted using the program fftsp500, which is listed in Appendix D.

It should be pointed out that, to accurately reproduce a signal, the Nyquist (sampling) theorem (Brigham 1974; Broesch 1997) states that the signal has to be sampled at a rate greater than twice the frequency of the highest frequency component existing in the signal, i.e., the number of sampling points per cycle has to be more than two for the highest frequency. This is equivalent to saying that the sampling circular frequency for the highest frequency has to be smaller than π radians, or the highest frequency detected in the Fast Fourier Transform is π radians.

Using the subroutine ifft (Inverse Fast Fourier Transform) in the MATLAB program on the fft data, we can retrieve the fft data back to the original S&P500 index. Figure 7.5 plots the original S&P500 index as a line, and the magnitude of ifft of fft as red +'s. The latter is exactly the same as the former. The magnitude of ifft is the same as the real of ifft, as the S&P500 data are real numbers. The phase of the ifft are 0's.

A program called fftsinewave is listed in Appendix D. The program calculates the Fast Fourier Transform of a pure sine wave of a certain frequency. The program would allow the readers to change the frequency, amplitude, phase shift, number of data points of the sine wave, or even combination of sine waves, and check the accuracy of the frequencies calculated from the Fast Fourier Transform. The program also computes the ifft of the fft of the sine wave, which would be exactly the same as the sine wave.

The readers can also write programs to find the fft of the real market signal after filtering by a technical indicator, as to gain further understanding what has been done to the signal by the indicator. If high frequency signals still remain after filtering, a trade can easily be terminated, as one would expect from the middle figure of Fig. 7.3 (compare with the middle figure of Fig. 7.2).

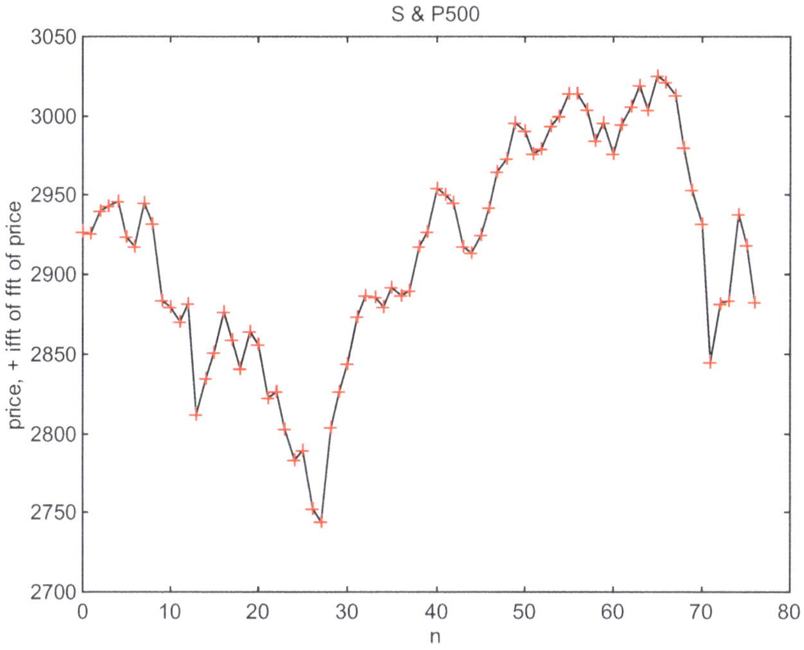

Fig. 7.5 The original S&P500 index is plotted s a line, and the magnitude of ifft of fft is plotted as red +'s. The figure can be plotted using the program fftsp500, which is listed in Appendix D.

7.2 Hang Seng Index

The Hang Seng index data are taken from March 1, 2019 to August 12, 2019 (n = 0 to n = 107, i.e. 108 data points). Profit % for each trading tactic can be computed using the program tradehangseng, by choosing different 'tactic' parameter in the program. Some of the examples are shown below.

7.2.1 Price − SMA10

The top figure of Fig. 7.6 shows the Hang Seng index. The middle figure shows the data being filtered by Price − SMA10. In the bottom figure, x shows when the index is bought, and + shows when it is sold. The vertical position of + also shows the total profit of all the trades, while the vertical position of the green circle shows the profit of each trade. High frequency trades can be seen when + is close to x. Seven trades are executed. The two low frequency trades are profitable, while the five high frequency trades are not. This would have been expected from Table 7.1, as the Unsure Profit Zone is $0.40 \leq \omega \leq \pi$, where a trade can make a profit or a loss. The total profit made is 664 points. As the minimum index is 25,824, and the maximum is 30,157, the profit % is 664 × (30,157 − 25,824) × 100% = 15%.

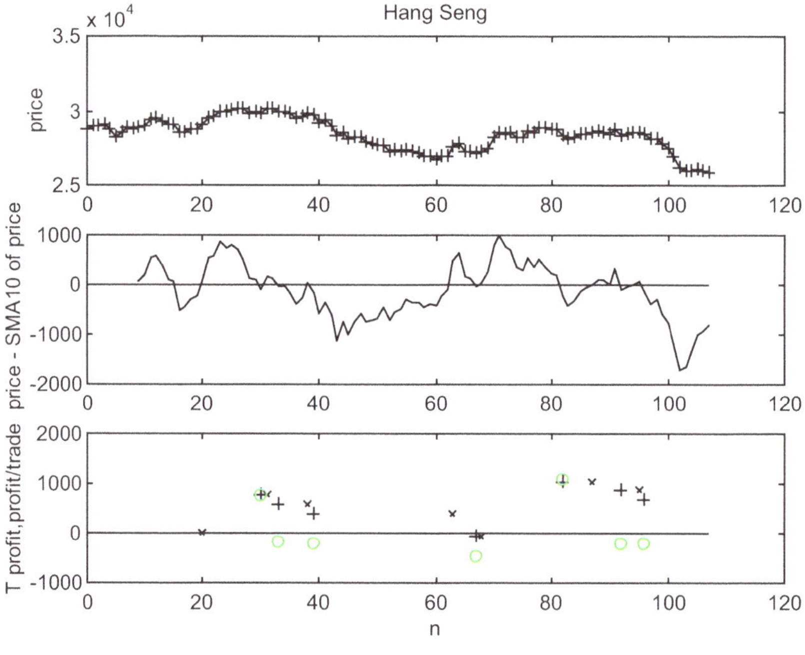

Fig. 7.6 The top figure shows the Hang Seng index. The middle figure shows the data being filtered by Price − SMA10. In the bottom figure, x shows when the index is bought, and + shows when it is sold. The vertical position of + also shows the total profit of all the trades, while the vertical position of the green circle shows the profit of each trade.

7.2.2 Awesome Oscillator

The top figure of Fig. 7.7 shows the Hang Seng index. The middle figure shows the data being filtered by Awesome Oscillator. In the bottom figure, x shows when the index is bought, and + shows when it is sold. The vertical position of + also shows the total profit of all the trades, while the vertical position of the green circle shows the profit of each trade. Only one trade is executed, making a total loss of 16%. We can compare the amplitudes of the frequency response H(ω) of the Awesome Oscillator in Fig. 5.3 with that of the (1 − SMA10) in Fig. 3.19. It can be seen that the latter can pick up high frequencies and the former is much more reserved in doing so. This is actually an advantage of the former as most high frequency trades are losers. Thus, only one low frequency trade is executed. However, the former has a much larger phase lag than the latter when low frequencies are picked up, contributing to a loss instead of a profit.

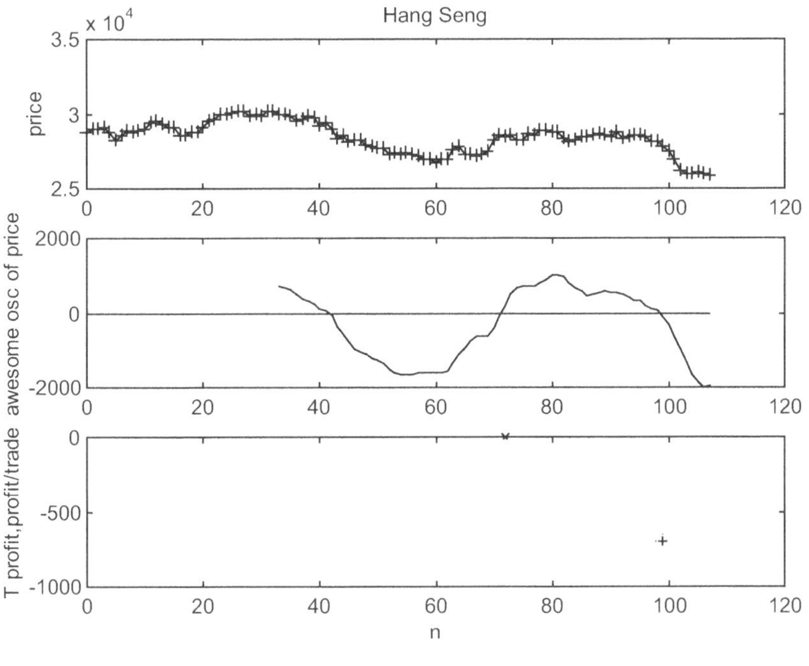

Fig. 7.7 The top figure shows the Hang Seng index. The middle figure shows the data being filtered by Awesome Oscillator. In the bottom figure, x shows when the index is bought, and + shows when it is sold. The vertical position of + also shows the total profit of all the trades, while the vertical position of the green circle shows the profit of each trade.

7.2.3 Accelerator Oscillator

The top figure of Fig. 7.8 shows the Hang Seng index. The middle figure shows the data being filtered by Accelerator Oscillator. In the bottom figure, x shows when the index is bought, and + shows when it is sold. The vertical position of + also shows the total profit of all the trades, while the vertical position of the green circle shows the profit of each trade. Two trades are executed, making a total profit of 18%. We can compare the phase of the frequency response H(ω) of the Accelerator Oscillator in Fig. 5.9 with that of the Awesome Oscillator in Fig. 5.4. It can be seen that the former has a much larger Sure Profit Zone than the latter. This is also obvious from Table 7.1. That explains why the former makes a profit, while the latter makes a loss.

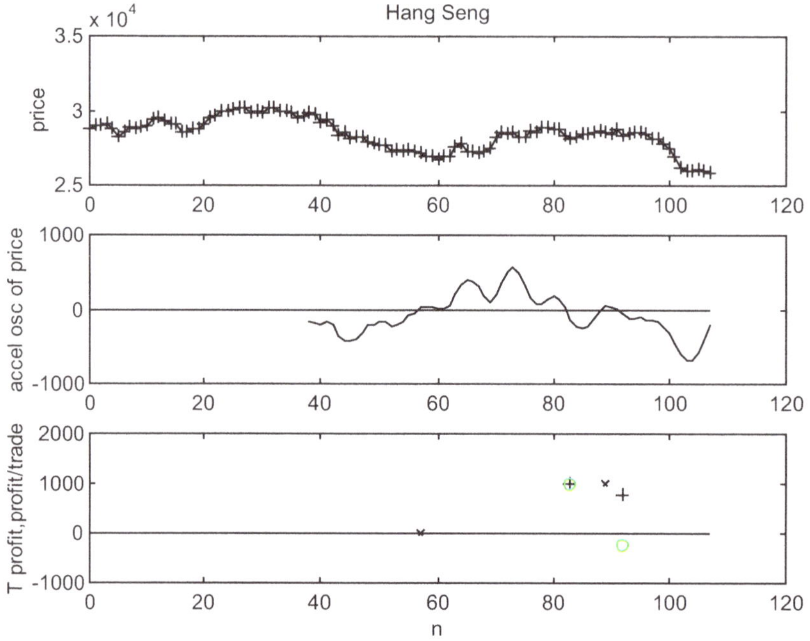

Fig. 7.8 The top figure shows the Hang Seng index. The middle figure shows the data being filtered by Accelerator Oscillator. In the bottom figure, x shows when the index is bought, and + shows when it is sold. The vertical position of + also shows the total profit of all the trades, while the vertical position of the green circle shows the profit of each trade.

7.2.4 Fast Fourier Transform of the Hang Seng index

The circular frequency in the Hang Seng index data can be calculated using the subroutine fft (Fast Fourier Transform) in the MATLAB program. Its magnitude is plotted in Fig. 7.9. The first point, corresponding to $\omega = 0$, is not plotted as it represents a constant in the signal. As mentioned in Chapter 2, this constant does not affect the calculation of the velocity and acceleration indicators. The interval of the circular frequency is calculated as $2\pi/108 = 0.058$ radian, as there are 108 data points. Figure 7.9 shows that most frequencies lie within $20 \times 0.058 \approx 1.2$ radian.

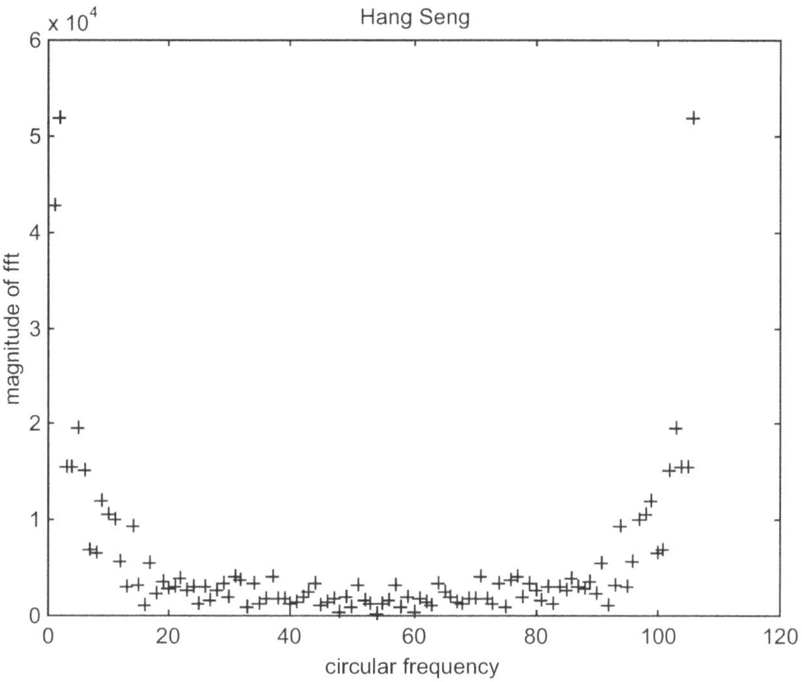

Fig. 7.9 Magnitude of the circular frequencies ω of the Hang Seng index calculated from Fast Fourier Transform (fft). The first point, corresponding to circular frequency $\omega = 0$, is not plotted as it represents a constant in the signal, and its magnitude is much larger than those of the rest of the frequencies. The magnitude of the fft is mirrored at the center of the plot. The figure can be plotted using the program ffthangseng, which is listed in Appendix D.

7.3 FTSE 100 Index

The FTSE 100 index data are taken from March 1, 2019 to August 14, 2019 ($n = 0$ to $n = 114$, i.e., 115 data points). Profit % for each trading tactic can be computed using the program tradeftse, by choosing different 'tactic' parameter in the program. Some of the examples are shown below.

7.3.1 Price − EMA6

The top figure of Fig. 7.10 shows the FTSE 100 index. The middle figure shows the data being filtered by Price − EMA6. In the bottom figure, x shows when the index is bought, and + shows when it is sold. The vertical position of + also shows the total profit of all the trades, while the vertical position of the green circle shows the profit of each trade. High frequency trades can be seen when + is close to x. Seven trades are executed, making a total profit of 512 points. Most profits came from low frequency trades. As the minimum index is 7104, and the maximum is 7686, the profit % is 512/(7686 − 7104) × 100% = 512/582 × 100% = 88%. This tactic has the advantage that it can make reasonable profit when the market is trending. Furthermore, it can respond to changes in a fast moving market, picking up a rise in a price movement, and getting out quickly in a market crash. As a matter of fact, in the last trade when there is a market crash, the position is bought at 7549 and sold at 7586, making a slight profit of 6% in 3 days.

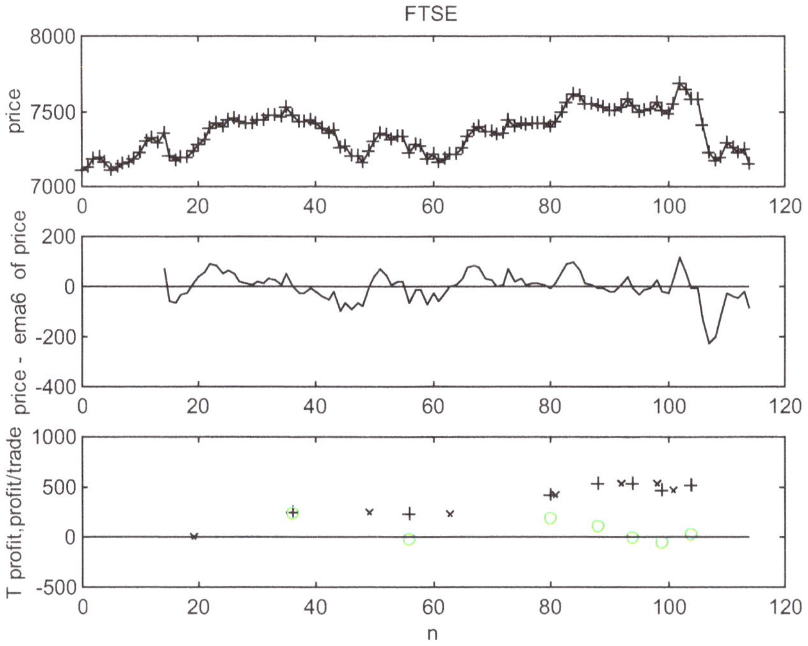

Fig. 7.10 The top figure shows the FTSE100 index. The middle figure shows the data being filtered by Price − EMA6. In the bottom figure, x shows when the index is bought, and + shows when it is sold. The vertical position of + also shows the total profit of all the trades, while the vertical position of the green circle shows the profit of each trade.

7.3.2 MACDH

The top figure of Fig. 7.11 shows the FTSE 100 index. The middle figure shows the data being filtered by MACDH. In the bottom figure, x shows when the index is bought, and + shows when it is sold. The vertical position of + also shows the total profit of all the trades, while the vertical position of the green circle shows the profit of each trade. Four trades are executed, the two low frequency trades are profitable while the two high frequency trades are not, and thus making a total loss of 15%. For the last trade, where a market crash occurred, buy indication was triggered at n = 102 at 7686, which is the peak of the index data. The position was sold 4 days later at 7407, losing 279 points, which is 48% (=279/582) of the whole range. There are two problems for this trade. Firstly, the phase lag causes the index to be bought too late. Secondly, the trade was also sold too late. Had the index been monitored on an hourly basis instead of a daily basis, and skipped convolution was applied, the position could have been closed at the hour when MACDH crossed from positive to negative at 7550, rather than at the end of the day at 7407, and thus losing only 136 (=7686 − 7550) index point, which amounts to 23% (=136/582) of the whole range, and resulting instead a total profit of 10% for the four trades.

MACDH, though described as a band pass filter, does allow some high frequencies to pass. It is these high frequency trades that led to the loss. As we can see in the time domain, as well as in the frequency spectrum of the FTSE 100 (Fig 7.12) in the next section, the data does contain more high frequencies than the S&P 500 index data, which is smoother.

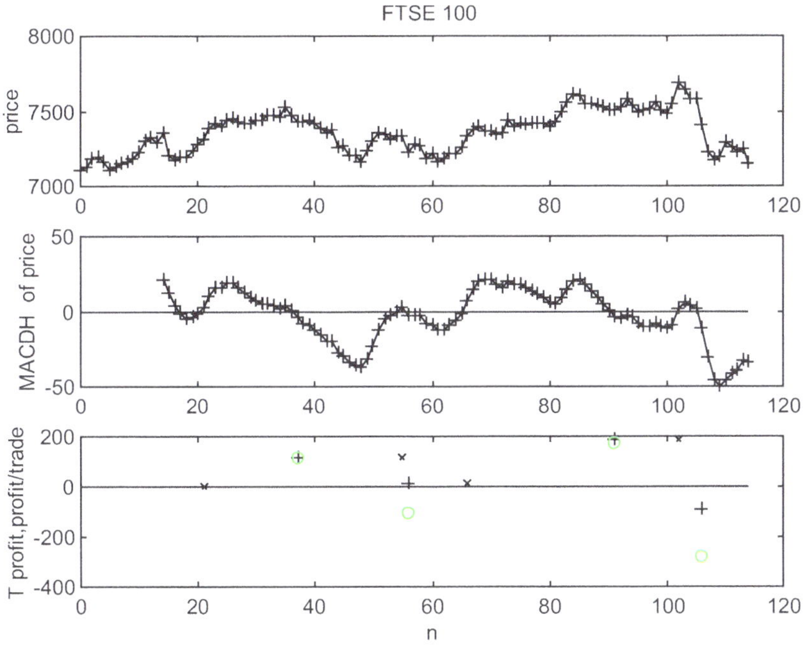

Fig. 7.11 The top figure shows the FTSE100 index. The middle figure shows the data being filtered by MACDH. In the bottom figure, x shows when the index is bought, and + shows when it is sold. The vertical position of + also shows the total profit of all the trades, while the vertical position of the green circle shows the profit of each trade.

7.3.3 Fast Fourier Transform of the FTSE 100 index

The circular frequency in the FTSE 100 data can be calculated using the subroutine fft (Fast Fourier Transform) in the MATLAB program. Its magnitude is plotted in Fig. 7.12. The first point, corresponding to $\omega = 0$, is not plotted as it represents a constant in the signal. As mentioned in Chapter 2, this constant does not affect the calculation of the velocity and acceleration indicators. The interval of the circular frequency is calculated as $2\pi/115 = 0.055$ radian, as there are 115 data points. Most of the signals lie within $20 \times 0.055 = 1.1$ radians.

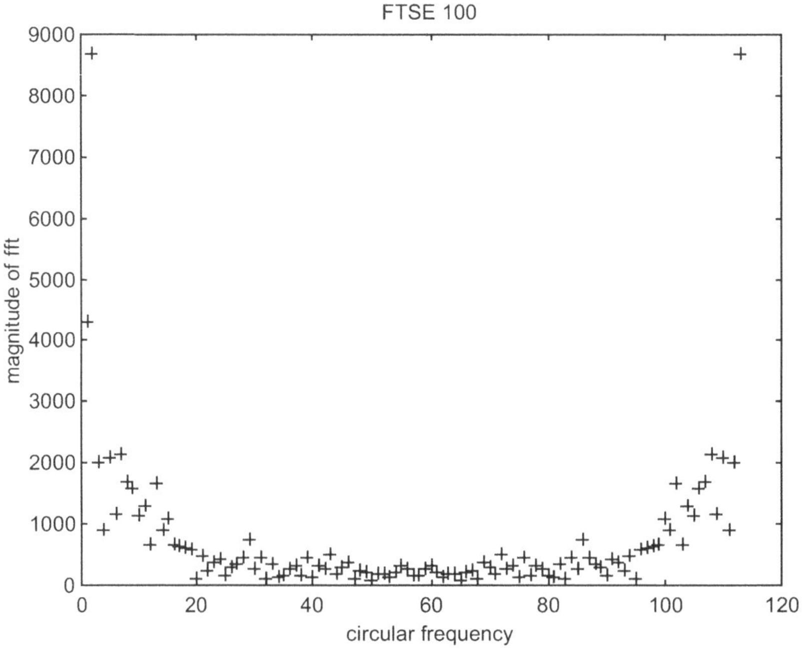

Fig. 7.12 Magnitude of the circular frequencies ω of the FTSE 100 index calculated from Fast Fourier Transform (fft). The first point, corresponding to circular frequency $\omega = 0$, is not plotted as it represents a constant in the signal, and its magnitude is much larger than those of the rest of the frequencies. The magnitude of the fft is mirrored at the center of the plot. The figure can be plotted using the program fftftse, which is listed in Appendix D.

7.4 CAC 40 Index

The CAC40 index data are taken from March 6, 2019 to August 21, 2019 (n = 0 to n = 117, i.e., 118 data points). Profit % for each trading tactic can be computed using the program tradecac40, by choosing different 'tactic' parameter in the program. Some of the examples are shown below.

7.4.1 MACDH

The top figure of Fig. 7.13 shows the CAC40 index. The middle figure shows the data being filtered by MACDH. In the bottom figure, x shows when the index is bought, and + shows when it is sold. The vertical position of + also shows the total profit of all the trades, while the vertical position of the green circle shows the profit of each trade. Two low frequency trades are executed, making a total profit of 320 points. As the minimum index is 5207, and the maximum is 5620, the profit % is 320/(5620 − 5207) × 100% = 77%.

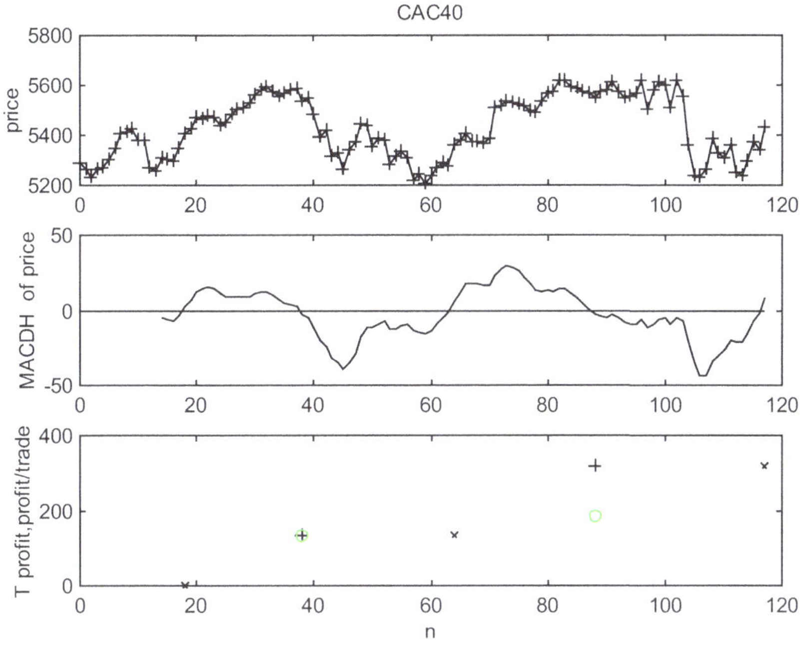

Fig. 7.13 The top figure shows the CAC40 index. The middle figure shows the data being filtered by MACDH. In the bottom figure, x shows when the index is bought, and + shows when it is sold. The vertical position of + also shows the total profit of all the trades, while the vertical position of the green circle shows the profit of each trade.

7.4.2 MACDH1

The top figure of Fig. 7.14 shows the CAC40 index. The middle figure shows the data being filtered by MACDH1. In the bottom figure, x shows when the index is bought, and + shows when it is sold. The vertical position of + also shows the total profit of all the trades, while the vertical position of the green circle shows the profit of each trade. Thirteen trades are executed, making a total loss of 155 points, which amounts to a loss of 38%. Most of the trades are high frequency trades and are losers. MACDH1 was originally designed by us to see whether profitability can be improved from that of MACDH. While it does eliminate the Loss Zone of MACDH, it has also turned into a high pass filter, and cannot filter off the high frequencies as MACDH can. Thus, it does not seem as if MACDH1 is a good idea.

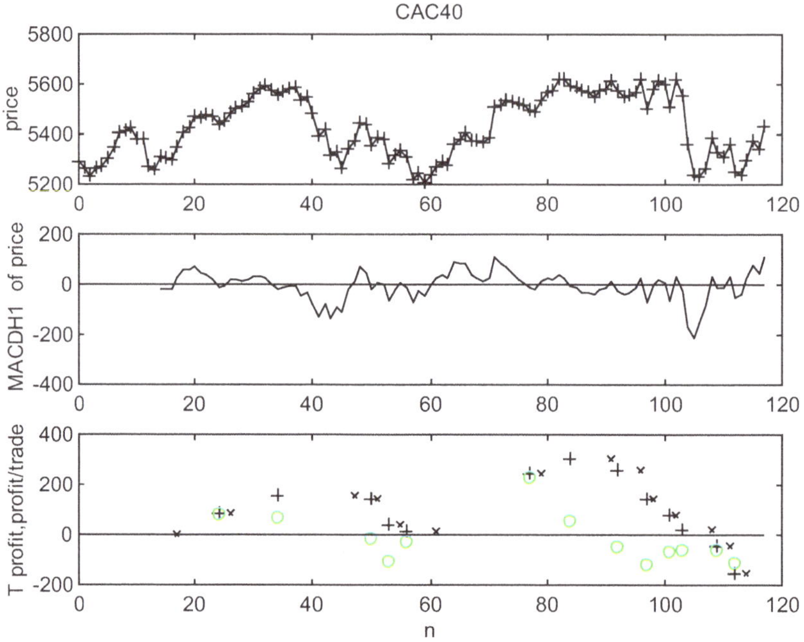

Fig. 7.14 The top figure shows the CAC 40 index. The middle figure shows the data being filtered by MACDH1. In the bottom figure, x shows when the index is bought, and + shows when it is sold. The vertical position of + also shows the total profit of all the trades, while the vertical position of the green circle shows the profit of each trade.

7.4.3 Fast Fourier Transform of CAC 40 index

The circular frequency in the CAC 40 data can be calculated using the subroutine fft (Fast Fourier Transform) in the MATLAB program. Its magnitude is plotted in Fig. 7.15. The first point, corresponding to $\omega = 0$, is not plotted as it represents a constant in the signal. As mentioned in Chapter 2, this constant does not affect the calculation of the velocity and acceleration indicators. The interval of the circular frequency is calculated as $2\pi/118 = 0.053$ radian, as there are 118 data points. Figure 7.12 shows that most frequencies lies within $20 \times 0.053 \approx 1.1$ radian. Compared to the previous S&P 500 data, the CAC 40 data is less smooth.

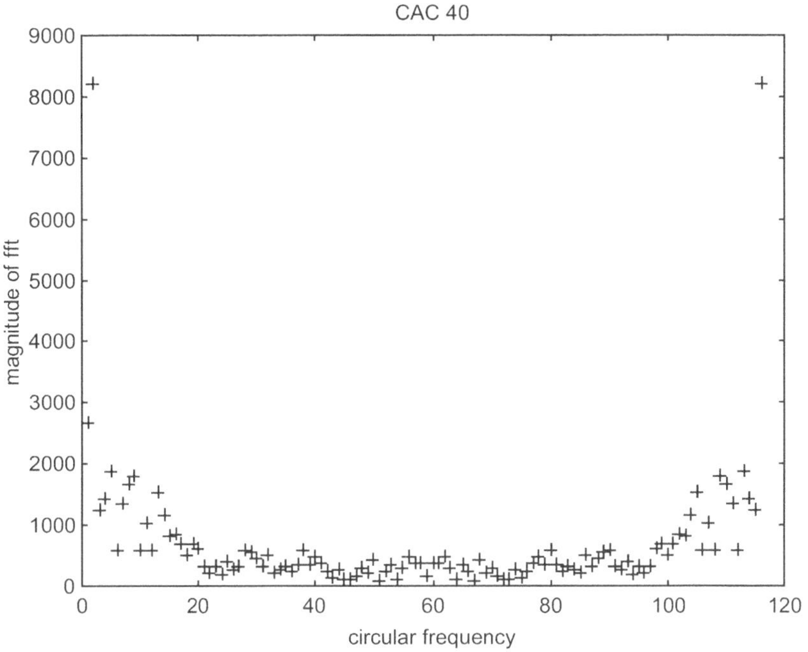

Fig. 7.15 Magnitude of the circular frequencies ω of the CAC 40 index calculated from Fast Fourier Transform (fft). The first point, corresponding to circular frequency $\omega = 0$, is not plotted as it represents a constant in the signal, and its magnitude is much larger than those of the rest of the frequencies. The magnitude of the fft is mirrored at the center of the plot. The figure can be plotted using the program fftcac40, which is listed in Appendix D.

7.5 Comparison of Different Trading Tactics

Table 7.2 shows the profit and loss of the S&P 500, Hang Seng, FTSE 100, and CAC 40 for the various trading tactics. The results are computed from the programs tradesp500, tradehangseng, tradeftse, and tradecac40 as listed in Appendix D. The final column in Table 7.2 shows the average profit % of the four markets using a particular trading tactic. The average is only a rough gauge as the number of markets averaged here is quite limited. The last row is the average profit % of the 11 trading tactics for each market. Again, this is meant to be a rough gauge, and is not meant to be a rigorous deduction. However, as will be shown in Table 7.3, it can imply that a certain market can be more profitable at certain times.

Table 7.2 Profit % of the S&P 500, Hang Seng, FTSE 100, and CAC 40 for the various trading tactics.

Trading tactic	S&P 500 Profit (%)	Hang Seng Profit (%)	FTSE 100 Profit (%)	CAC 40 Profit (%)	Average market profit (%)
Price – SMA10	22	15	13	−4	11.5
Price – SMA20	49	7	−4	−1	12.75
Awesome Oscillator	−12	−16	−30	−4	−15.5
Accelerator Oscillator	−7	18	−32	−6	−6.75
Price – EMA3	42	31	37	17	31.75
Price – EMA6	28	9	88	15	35
EMA3 – EMA6	37	10	10	17	18.5
EMAACCEL	33	−7	30	17	18
MACD	−15	−34	−30	−65	−36
MACDH	54	11	−15	77	31.75
MACDH1	2	25	48	−38	9.25
Average profit %	21.2	6.3	10.5	2.3	

The final column shows the average profit % of the four markets using a particular trading tactic.

In spite of the limited data shown in Table 7.2, a few points can be noted.

1. Of all the trading tactics listed, only the Awesome Oscillator (AO), and MACD lose money in all markets. This is actually somewhat consistent with Table 7.1, which shows that both of them have the narrowest Sure Profit Zones, the former having $0 \leq \omega < 0.12$, and the latter having $0 \leq \omega < 0.11$. As well, both of them have the longest Loss Zones, with the former having $0.13 < \omega < \pi$, and the latter having $0.12 < \omega < \pi$.
2. Price – EMA3, Price – EMA6, and EMA3 – EMA6 make money in all markets, with the first two doing particularly very well. Again, this is consistent with Table 7.1, which shows that the first two trading tactics have the longest Sure Profit Zones, the first one having $0 \leq \omega < 0.72$ and the second one having $0 \leq \omega < 0.54$. Both of them do not have any Loss Zones.
3. Price – EMA3, Price – EMA6, and MACDH are the top three trading tactics that make the highest average profit. For the first two, this is not unexpected because of the reasons given in (2). And for MACDH, as discussed in the last chapter, it is a band pass filter that filters off high frequencies, whose trades often result in losses. MACDH can make good profit when the market is trending, where its phase can have a phase lead close to the optimal phase lead of $\pi/2$. While Price –

EMA3 and Price – EMA6 make money in all four markets, MACDH makes money only in three of the markets, and not in FTSE 100. However, as described earlier, had skipped convolution been used, thus allowing the trader to be alert of a market crash earlier, MACDH could have made a total profit of 10% for FTSE 100, instead of a loss. Of course, the trader can also put a stop loss order in the trade, and cuts down his loss in case of a market crash.

Table 7.3 lists the average profit % from the 11 trading tactics for each of the four markets. In the second column, the range of frequencies with the larger amplitudes is listed for each market. Those numbers, are, of course, quite hand-waving. In spite of that, it can be implied that the lesser the higher number in the range, the more trending the market is. Thus, S&P 500 appears to be more trending than the other markets. This seems to be correct if we compare the top figures of Figs 7.1, 7.6, 7.10 and 7.13.

The third column of Table 7.3 are copied from the last row of Table 7.2. There appears to be a correlation between the second column and the third column. The more trending the market, the more profitable it can be, no matter what trading tactic is used. Intuitively, that seems to be a reasonable deduction. As a matter of fact, it surely is consistent with the results of our Fourier Analysis, where all velocity indicators described would retain some of the lowest frequency components of the price data, where most profits are made. Thus, it would be beneficial for the trader to pick a market which is less volatile than others for trading. He can look and compare the frequency spectrum of various markets to find the ones that are not very volatile. And then again, if he believes that the market is going to be volatile because of uncertain economic environment, he can choose to stay out of the market.

Table 7.3 Average profit % from the 11 trading tactics for each market.

Market	Most frequencies, ω, lie within (radian)	Average profit % from the 11 trading tactics
S&P500	$0 < 0.8$	21.2
Hang Seng	$0 < 1.2$	6.3
FTSE100	$0 < 1.1$	10.5
CAC 40	$0 < 1.1$	2.3

The current study is limited by the small sample size in real market data. A much larger sample size would be needed to substantiate the deductions. Randomized samples, in terms of various markets and time duration should be used.

Analysis of the Trading Tactics 8

There is no one size fits all trading tactics, just as there is no one size fits all knife in the kitchen. Depending on what you would like to cut in the kitchen, you need to use different kinds of knife to do the job. While you would know what you want to cut, you would not know how the market would behave in the future. If the market is moving along slowly with ripples, you may think that it may continue as such, and choose a tactic which would capture the slow movement. If the market is volatile, you may think that it may carry on as such, and pick a tactic to make some profit. We will analyze some of the trading tactics below, and noticeably, point out some of the tactics that should be avoided.

8.1 Profit Zone and Loss Zone

The phase and amplitude characteristics, and especially the former, of technical indicators used as velocity indicators in the trading tactics are significant. As we pointed out before, in order for a trade to be profitable, the phase of the price signal after operated on by the technical indicator, needs to have a phase lead lying between π and 0 from the price signal. The region where the velocity indicator satisfies this condition will be called the Profit Zone. If the phase lead lies between 0 and $-\pi$, the trade will not be profitable. That corresponding region will be called the Loss Zone. Within the Profit zone, a trade can still lose money due to sampling delay, as the data are not continuous. Thus, the Profit Zone can be further divided into Sure Profit Zone, and Unsure Profit Zone. For the former, profit is guaranteed, and for the latter, profit or loss can be made.

8.2 Price − EMA of Price Compared to Price − SMA of Price

Both trading tactics have zero Loss Zones. However, they have their differences.

Simple Moving Averages (SMA) of a signal can be zero for certain frequencies of the signal. That means, for those frequencies, the signal disappears. The phases of

D. K. Mak, *Trading Tactics in the Financial Market*, Management for Professionals,
https://doi.org/10.1007/978-3-030-70622-7_8

Price − SMA at those frequencies are zero. In addition, the wrapped phases of SMA at some other frequencies can be zero. These would again lead to the phases of Price − SMA at those frequencies to be zero. As losses usually occur when the phase is close to zero due to sampling delay, Price − SMA would not be considered as very profitable trading tactics.

SMA is a very common smoothing indicator used by traders. However, it simply adds up the last N bars of data, and ignores the ones before them. By contrast, EMA uses many more data than SMA, and it puts greater weight to most recent data than older ones. The amplitude response of the EMA is always greater than 0 (see Chapter 4). Furthermore, the phase of Price − EMA is positive for $0 \leq \omega < \pi$, and 0 only when $\omega = \pi$.

We will compare (Price − EMA, M = 6, of Price) with (Price − SMA, N = 10, of Price). Their amplitude responses are shown in Fig. 8.1. The former shows a much smoother function than the latter. Figure 8.2 shows the phase of Price − EMA (M = 6) of Price compared to the phase of Price − SMA (N = 10) of Price. The phase of the former is larger than that of the latter except in the region $2.9 < \omega < \pi$, thus making the former more advantageous in making profits.

We will also compare the phase of Price − EMA (M = 6) of Price with the phase of Price − SMA (N = 20) of Price (Fig. 8.3). The phase of the former is larger than that of the latter except in the region $3.0 < \omega < \pi$, thus making the former more advantageous in making profits.

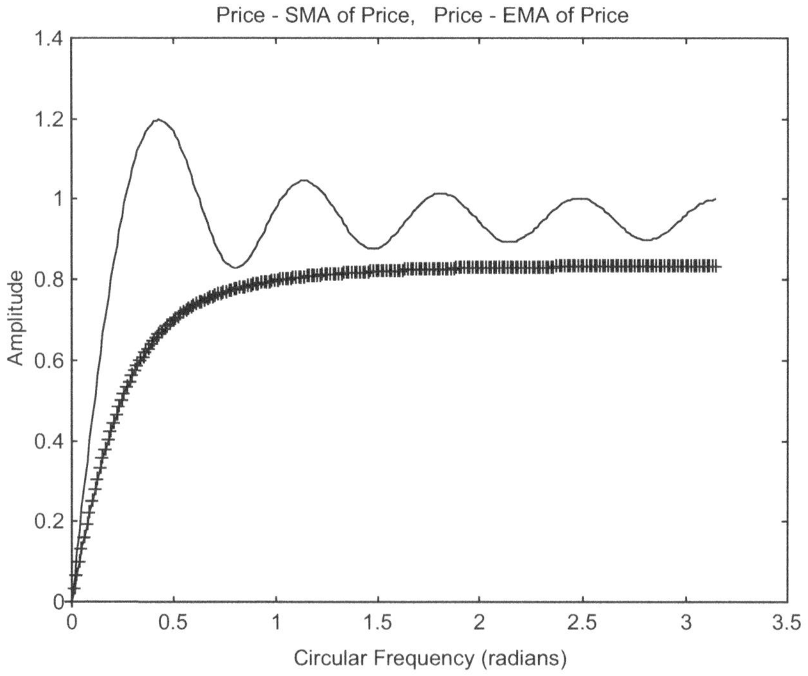

Fig. 8.1 Amplitude response of (1 − EMA, M = 6), plotted as +, compared to (1 − SMA, N = 10), plotted as a line. The program pmsmapmema has been used to draw this figure.

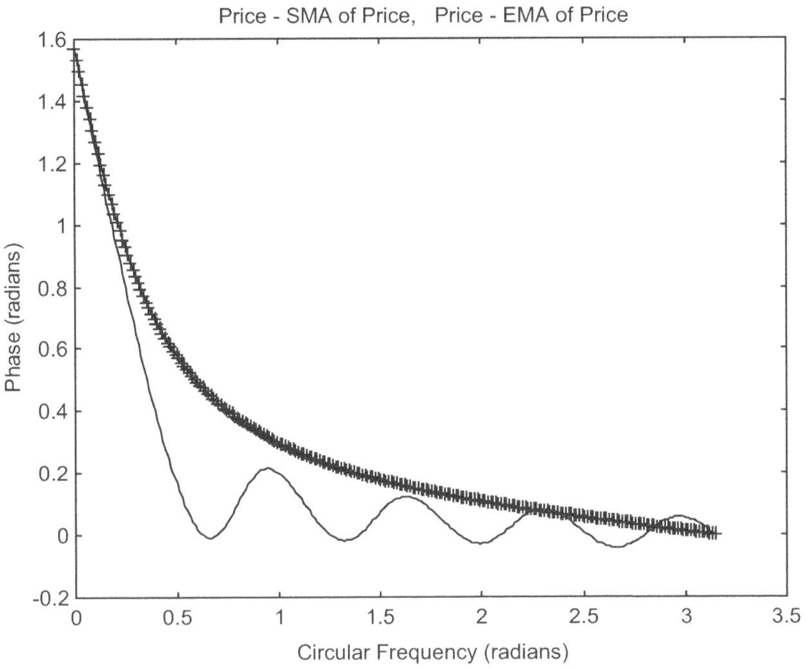

Fig. 8.2 Phase response of (1 − EMA, M = 6), plotted as +, compared to (1 − SMA, N = 10), plotted as a line. The program pmsmapmema has been used to draw this figure.

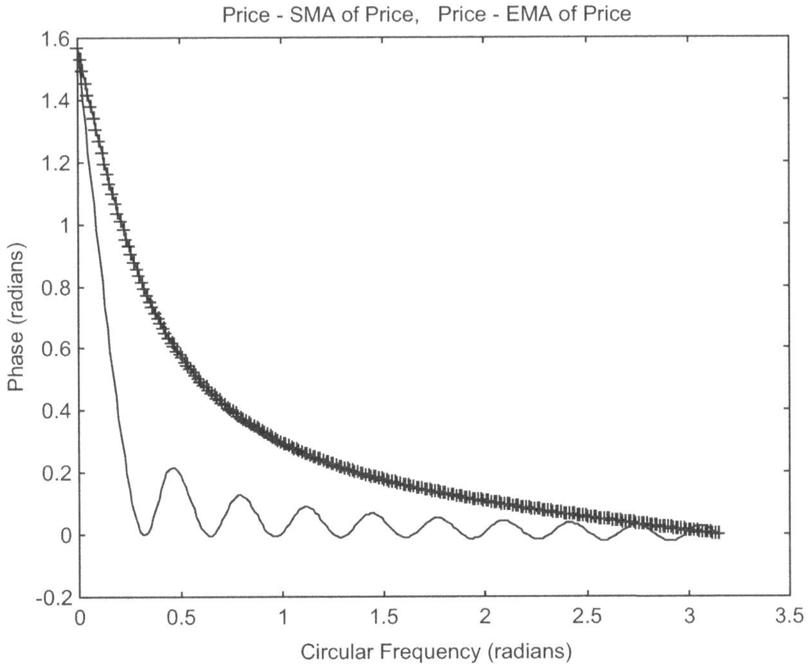

Fig. 8.3 Phase response of (1 − EMA, M = 6), plotted as +, compared to (1 − SMA, N = 20), plotted as a line. The program pmsmapmema has been used to draw this figure.

In addition, the Sure Profit Zones of Price − EMA for both M = 3 and 6 are longer than those of Price − SMA for both 10 and 20 (see Table 7.1). Thus, Price − EMA should be used instead of Price − SMA in order to increase the probability of the profitability of the trades. Obviously, Price − EMA(M = 6) is a smoother function than Price − EMA(M = 3), and will thus create less buy and sell indications.

8.3 Awesome Oscillator (AO) and Moving Average Convergence Divergence (MACD)

From Table 7.1, it can be seen that both Awesome Oscillator (SMA5 − SMA34) and MACD (EMA12 − EMA26) have very narrow Profit Zones, with $0 \leq \omega < 0.13$ radian for the former, and $0 \leq \omega < 0.12$ radian for the latter. In addition, for $\omega > 1.19$ radians, the wrapped phase of AO is different from the unwrapped phrase, which represents the real time delay, thus causing a systematic error in the AO. Thus, both AO and MACD are not recommended as velocity indicators, as the probability of their profitability is low.

Both AO and MACD have been used in other trading tactics—as alerts in trend reversals, e.g., when they are divergent with price (Pring 1991; Elder 1993; Mak 2003). It should be noted, however, that they are still functioning as velocity indicators, which thus would have the same intrinsic weaknesses.

8.4 Accelerator Oscillator (AC)

The Accelerator Oscillator is an acceleration indicator, but it can be used as a velocity indicator. Being an acceleration indicator, it does have certain advantage over velocity indicators as its phase is π at $\omega = 0$, and thus can possibly pick up some low frequency components at or near $\omega = 0.14$ radian where its phase lead ϕ is $\pi/2$, thus making maximal profit. Furthermore, its Profit Zone lies between 0 and 0.47, where most low frequencies of market price reside.

However, in the Loss Zones of the Accelerator Oscillator, the wrapped phase lead goes as low as $-\pi$, and includes the phase lead of $-\pi/2$, where maximum loss occurs. Furthermore, just like AO, for $\omega > 1.19$ radians, the wrapped phase of AC is different from the unwrapped phrase, which represents the real time delay, thus causing a systematic error in the AC. Thus, it would seem that AC, which is derived from SMA's is not a very profitable velocity indicator. It can possibly be replaced with another acceleration indicator, MACDH, which is derived from EMA's.

8.5 MACDH

MACDH is an acceleration indicator, but it has been said that it has been used as a velocity indicator in aggressive trading. Being an acceleration indicator, its phase is π at $\omega = 0$, and thus can possibly pick up some low frequency components at or near $\omega = 0.081$ radian ($=\pi/39$) where its phase lead ϕ is $\pi/2$, thus making maximal profit. Furthermore, its Profit Zone lies between 0 and 0.29 radian, where low frequencies of market price reside. Its Loss Zone ranges from 0.29 to π radians. Its phase decreases from 0 radian at $\omega = 0.29$ radian to the minimum phase lead of -0.65 ($= -\pi/4.8 > -\pi/2$) radian at $\omega = 0.99$ radian and then slowly increases to 0 at $\omega = \pi$ radians. That is, the phase remains negative for $0.29 < \omega < \pi$ radians. As MACDH is somewhat like a band pass filter, filtering off the high frequency components, and its minimum phase lead is only -0.65 radian, it proves to be a very profitable velocity indicator, especially when the market is trending.

Furthermore, while MACDH has been described as a band pass filter, it does allow some high frequency signals to pass through (see Fig. 6.3 in Chapter 6). The amplitude of high frequency signals is much reduced, but not completely eliminated. The effect is that the trade will not be sold when some high frequency noise of low amplitude occurs, but the position will be sold when the high frequency component in the signal has a large amplitude, such as in a market crash.

8.6 Recommendations

Traders would preferably like to employ trading tactics that have high probability of making a profit, and definitely would try to avoid using the ones that have high probability of losing money.

Simple Moving Average (SMA) has the disadvantage that it uses limited past data, which are all of equal weighting. As a result, this definition renders some of the frequencies of a signal to disappear completely. Thus, trading tactics employing SMA are not reliable. One popular tactic that should be avoided is the Awesome Oscillator, as its chance of making a profit is slim. In addition, Accelerator Oscillator, which also employs SMA's, should not be encouraged.

Tactics that use SMA can always be replaced by better ones that use Exponential Moving Average (EMA), which puts more weights into recent data. However, not all tactics using EMA are profitable. One popular tactic that employs EMA, the MACD, should be avoided as its probability of making a profit is low.

For slow moving trending market, MACDH provides a good trading tactic, making reasonable profits with few trades. Nevertheless, it definitely should not be used in volatile markets.

Price − EMA6 of Price has demonstrated itself to be an all versatile tactic for both slow-moving and volatile markets. It has the potential of making good profits when the market is trending, and it can also respond quickly in a fast moving market.

Price − EMA3 of Price has similar characteristics as Price − EMA6 of Price. The former may make more profit than the latter sometimes. However, it would involve taking more trades.

We should caution that the profit percentage of each trading tactic has been calculated with the assumption that the price signal consists of a single frequency. However, the signal is actually composed of a summation of several frequencies, and velocity indicator acting on the signal should have been a combination of different phase leads, which thus would affect the buy and sell indications. For example, of all the trading tactics mentioned in Chapter 7, Price − SMA20 attains the highest profit of 49% for S&P500, even though it performs rather poorly for the other markets. Nevertheless, we believe that emulating the real market signal as a single frequency signal would b e a good approximation to start. And then the lengths of the Profit Zone, the Sure Profit Zone and the Loss Zone would cast light onto which trading tactics can provide a higher probability of profitability, and which trading tactics should be avoided. The probability can also be gauged by integrating the phase plot over the frequency spectrum of the different zones.

It should also be noted that the financial market can be described as a complex adaptive system, which is studied under the discipline of complexity theory (Waldrop 1992; Casti 1995, 1997). In a complex system, every agent acts independently, and has his own rules. He can decide whether to trade or stay away, when to execute, and when to get out. He is also adaptive, and will modify his rules and systems on the basis of new knowledge (Mak 2003).

In a complex system, if every person uses the same rule, the rule will not work. An example is the fast lane on a highway, which is the leftmost lane. If every driver moves to the fast lane, the leading drivers would find the lane to be fast enough, while the rearmost drivers would consider it to be a slow lane. Similarly, if every trader uses the same rule, the first of the traders who get into the market would find the rule self-fulfilling, while the last of the traders would find the rule self-defeating. Fortunately, and in reality, not all traders would believe in the same thing, nor would they know some of the tactics proposed. Thus, a trading tactic that has a higher probability of making a profit can prevail.

9 Epilogue

Trading tactics abound. Trading gurus would advocate the tactics that they prefer, and demonstrate examples of trades that are profitable using those tactics. As the market is random or pseudo-random (Mak 2006), it is definitely possible to find examples that a trading tactic is profitable at certain times. However, presumably, traders would like to know which tactic would have a higher probability of making a profit.

It has been shown in this book that, even though the traders may not have realized it, quite a number of trading tactics employ indicators that are velocity indicators, and they actually follow one trading rule: buy when velocity crosses from negative to positive, and sell when velocity crosses from positive to negative. Velocity can be defined as the slope of the price data. If the velocity is positive, price is trending up. If it is negative, price is trending down. The difference among the trading tactics is that they employ different velocity indicators to emulate velocity, with some of them much better than others.

The whole problem would thus narrow down to how good the velocity indicators are in emulating velocity. Examples of velocity indicators are: Awesome Oscillator (AO), and Moving Average Convergence-Divergence (MACD), both of them are popular among traders. To compare the indicators, we mathematically analyze them and compare their characteristics. The indicators are Fourier Transformed to find out their amplitude and phase. By looking at the amplitude and phase, and especially the latter, one can easily see that some indicators are more profitable than others, and some of them should definitely be avoided. Artificial data have been used to substantiate the result of the mathematical analysis. Real market data tend also to support the findings.

Phases of indicators play an important role in market timing, and they are related to frequencies of the price signal. Reciprocal of frequency is simply period of a cycle. And any market price signal can be considered to be a summation of waves of various cycles with different periods. We have shown that if the frequency of the velocity indicator has a phase lead that lies between 0 and π radians of the same frequency of the signal, the trade would be profitable, otherwise it would be losing

D. K. Mak, *Trading Tactics in the Financial Market*, Management for Professionals,
https://doi.org/10.1007/978-3-030-70622-7_9

money. We define the profitable frequency range of the velocity indicator to be the Profit Zone, and the rest the Loss Zone. As the signal is sampled, and therefore not a continuous curve, sampling delay can cause losses even in the Profit Zone, which is thus further divided into the Sure Profit Zone and Unsure Profit Zone. Within the Sure Profit Zone, profit is guaranteed. Within the Unsure Profit Zone, a profit or a loss can result. Obviously, the larger the Profit Zone, and the larger the Sure Profit Zone of a trading tactic, the higher the probability that the tactic can make money. The probability can also be gauged by integrating the area under the phase plot using Calculus.

A signal can be smoothed by using Simple Moving Average (SMA), which, unfortunately can completely disappears when the signal are at certain frequencies. The more data points the SMA is averaging, the more frequencies disappear, and the smaller is the Profit Zone. Furthermore, SMA puts equal weighting on past data. Thus, velocity indicators employing SMA are not very reliable, and their relevant trading tactics should be avoided. More noticeably is the Awesome Oscillator. It can perform rather poorly.

A signal can also be smoothed by using Exponential Moving Average (EMA). Velocity indicators employing EMA would have advantages over those employing SMA, as EMA uses more data points than SMA, and it also puts greater weight to the most recent data than older data. One velocity indicator, Price − EMA of Price, i.e., when price crosses over its EMA, and especially Price − EMA6 (EMA, M = 6) of Price, has demonstrated that it is quite a profitable indicator. However, the Moving Average Convergence-Divergence (MACD), even though it employs EMA, has been shown to be quite a poor performer. More surprisingly, we have shown that the Moving Average Convergence-Divergence Histogram (MACDH), which is actually an acceleration indicator utilizing EMA, and is said to be used mostly by aggressive traders, provides good market timing when used as a velocity indicator. MACDH has the characteristics that it filters off high frequency signals. It is particularly profitable when the real market data contains low frequency components.

Some of the times, market can drop very quickly, rendering huge losses for traders. A technique, called skipped convolution can be used. It uses a lower time frame to monitor details of market movement. In market crashes, the traders can get out of the market as soon as the velocity indicator crosses from positive to negative, thus avoiding huge losses.

Trading gurus always brag about their trading tactics, and how profitable they can be. What we would like to know is which tactic has a higher probability of making a profit. We have shown, for the first time, by using Fourier Analysis, that some tactics are actually better than others, while some, including a few popular ones, should be avoided. Furthermore, Fourier Analysis can help to identify which market is trending, and which market is volatile. The trader should pick the trending market to trade, as there appears to be a higher probability that it is more profitable, no matter which trading tactic he chooses. We hope the ideas presented in this book can help traders make more profitable trades.

Happy trading, and enjoy.

Appendix A: Sure and Unsure Profit and Loss Zones

The frequency spectrum of the velocity indicator of a trading tactic can be divided into a Profit Zone and a Loss Zone. If the frequencies of the price signal lie within the Profit Zone, the trade will make a profit. If the frequencies of the price signal lie within the Loss Zone, the trade will make a loss.

As the price signal is not continuous, but is sampled, sampling delay can cause losses in the Profit Zone, or profit in the Loss Zone. Thus, Profit Zone can be divided into Sure Profit Zone and Unsure Profit Zone. Within the former, the trade will definitely make a profit. Within the latter, the trade can make a profit or a loss.

Similarly, the Loss Zone can be divided into Sure Loss Zone, and Unsure Loss Zone. Within the former, the trade will definitely make a loss. Within the latter, the trade can make a profit or a loss.

A.1 Profit Zone

In Table A.1 (which is the same as Table 2.3), ω is the circular frequency, or the sampling rate of the price signal, which is a sine wave of a single frequency. ϕ is the phase lead of the velocity indicator from the signal, where $0 < \phi < \pi$. μ is the phase shift of the original price signal caused by sampling delay.

Table A.1 Sure Profit Zone and Unsure Profit Zone

Sure Profit Zone	$\phi > \omega$	Always makes a profit
Unsure Profit Zone	$\phi < \omega$	$\mu < \phi$ $(\mu > 0)$ makes a profit $\mu \geq \phi$ $(\mu > 0)$ makes a loss

(See Fig. 3.22 to find out how the Profit Zone can be divided into Sure and Unsure Profit Zone)

In the Profit Zone, $0 < \phi < \pi$.
Maximum of μ is ω, the circular frequency, i.e., $\mu \leq \omega$.

In the Sure Profit Zone, $\phi > \omega > \mu$.

In the Unsure Profit Zone, $\phi < \omega$.

D. K. Mak, *Trading Tactics in the Financial Market*, Management for Professionals,
https://doi.org/10.1007/978-3-030-70622-7

When $0 < \mu \leq \phi$, the trade would make a profit
When $\phi < \mu < \omega$, the trade would make a loss

A.1.1 Unsure Profit Zone

Examples

We will take a look at two examples with the original price signal represented by

$$\text{Price} = \sin(\omega n + \theta_0) = \sin(\omega n + (\omega - \mu)) \tag{A.1}$$

where the original phase offset (phase lead, in this case) $\theta_0 = \omega - \mu > 0$

The filtered price from the velocity indicator would then be written as

$$\text{Filtered price} = \sin(\omega n + \theta_0 + \phi) = \sin(\omega n + (\omega - \mu) + \phi) \tag{A.2}$$

Example A.1

$$\text{Price} = \sin(\pi/6\, n + (\pi/6 - \mu))$$

where the circular frequency $\omega = \pi/6$ and the original phase offset $\theta_0 = \pi/6 - \mu$.

A filtered price is arbitrarily set to have a phase lead ϕ of $\pi/12$ from the price signal.

The filtered price would then be

$$\text{Filtered Price} = \sin(\pi/6\, n + (\pi/6 - \mu) + \pi/12)$$

Using the program tradeartif (with the parameter tactic = 12), it can be shown that the trade makes a profit for $0 < \mu \leq \pi/12$, and makes a loss for $\pi/12 < \mu < \pi/6$. The computational results also agree with the theoretical calculations from the program buysellprice.

Example A.2

$$\text{Price} = \sin(\pi/3\, n + (\pi/3 - \mu))$$

where the circular frequency $\omega = \pi/3$ and the original phase offset $\theta_0 = \pi/3 - \mu$.

A filtered price (filtered by a velocity indicator) is arbitrarily set to have a phase lead ϕ of $\pi/12$ from the price signal.

The filtered price would then be

$$\text{Filtered Price} = \sin(\pi/3\, n + (\pi/3 - \mu) + \pi/12)$$

Using the program tradeartif (with the parameter tactic = 12), it can be shown that the trade makes a profit for $0 < \mu \leq \pi/12$, and makes a loss for $\pi/12 < \mu < \pi/3$. The computational results also agree with the theoretical calculations from the program buysellprice.

The above two examples just show that, in the Unsure Profit Zone, a trade makes a profit for $0 < \mu \leq \phi$, and makes a loss for $\phi < \mu < \omega$, in agreement with Table A.1.

μ can actually be extended to less than 0 ($\mu < 0$) or larger than ω ($\mu > \omega$) for Eq. (A.1) and (A.2) to include larger original phase offset.

μ is less than 0 for the two examples below:

In Example 2.4 in Chapter 2, where $\phi = 0$
The phase offset $\theta_0 = \pi/4$ can be written as $\pi/6 + \pi/12 = \pi/6 - (-\pi/12)$
Thus, $\mu = -\pi/12$.

In Example 2.5 in Chapter 2, where $\phi = \pi/12$
The phase offset $\theta_0 = \pi/4$ can be written as $\pi/6 + \pi/12 = \pi/6 - (-\pi/12)$
Thus $\mu = -\pi/12$

Plots

As in Chapter 2, we can set

$$\text{nbuy} = \text{Integer}\left((2\pi - \theta_0 - \phi)/\omega\right) + 1 \tag{2.1}$$

$$\text{Buy price} = \sin\left(\text{nbuy x } \omega + \theta_0\right) \tag{2.2}$$

And, as sine wave is an odd function,

$$\text{Sell price} = -\text{Buy price} \tag{2.5}$$

$$\text{Profit} = 2 \text{ x Sell Price} \tag{2.6}$$

$$\text{Profit\%} = \text{Profit}/2 \text{ x } 100\% \tag{2.7}$$

where

nbuy = n where the buying indication is triggered
$\theta_0 = \omega - \mu$ = the initial phase offset of the price signal,
μ is the phase shift of the price signal due to sampling
ϕ is the phase lead of the velocity indicator from the price signal, and
Integer is the integer portion of the argument.

In Eq. (2.7), 2 = peak − valley of the sine wave, whose amplitude equals 1.

The above equations form the basis of the program unsure, which plots profit % versus μ.

Given $\omega = \pi/6$ and $\phi = \pi/12 \approx 0.26$, Fig. A.1 shows a plot of profit % versus μ. The figure shows that

When $\mu = 0$, profit % = 0, and as μ increases, profit % slowly increases to 25.9%
When $\mu <$ and $\approx \pi/12$, profit % $\approx$ 25.9
But, when $\mu >$ and $\approx \pi/12$, profit % ≈ -25.9

This simply means that a very slight change in μ at $\phi = \pi/12$ can change a trade from taking a profit to taking a loss.

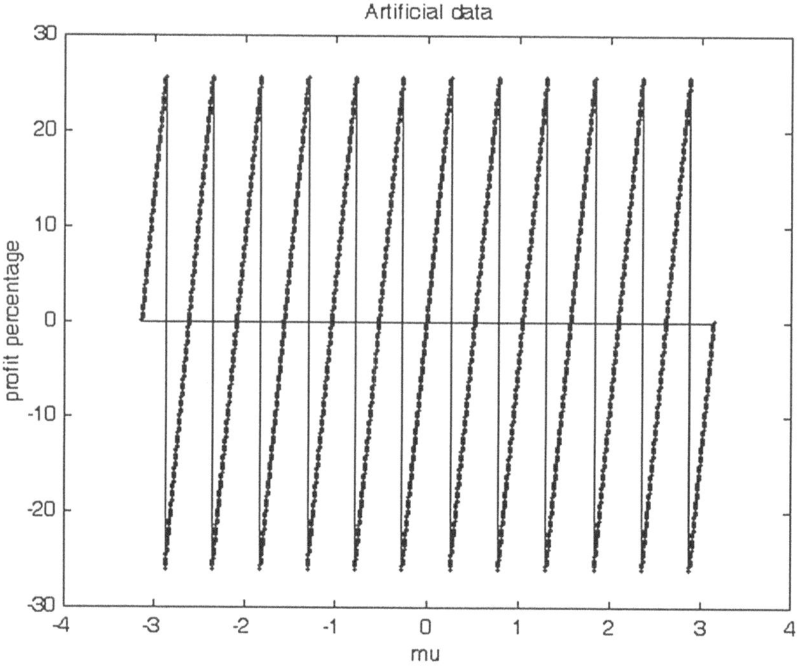

Fig. A.1 Profit % of a trade is plotted versus μ, the phase shift of the price signal due to sampling. $\omega = \pi/6$ and $\phi = \pi/12$, i.e., $\phi < \omega$, which is the Unsure Profit Zone, where a trade can make a profit or a loss. This figure is plotted by the program unsure.

A.1.2 Sure Profit Zone

The program unsure can also be used to plot profit percentage in the Sure Profit Zone, when $\phi > \omega$.

Example A.3
Given $\omega = \pi/6$ and $\phi = \pi/4$, Fig. A.2 shows a plot of profit % versus μ.

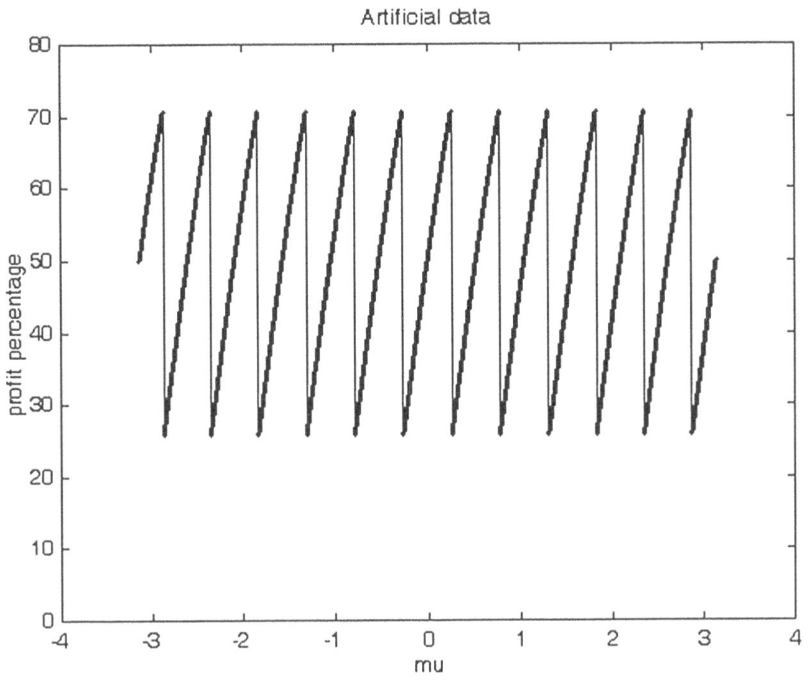

Fig. A.2 Profit % of a trade is plotted versus μ, the phase shift of the price signal due to sampling. $\omega = \pi/6$ and $\phi = \pi/4$, i.e., $\phi > \omega$, which is the Sure Profit Zone.

Figure A.2 shows that when $\phi > \omega$, the trade is profitable all the time, in agreement with Table A.1. However, variation in μ does affect the profit %.

Example A.4
Given $\omega = \pi/6$ and $\phi = \pi/2$, Fig. A.3 shows a plot of profit % versus μ.

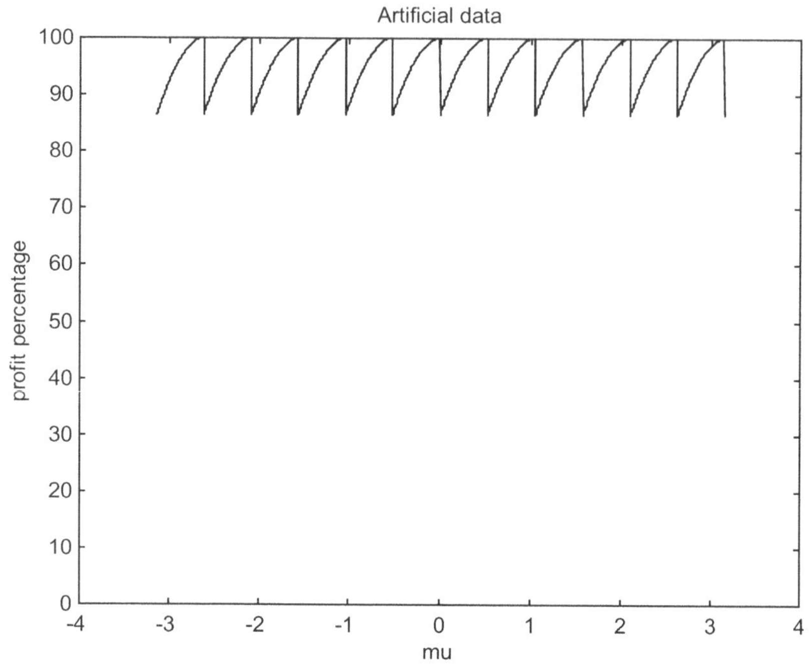

Fig. A.3 Profit % of a trade is plotted versus μ, the phase shift of the price signal due to sampling. $\omega = \pi/6$ and $\phi = \pi/2$, i.e., $\phi > \omega$, which is the Sure Profit Zone.

Figure A.3 shows that when $\phi > \omega$, the trade is profitable all the time, in agreement with Table A.1. As $\phi = \pi/2$, the optimal phase lead for a velocity indicator, profit % can achieve 100%. However, variation in μ can reduce the profit %.

A.2 Loss Zone

In Table A.2, ω is the circular frequency, or the sampling rate of the price signal, which is a sine wave of a single frequency. ϕ is the phase lead of the velocity indicator from the signal, where $0 > \phi > -\pi$. μ is the phase shift of the original price signal caused by sampling delay.

Table A.2 Sure Loss Zone and Unsure Loss Zone

Sure Loss Zone	$\phi > -\pi + \omega$	always makes a loss
Unsure Loss Zone	$\phi < -\pi + \omega$	$\mu < \phi + \pi \quad (\mu > 0)$ makes a loss $\mu \geq \phi + \pi \quad (\mu > 0)$ makes a profit

The original price signal is represented by

$$\text{Price} = \sin\ (\omega\,n + \theta_0) = \sin\ (\omega\,n + (\omega - \mu)) \tag{A.1}$$

where the original phase offset (phase lead, in this case) $\theta_0 = \omega - \mu$.

The filtered price from the velocity indicator would then be written as

$$\text{Filtered price} = \sin\ (\omega\,n + \theta_0 + \phi) = \sin\ (\omega\,n + (\omega - \mu) + \phi) \tag{A.2}$$

A.2.1 Unsure Loss Zone

Example

Example A.5

$$\text{Price} = \sin\ (\pi/6\,n + (\pi/6 - \mu))$$

where the circular frequency $\omega = \pi/6$ and the original phase offset $\theta_0 = \pi/6 - \mu$.

A filtered price is arbitrarily set to have a phase lead ϕ of $-\pi + \pi/12$ from the price signal.

The filtered price would then be

$$\text{Filtered Price} = \sin\ (\pi/6\,n + (\pi/6 - \mu) - \pi + \pi/12)$$

Using the program tradeartif (with the parameter tactic = 12), it can be shown that the trade makes a profit for $\pi/12 < \mu \leq \pi/6$, and makes a loss for $0 < \mu < \pi/12$. The computational results also agree with the theoretical calculations from the program buysellprice, as shown in Fig. A.4.

Also, in Example 2.8 in Chapter 2, $\mu = \pi/9$. And the trade makes a profit.

Plots

Example A.6

Given $\omega = \pi/6$ and $\phi = -\pi + \pi/12$, Fig. A.4 shows a plot of profit % versus μ.

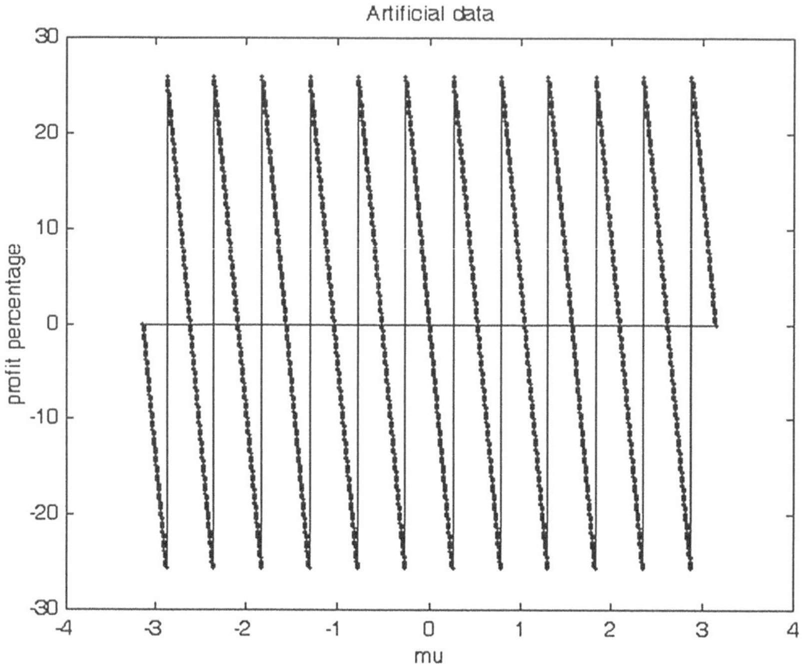

Fig. A.4 Profit % of a trade is plotted versus μ, the phase shift of the price signal due to sampling. $\omega = \pi/6$ and $\phi = -\pi + \pi/12$, i.e., $\phi < -\pi + \omega$, which is the Unsure Loss Zone, where a trade can make a profit or a loss. This figure is plotted by the program unsure.

Example A.7

Given $\omega = \pi/6$ and $\phi = -\pi + \pi/7$, Fig. A.5 shows a plot of profit % versus μ.

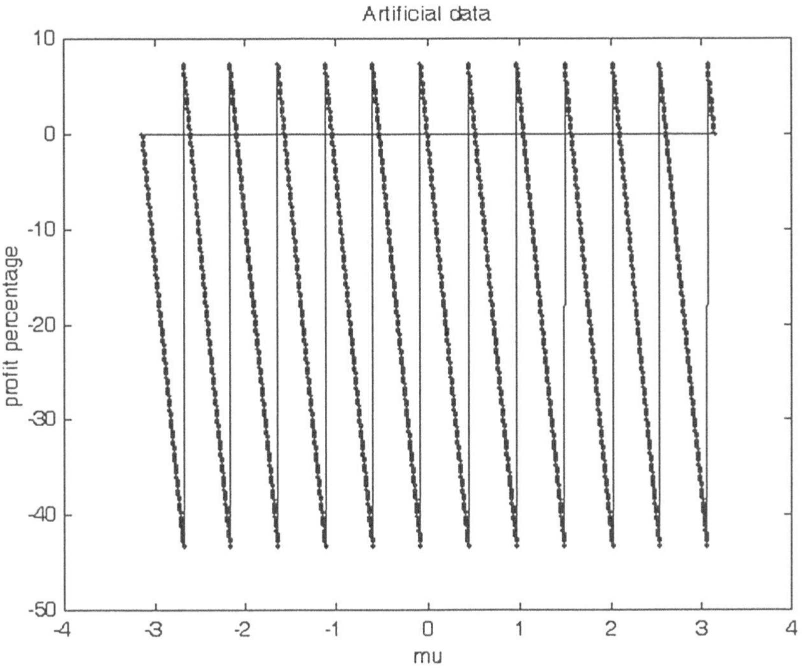

Fig. A.5 Profit % of a trade is plotted versus μ, the phase shift of the price signal due to sampling. $\omega = \pi/6$ and $\phi = -\pi + \pi/7$, i.e., $\phi < -\pi + \omega$, which is the Unsure Loss Zone, where a trade can make a profit or a loss.

A.2.2 Sure Loss Zone

Example A.8

Given $\omega = \pi/6$ and $\phi = -\pi + \pi/5$, Fig. A.6 shows a plot of profit % versus μ.

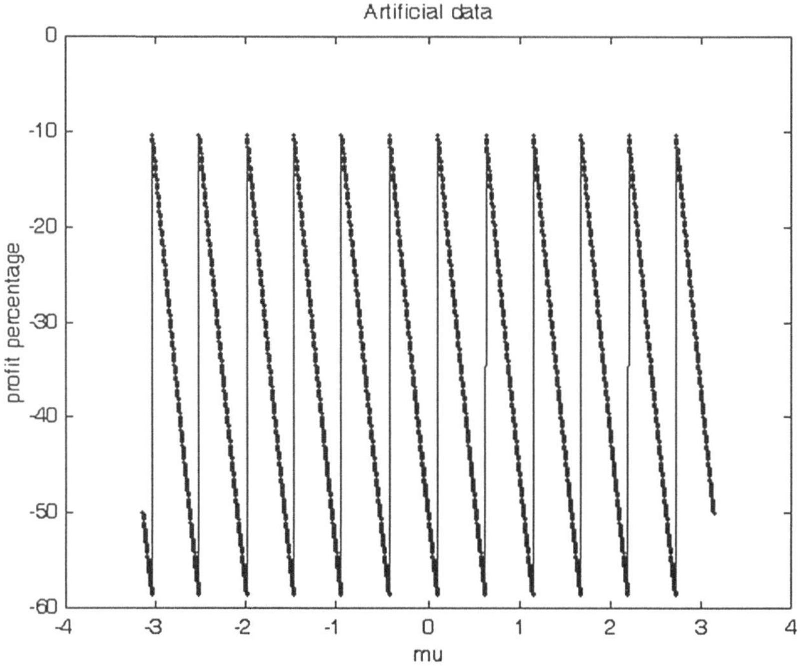

Fig. A.6 Profit % of a trade is plotted versus μ, the phase shift of the price signal due to sampling. $\omega = \pi/6$ and $\phi = -\pi + \pi/5$, i.e., $\phi > -\pi + \omega$, which is the Sure Loss Zone, where a trade always makes a loss.

Appendix B: Simple Moving Average

B.1 Simple Moving Average (SMA)

A simple N-day average is created by adding the prices over N days and dividing by N. It becomes a simple moving average when the next day's weighted price is added to the sum and the weighted first day's price is dropped off (Mak 2003). Thus the unit sample (or impulse) response, h(k) = 1/N, where k = 0, 1, 2, ..., N−1.

Day, of course, can be replaced by any time unit. For example, a time unit can be 1 hour.

The frequency response function, $H(\omega)$, can be written as

$$H(\omega) = \sum_{k=0}^{N-1} h(k) \exp\left(-ik\omega\right) \tag{B.1}$$

Thus, the frequency response function, $H(\omega)$, of an SMA is given by

$$H(\omega) = \frac{1}{N} \sum_{k=0}^{N-1} exp\left[-ik\omega\right] = \frac{1}{N} \frac{1 - exp\left[-iN\omega\right]}{1 - exp\left[-i\omega\right]} \tag{B.2}$$

At ω = 0, $H(\omega)$ is indeterminate. However, using the De l'Hopital's Rule (e.g. Kaplan 1959, p. 27), it can be shown that when

$$\omega \rightarrow 0, H(\omega) \rightarrow 1$$

From (B.2), $H(\omega)$ and its magnitude = 0, when

$$exp\left[-iN\omega\right] = \cos\ (N\ \omega) - i\ \sin\left(N\ \omega\right) = 1 \tag{B.3}$$

i.e., $N\ \omega = 2m\pi$

$$\text{And}\quad \omega = 2m\pi/N, \text{where m} = 1, 2, 3, 4, \ldots . \tag{B.4}$$

D. K. Mak, *Trading Tactics in the Financial Market*, Management for Professionals,
https://doi.org/10.1007/978-3-030-70622-7

For N odd,

$$H(\omega) = \frac{1}{N} exp\left[-i\frac{N-1}{2}\omega\right]\left[1 + 2cos\omega + \ldots + 2\,cos\,\frac{N-1}{2}\omega\right]$$
$$= \frac{1}{N} exp\left[-i\frac{N-1}{2}\omega\right]\left[1 + \sum_{l=1}^{(N-1)/2} 2\cos\left(l\omega\right)\right] \tag{B.5}$$

For N even

$$H(\omega) = \frac{1}{N} exp\left[-i\frac{N-1}{2}\omega\right]\left[2\,cos\,\frac{\omega}{2} + \ldots + 2\,cos\,\frac{N-1}{2}\omega\right]$$
$$= \frac{1}{N} exp\left[-i\frac{N-1}{2}\omega\right]\sum_{l=1}^{N/2} 2\,cos\,\frac{2l-1}{2}\omega \tag{B.6}$$

Thus, for all N, the unwrapped phase of H(ω) is given by (Mak 2003)

$$\phi(\omega) = -\frac{N-1}{2}\omega \tag{B.7}$$

which is linear with respect to ω.

As mentioned in (B.4), magnitude of H(ω) = 0 when $\omega = 2m\pi/N$, where m = 1, 2, 3, 4,... Thus, using (B.7), at those points

$$\phi(\omega) = -\frac{N-1}{N}m\pi \tag{B.8}$$

The larger the number of points, N, the smoother the output response is. However, it will also yield a larger phase lag, according to Eq. (B.7).

The bar lag $b(\omega)$, i.e., the number of bars lagging behind the signal is given by

$$b(\omega) = \phi(\omega)/\omega = -(N-1)/2 \tag{B.9}$$

and is independent of ω.

B.2 SMA(M) – SMA(N), Fast SMA – Slow SMA

The difference of two SMA's can form a velocity indicator. From Eqs. (B.5) and (B.6)

$$H(\omega) = \frac{1}{N} exp\left[-i\frac{N-1}{2}\omega\right] C \tag{B.10}$$

$$= \frac{C}{N}\left[cos\left(\frac{N-1}{2}\omega\right) - isin\left(\frac{N-1}{2}\omega\right)\right] \tag{B.11}$$

where

$$C = \left[1 + \sum_{l=1}^{\frac{N-1}{2}} 2\cos(l\omega)\right] \qquad \textit{for N odd} \tag{B.12}$$

$$= \sum_{l=1}^{N/2} 2\cos\frac{2l-1}{2}\omega \qquad \textit{for N even} \tag{B.13}$$

The frequency response of the difference between two SMA's is given by

$$H_M(\omega) - H_N(\omega) = \frac{1}{M}exp\left[-i\frac{M-1}{2}\omega\right]C_M - \frac{1}{N}exp\left[-i\frac{N-1}{2}\omega\right]C_N$$
$$= \frac{C_M}{M}\cos\frac{M-1}{2}\omega - \frac{C_N}{N}\cos\frac{N-1}{2}\omega - i\frac{C_M}{M}\sin\frac{M-1}{2}\omega + i\frac{C_N}{N}\sin\frac{N-1}{2}\omega \tag{B.14}$$

At $\omega = 0$, since both $H_M(\omega)$ *and* $H_N(\omega) = 1$, $H_M(\omega) - H_N(\omega) = 0$.
The phase of $H_M(\omega) - H_N(\omega)$ is given by

$$\phi(\omega) = tan^{-1}\left(\frac{\frac{C_N}{N}\sin\frac{N-1}{2}\omega - \frac{C_M}{M}\sin\frac{M-1}{2}\omega}{\frac{C_M}{M}\cos\frac{M-1}{2}\omega - \frac{C_N}{N}\cos\frac{N-1}{2}\omega}\right) \tag{B.15}$$

At $\omega = 0$, both the numerator and denominator of argument of tan^{-1} are 0. Thus, the phase of the $\phi(\omega)$ at $\omega = 0$ is of the indeterminate form. However, using the De l'Hopital's Rule (e.g. Kaplan 1959, p. 27), it can be shown that when

$\omega \to 0, \phi(\omega) \to \pi/2$

An example of the fast SMA minus the slow SMA is the Awesome Oscillator, where the length of the fast SMA is 5, and that of the slow SMA is 34.

Equation (B.15) yields the wrapped phase of $H_M(\omega) - H_N(\omega)$. The unwrapped phase can be different from the wrapped phase. Both the wrapped phase and unwrapped phase of the Awesome Oscillator are shown in Chapter 5.

B.3 Price − SMA

When the signal (e.g., price) is used instead of the fast SMA, the signal would be equivalent to an SMA with M = 1 of the signal, and therefore $C_M = 1$. Equation (B.14) becomes

$$1 - H_N(\omega) = 1 - \frac{C_N}{N}\cos\frac{N-1}{2}\omega + i\frac{C_N}{N}\sin\frac{N-1}{2}\omega \tag{B.16}$$

And Eq. (B.15) becomes

$$\phi(\omega) = tan^{-1}\left(\frac{\frac{C_N}{N}\sin\frac{N-1}{2}\omega}{1 - \frac{C_N}{N}\cos\frac{N-1}{2}\omega}\right) \tag{B.17}$$

When $(N-1)/\omega = \pi, 2\pi, 3\pi, \ldots$, $\sin[(N-1)/\omega] = 0$. From Eq. (B.11), the phase of $H_N(\omega) = 0$. From Eq. (B.16), the phase of $1 - H_N(\omega)$, i.e., $\phi(\omega)$ in Eq. (B.17), would thus also equal to 0.

When the amplitude of $H_N(\omega) = 0$, from Eq. (B.11), it would imply that both $\cos((N-1)/\omega)$ and $\sin((N-1)/\omega)$ equals 0. From Eq. (B.16), the phase of $1 - H_N(\omega)$, i.e., $\phi(\omega)$ in Eq. (B.17), would thus also equal to 0.

Appendix C: Exponential Moving Average, Moving Average Convergence-Divergence

C.1 Exponential Moving Average, EMA

The frequency response function of the exponential moving average, H(ω), is given by

$$H(\omega) = \frac{\alpha}{1 - (1 - \alpha)\exp(-i\omega)} \tag{C.1}$$

where $\alpha = 2/(M + 1)$

M is a positive integer chosen by the trader and is often called the length of EMA. Thus, α has to be equal or less than 1.

The magnitude of H(ω) is given by Lyons (1997), Mak (2006, p. 15).

$$|H(\omega)| = \frac{\alpha}{\left[1 - 2(1 - \alpha)cos\omega + (1 - \alpha)^2\right]^{1/2}} \tag{C.2}$$

The phase is given by

$$\phi(\omega) = tan^{-1}\left[\frac{-(1 - \alpha)sin\omega}{1 - (1 - \alpha)cos\omega}\right] \tag{C.3}$$

The bar lag, b(ω), i.e., the number of bars lagging behind the signal is given by

$$\mathrm{b}(\omega) = \phi(\omega)/\omega \tag{C.4}$$

As $\omega \to 0$, $\mathrm{b}(\omega) \to -(1/\propto - 1) = -(M - 1)/2$

This is in consistent with

As $\omega \to 0$, $d\phi(\omega)/d\omega \to -(M - 1)/2$

When $\omega = \pi$, $\phi(\omega) = 0$, $\mathrm{b}(\omega) = 0$

It can be shown that the slope of b(ω), *i. e.* , $d\mathrm{b}(\omega)/d\,\omega$ when $\omega \to 0$ is 0.

This is in consistent with the slope of the slope of $\phi(\omega)$, i.e.,

$\mathrm{d}^2\,\phi(\omega)/\,d\,\omega^2$ is 0 when $\omega \to 0$.

D. K. Mak, *Trading Tactics in the Financial Market*, Management for Professionals,
https://doi.org/10.1007/978-3-030-70622-7

C.2 Moving Average Convergence-Divergence, MACD

MACD was created by Gerald Appel in the late 1970's. It is the difference between the fast EMA (M = 12) and the slow EMA (N = 26)

The frequency response of an EMA can be written as

$$\begin{aligned} H(\omega) &= \frac{\propto}{1-(1-\propto)\exp(-i\omega)} \\ &= \frac{\propto[1-(1-\propto)\exp(i\omega)]}{1-2(1-\propto)\cos(\omega)+(1-\propto)^2} \end{aligned} \quad \text{(C.5)}$$

Defining $$\beta = 1-2(1-\propto)\cos(\omega)+(1-\propto)^2 \quad \text{(C.6)}$$

$$H_M(\omega) = \frac{\propto_M[1-(1-\propto_M)\exp(i\omega)]}{\beta_M} \quad \text{(C.7)}$$

$$H_N(\omega) = \frac{\propto_N[1-(1-\propto_N)\exp(i\omega)]}{\beta_N} \quad \text{(C.8)}$$

where $\propto_M = 2/(M+1)$
$\propto_N = 2/(N+1)$

The frequency response of the difference of two EMA's can be written as

$$\begin{aligned} & H_M(\omega) - H_N(\omega) \\ &= \frac{\propto_M\beta_N[1-(1-\propto_M)\exp(i\omega)] - \propto_N\beta_M[1-(1-\propto_N)\exp(i\omega)]}{\beta_M\beta_N} \end{aligned} \quad \text{(C.9)}$$

And the phase

$$\begin{aligned} & \phi(\omega) \\ &= tan^{-1}\left\{\frac{[\propto_N\beta_M(1-\propto_N)-\propto_M\beta_N(1-\propto_M)]sin\omega}{\propto_M\beta_N-\propto_M\beta_N(1-\propto_M)cos\omega-\propto_N\beta_M+\propto_N\beta_M(1-\propto_N)cos\omega}\right\} \end{aligned} \quad \text{(C.10)}$$

At $\omega = 0$, both the numerator and denominator of argument of tan^{-1} are 0. Thus, the phase of $\phi(\omega)$ at $\omega = 0$ is of the indeterminate form. However, using the De l'Hopital's Rule (e.g. Kaplan 1959, p. 27), it can be shown that when $\omega \to 0$, $\phi(\omega) \to \pi/2$.

C.3 Price − EMA

When the signal (e.g., price) is used instead of the fast EMA, the signal would be equivalent to an EMA with M = 1 of the signal, and therefore $\propto_M = 1$, $\beta_M = 1$.

$$H_M(\omega) - H_N(\omega) = \frac{\beta_N - \propto_N [1 - (1 - \propto_N) \exp(i\omega)]}{\beta_N} \tag{C.11}$$

And

$$\phi(\omega) = tan^{-1}\left\{\frac{[\propto_N(1 - \propto_N)]sin\omega}{\beta_N - \propto_N + \propto_N(1 - \propto_N)cos\omega}\right\} \tag{C.12}$$

C.4 Comparison of SMA with EMA

In an N period SMA, the weights are equally distributed in the last N bars. To emphasize the influences from the recent data, the M period exponential moving average (EMA) is defined as

$$\begin{aligned} y(n) &= \alpha x(n) + (1 - \alpha)y(n - 1) \\ &= \alpha \sum_{k=0}^{\infty} (1 - \alpha)^k x(n - k) \\ &= \frac{2}{M+1} \sum_{k=0}^{\infty} \left(\frac{M-1}{M+1}\right)^k x(n - k) \end{aligned} \tag{C.13}$$

where $\alpha = 2/(M + 1)$

Note that, for the EMA, infinite number of data points can be used for M > 1. Equation (C.13) is exactly the same as Eq. (4.3) in Chapter 4, but written in a slightly different form.

It can be shown that at $\omega = 0$, if N = M, the bar lag of the SMA and EMA is the same and is equal to (M − 1)/2. However, while the bar lag remains the same for all ω for SMA, the bar lag slowly decreases to 0 when ω approaches π for the EMA. Thus, EMA has a definite advantage over SMA.

Appendix D: MATLAB Programs

The Matlab programs are listed in alphabetical order.

D.1 accelosc

```
%accelosc,   Plot Amplitude and Phase of  accelerator oscillator
%  unwrap phase,   Find Sure and Unsure Profit Zones
clear
NN=240;  %240
intomega=pi/NN;
M1=5;

M2=34;

for I= 1: NN+1
   omegavector(I) = (I-1)*intomega;

    H1vector(I)=1/M1*( 1- exp(-i*M1*omegavector(I)) )  /( 1 -
exp(-i*omegavector(I) )  );
     mag1(I)=abs(H1vector(I));
     phase1(I)= angle(H1vector(I));

     H2vector(I)= 1/M2*( 1- exp(-i*M2*omegavector(I)) )  /( 1 -
exp(-i*omegavector(I) )  );
     mag2(I)=abs(H2vector(I));
     phase2(I)= angle(H2vector(I));

      H3vector(I)= H1vector(I)  - H2vector(I); % awesome oscillator
```


D. K. Mak, *Trading Tactics in the Financial Market*, Management for Professionals,
https://doi.org/10.1007/978-3-030-70622-7

```
    mag3(I)=abs(H3vector(I));
    phase3(I)= angle(H3vector(I));

    H5vector(I) =H1vector(I) *H3vector(I);  % SMA(5)*awesome oscillator
  mag5(I)=abs(H5vector(I));
    phase5(I)= angle(H5vector(I));

    H6vector(I) = H3vector(I) - H5vector(I); % accelerator oscillator
(AC)
   mag6(I)=abs(H6vector(I));
    phase6(I)= angle(H6vector(I));

   end
  mag(1) = 1;
  phase1(1) = 0;
  mag2(1) = 1;
   phase2(1) = 0;
   mag3(1) = 0;
 phase3(1) = pi/2;
   mag5(1) = 0;
 phase5(1) = pi/2;
    mag6(1) = 0;
  phase6(1) = pi;

  phase6unwrap = unwrap(phase6);
   for I= 1: NN+1
    barlag(I) = phase6unwrap(I)/omegavector(I);
  end
     figure(1)
     plot(omegavector, mag3, 'k+-' , omegavector, mag5,  'kx-'  )
     xlabel('Circular Frequency (radians)')
     ylabel('Amplitude')
     title('Awesome oscillator and SMA(5)*Awesome oscillator')

  figure(2)
     plot(omegavector, phase3, 'r+-' , omegavector, phase5, 'kx-'  )
     xlabel('Circular Frequency (radians)')
     ylabel('Phase (radians)')
    title('Awesome oscillator and SMA(5)*Awesome oscillator')
```

```
figure(3)
plot(omegavector, mag6, 'k-' )
xlabel('Circular Frequency (radians)')
ylabel('Amplitude')
title('Accelerator oscillator')

figure(4)
plot(omegavector, phase6, 'k-' )
xlabel('Circular Frequency (radians)')
ylabel('Wrapped Phase (radians)')
title('Accelerator oscillator')

% to find intersection point of phase3 and omegavector, to find
Sure Profit Zone and Unsure Profit Zone
for I = 1: NN
if ( phase6(I) - omegavector(I) ) > 0 & ( phase6(I+1)
- omegavector(I+1) ) < 0
intersectomega = omegavector(I)
intersectphase =phase6(I)
end
end
figure(5)
plot( omegavector, phase6unwrap, 'k.' )
xlabel('Circular Frequency (radians)')
ylabel('Unwrapped Phase (radians)')
title('Accelerator oscillator')

figure(6)
plot(omegavector, barlag, 'k+-' )
xlabel('Circular Frequency (radians)')
ylabel('bars lag)')
title('Accelerator oscillator')

figure(7)
plot(omegavector, mag3, 'r+-' , omegavector, mag5, 'bx-' ,
omegavector, mag6, 'k.-' ) % 3 awesome, 6 wrapped AC
xlabel('Circular Frequency (radians)')
ylabel('Amplitude')
title('Awesome oscillator, SMA(5)*Awesome oscillator and
Accelerator Oscillator')
```

```
 figure(8)
plot(omegavector, phase3, 'k-' , omegavector, phase6, 'r.')
xlabel('Circular Frequency (radians)')
ylabel('wrapped Phase (radians)')
  title('Awesome Oscillator, Accelerator oscillator')
```

D.2 acceloscsig

```
% acceloscsig, plot accelerator oscillator(AO) of a dummy signal, plot
signal with 2 frequencies, plot signal of 1 frequency when amp2 = 0
% set profit = 0 if first data point of accelerator oscillator is greater
than 0
clear
factor = 30 ; % factor = 20.83, 9, 6.283 , 5, 9/2, 9/3, 9/4
% check profit, 31.4, 15.7, 10.47, 7.85, 6.28
%  check profit, take approx 30, 15, 10, 8, 6


factor2 = factor/4 ;
omega = pi/factor;
omega2 = pi/factor2;
NN = 10 * factor; %  NN = 10*factor


% define original signal
amp2 = 0  ; % 0.4
theta0 = 0 ; % add to price signal  0, pi/2, pi, 3*pi/2
  for I= 1: NN+1
     zero(I)=0;
      xvector(I) = I-1;
      yvector(I)= sin( omega*xvector(I)  + theta0 ) + amp2*
sin( omega2*xvector(I) );
   end

   % set parameters of awesome oscillator and accelerator oscillator
N1= 5;
N2=34;
N3=5;
```

```
  % calculate technical indicators on signal
    for I = N1 : NN+1
       sma1signal(I) = 0;
       for J = 1:N1
          sma1signal(I) = sma1signal(I ) + 1/N1 * yvector(I+1 - J);
          end
    end
     for I = N2 : NN+1
       sma2signal(I) = 0;
       for J = 1:N2
          sma2signal(I) = sma2signal(I ) + 1/N2 * yvector(I+1 - J);
          end
    end
    for I = N2 : NN+1
     aweosc(I) = sma1signal(I) - sma2signal(I); % calculate awesome
oscillator
     end
     N2PN3 = N2+N3;
      for I = N2PN3 : NN+1
     signalline(I) = 0;
     for J = 1:N3
        signalline(I) = signalline(I ) + 1/N3 * aweosc(I+1 - J);
        end
  end
  for I = N2PN3 : NN+1
     accelosc (I) = aweosc(I) - signalline(I); %calculate aceleraator
oscillator
     end
  % To calculate buy price and sell price, and profit of acceleration
oscillator
  B = 0; % Buy originally set to 0
   Iprofit=1;
     if    accelosc(N2PN3)   >  0  % first data point  greater than 0,
we do not buy
        Iprofit = 0;
     end
```

```
      for I = N2PN3: NN+1
       if   B == 0  &   accelosc(I)   >  0
        I  ,          ybuy = yvector(I)
        B = 1
              else
        if  B == 1   &    accelosc(I)  < 0
           I,    ysell = yvector(I)
           switch Iprofit
           case {0}
              profit = 0
     Iprofit=1;
              case{1}
               profit = ( (ysell - ybuy)/2  ) *100
                 end
             B = 0
              end
         end
  end
   figure(1)
     plot(xvector, yvector, 'kx-',   xvector(N2: NN+1), aweosc(N2 :
NN+1), 'r+-', xvector(N2PN3: NN+1),signalline(N2PN3 : NN+1), 'b+-',
xvector, zero, 'k' )
     xlabel('t')
     ylabel('price, awesome oscillator,  signal line')
           figure(2)
     plot(xvector, yvector, 'kx-',  xvector(N2PN3: NN+1),
accelosc(N2PN3 : NN+1), 'k+-',   xvector, zero, 'k' )
     xlabel('t')
     ylabel('price,  accelerator oscillator of price')
```

D.3 awesig

```
% % awesig,  plot awesome oscillator(AO) of a dummy signal, plot signal
with 2 frequencies,  plot signal of 1 frequency when amp2 = 0
%  set profit = 0 if first data point of awesome oscillator is greater
than 0
clear
factor = 30 ;  % factor =  20.83, 9, 6.283 , 5, 9/2, 9/3, 9/4
% factor = 24.166, AO of signal is in phase with signal
```

```
%   check profit,  31.4, 15.7, 10.47, 7.85, 6.28
%   check profit, take approx  30, 15, 10, 8, 6
factor2 = factor/4 ;
omega = pi/factor;
omega2 = pi/factor2;
NN = 8 * factor; %  NN = 8*factor
% define original signal
amp2 = 0  ; % 0.4
theta0 = 0   ;  %  add to price signal   0,  pi/2 pi, 3*pi/2
  for I= 1: NN+1
     zero(I)=0;
      xvector(I) = I-1;
      yvector(I)= sin( omega*xvector(I)   +  theta0 ) + amp2*
sin( omega2*xvector(I) );
   end
   % set parameters of awesome oscillator and accelerator oscillator
N1= 5;
N2=34;
N3=5;
 % calculate technical indicators on signal
   for I = N1 : NN+1
      sma1signal(I) = 0;
      for J = 1:N1
         sma1signal(I) = sma1signal(I ) + 1/N1 * yvector(I+1 - J);
         end
   end
     for I = N2 : NN+1
      sma2signal(I) = 0;
      for J = 1:N2
         sma2signal(I) = sma2signal(I ) + 1/N2 * yvector(I+1 - J);
         end
   end
   for I = N2 : NN+1
      aweosc(I) = sma1signal(I) - sma2signal(I); % calculate awesome
oscillator of signal
      end
```

```
N2PN3 = N2+N3;
 for I = N2PN3 : NN+1
signalline(I) = 0;
for J = 1:N3
   signalline(I) = signalline(I ) + 1/N3 * aweosc(I+1 - J);
   end
end

for I = N2PN3 : NN+1
   accelosc (I) = aweosc(I) - signalline(I); %calculate aceleraator
oscillator of signal
   end
% To calculate buy price and sell price, and profit of awesome oscillator
B = 0; % Buy originally set to 0

 Iprofit=1;
if    aweosc(N2)    > 0 % first data point greater than 0, we do
not buy
   Iprofit = 0;
end
 for I = N2: NN+1
  if  B == 0 &  aweosc(I)  > 0
  I ,          ybuy = yvector(I)
  B = 1
       else
  if B == 1  &   aweosc(I)  < 0
    I,   ysell = yvector(I)

    switch Iprofit
    case {0}
       profit = 0
Iprofit=1;
       case{1}
        profit = ( (ysell - ybuy)/2  ) *100
          end

      B = 0
       end
    end
end
```

```
    figure(1)
     plot(xvector, yvector, 'kx-',   xvector(N1: NN+1), sma1signal(N1 :
NN+1), 'r+-', xvector(N2: NN+1),sma2signal(N2 : NN+1), 'b+-',   xvector,
zero, 'k' )
     xlabel('t')
     ylabel('price, sma5, sma34')

         figure(2)
     plot(xvector, yvector,'kx-', xvector(N2: NN+1), aweosc(N2 : NN+1),
'r+-',   xvector, zero, 'k' )
     xlabel('t')
     ylabel('price,awesome oscillator of price')
```

D.4 awesome

```
% awesome,  Plot Amplitude and Phase of simple moving averages and awesome
oscillator
% unwrap phase, Find Sure and Unsure profit Zone
clear
NN= 240 ;  % 240
intomega=pi/NN;
M1=5 ; % 5
M2=34;  % 34

for I= 1: NN+1
   omegavector(I) = (I-1)*intomega;

    H1vector(I)=1/M1*( 1- exp(-i*M1*omegavector(I)) )  /( 1 -
exp(-i*omegavector(I) )  );
     mag1(I)=abs(H1vector(I));
     phase1(I)= angle(H1vector(I));

     H2vector(I)= 1/M2*( 1- exp(-i*M2*omegavector(I)) )  /( 1 -
exp(-i*omegavector(I) )  );
     mag2(I)=abs(H2vector(I));
     phase2(I)= angle(H2vector(I));

       H3vector(I)= H1vector(I)  - H2vector(I); % awesome oscillator
     mag3(I)=abs(H3vector(I));
     phase3(I)= angle(H3vector(I));

  end
```

```
 phase3unwrap = unwrap(phase3); % unwrap phase
for I= 1: NN+1
   barlag(I) = phase3unwrap(I)/omegavector(I);
end
mag(1) = 1;
phase1(1)=0;
mag2(1) = 1;
phase2(1)=0;
 mag3(1) = 0;
phase3(1) = pi/2;
phase3unwrap(1) = pi/2;
    figure(1)
    plot(omegavector, mag1, 'k+-' , omegavector, mag2, 'kx-' )
    xlabel('Circular Frequency (radians)')
    ylabel('Amplitude')
    title('Simple Moving Average')

figure(2)
    plot(omegavector, phase1, 'k+-' , omegavector, phase2, 'kx-' )
    xlabel('Circular Frequency (radians)')
    ylabel('Phase (radians)')
    title('Simple Moving Average')
     figure(3)
    plot(omegavector, mag3, 'k-' )
    xlabel('Circular Frequency (radians)')
    ylabel('Amplitude')
    title('Awesome Oscillator')
        figure(4)
    plot(omegavector, phase3, 'k-'   )
    xlabel('Circular Frequency (radians)')
    ylabel('Wrapped Phase (radians)')
    title('Awesome Oscillator')

    % to find intersection point of phase3 and omegavector, to find Sure
Profit Zone and Unsure Profit Zone
       for I = 1: NN
                     if ( phase3(I) - omegavector(I) ) > 0  & ( phase3(I+1)
```

```
        - omegavector(I+1) ) < 0
                    intersectomega = omegavector(I)
            intersectphase =phase3(I)
                end
              end

          figure(5)
               plot( omegavector, phase3unwrap, 'k-' )
            xlabel('Circular Frequency (radians)')
            ylabel('Unwrapped Phase (radians)')
            title('Awesome Oscillator')

        figure(6)
            plot(omegavector, barlag, 'k+-' )
            xlabel('Circular Frequency (radians)')
            ylabel('bars lag)')
             title('Awesome Oscillator')
```

D.5 buysellprice

```
%buysellprice, to calculate theoretical buy and sell price where price
is a signal of a single sine wave.
% omega, theta0 and phi are given
% As sine wave is an odd function with respect to the horizontal axis,
sell price = - buy price
clear

omega = pi/6 % circular frequency
theta0 = 0 ;% theta0 = initial phase shift of price signal, e.g. pi/4,
pi/2
phi = -0.4718 ; % phi = phase lead of velocity indicator, e.g., pi/2
nbuy = fix( (2*pi - theta0 - phi)/omega ) + 1
buyprice = sin (nbuy *omega + theta0 )
nsell = fix( (3*pi - theta0 - phi)/omega ) + 1
sellprice = sin (nsell *omega + theta0 )
profit = sellprice - buyprice
profitpercent = profit/2 *100
```

D.6 ema

```
% ema,  Plot Amplitude and Phase and bar lag of exponential moving average
clear
NN=180;  %60
intomega=pi/NN;
N = 3;
alpha = 2/(N+1);

for I= 1: NN+1
  omegavector(I) = (I-1)*intomega;

   H1vector(I)= alpha/ (1 -(1- alpha)*  exp (-i * omegavector(I) ) ) ;
    mag1(I)=abs(H1vector(I));
    phase1(I)= angle(H1vector(I));
    barlag1(I) = phase1(I) / omegavector(I);

   end

   barlag1(1) = -(N-1)/2;

  figure(1)
  subplot(1, 1, 1)
     plot(omegavector, mag1, 'kx-'  )
     xlabel('Circular Frequency (radians)')
     ylabel('Amplitude')
     title('Exponential Moving Average')

     figure(2)
     subplot(1, 1, 1)
     plot(omegavector, phase1, 'kx-'   )
     xlabel('Circular Frequency (radians)')
     ylabel('Phase (radians)')
    title('Exponential Moving Average')

 figure(3)
     subplot(1, 1, 1)
     plot(omegavector, barlag1, 'kx-'  )
     xlabel('Circular Frequency (radians)')
     ylabel('bar lag')
      title('Exponential Moving Average')
```

D.7 emaaccel

```
%emaaccel ,  Plot Amplitude and Phase of  ema3 - ema6,  ema9(ema3 - ema6),
emaaccel = (ema3 - ema6) - ema9(ema3 - ema6)
clear
NN=240;
intomega=pi/NN;
M1=3 ;  % 12
alpha1=2/(M1+1);
M2= 6; %26
alpha2=2/(M2+1);
M3=9 ; %9
alpha3=2/(M3+1);

for I= 1: NN+1
   omegavector(I) = (I-1)*intomega;

    H1vector(I)= alpha1/ ( 1-(1-alpha1)*exp(-i*omegavector(I)));
     mag1(I)=abs(H1vector(I));
     phase1(I)= angle(H1vector(I));

     H2vector(I)= alpha2/ (1-(1-alpha2)*exp(-i*omegavector(I)));
     mag2(I)=abs(H2vector(I));
     phase2(I)= angle(H2vector(I));

     H4vector(I) = H1vector(I) - H2vector(I); %ema3 - ema6
     mag4(I)=abs(H4vector(I));
     phase4(I)= angle(H4vector(I));

     H3vector(I)= alpha3/ ( 1-(1-alpha3)*exp(-i*omegavector(I)));
     H6vector(I) = H3vector(I)*H4vector(I);% signal line - ema9(ema3 -
ema6)
     mag6(I)=abs(H6vector(I));
     phase6(I)= angle(H6vector(I));

          H5vector(I) = H4vector(I) - H6vector(I); %  (ema3 - ema6) -
ema9(ema3 - ema6)

     mag5(I)=abs(H5vector(I));
     phase5(I)= angle(H5vector(I));
      end
```

```
mag1(1) = 1;
phase1(1) = 0;
mag2(1) = 1;
phase2(1) = 0;
mag4(1) = 0; % (ema3 - ema6)
phase4(1) = pi/2;
  mag6(1) = 0; % signal line
 phase6(1) = pi/2;
 mag5(1) = 0; %(ema3 - ema6) - ema9(ema3 - ema6)
 phase5(1) = pi;
 figure(1)
   subplot(1, 1, 1)
   plot( omegavector, mag5, 'k-' )  % emaaccel
   xlabel('Circular Frequency (radians)')
   ylabel('Amplitude')
   title('EMAACCEL')  % emaaccel =  (ema3 - ema6) - ema9(ema3 - ema6)
     figure(2)
   subplot(1, 1, 1)
   plot( omegavector, phase5, 'k-'  )   % emaaccel
   xlabel('Circular Frequency (radians)')
   ylabel('Phase (radians)')
      title('EMAACCEL')  % emaaccel =  (ema3 - ema6) - ema9(ema3 - ema6)
 % to find intersection point of phase3 and omegavector
      for I = 1: NN
                 if ( phase5(I) - omegavector(I) ) > 0  & ( phase5(I+1)
- omegavector(I+1) ) < 0
            intersectomega = omegavector(I)
   intersectphase =phase5(I)
        end
      end
   figure(3)
   plot(omegavector, mag4, 'r+-' , omegavector, mag6, 'bx-' ,
omegavector, mag5, 'k.-' )  % (ema3 - ema6), signal line, emaaccel
   xlabel('Circular Frequency (radians)')
   ylabel('Amplitude')
  title('EMAACCEL')  % emaaccel =  (ema3 - ema6) - ema9(ema3 - ema6)
```

```
 figure(4)
subplot(1, 1, 1)
plot(omegavector, phase4, 'r+-' , omegavector, phase6, 'bx-' ,
omegavector, phase5, 'k-'  )  % 4  (ema3 - ema6),   6  ema9(ema3 - ema6),
5  emaaccel
    xlabel('Circular Frequency (radians)')
    ylabel('Phase (radians)')
    title('EMAACCEL')  % emaaccel =  (ema3 - ema6) - ema9(ema3 - ema6)
```

D.8 emaaccelsig

```
% % emaaccelsig,  plot emaaccel of a dummy signal, plot signal with 2
frequencies,  plot signal of 1 frequency when amp2 = 0
%  set profit = 0 if first data point of emaaccel is greater than 0
clear
factor = 6 ; % factor =  20.83, 9, 6.283 , 5, 9/2, 9/3, 9/4
%   check profit, take approx  30, 15, 10, 8, 6
factor2 =  factor/4  ;
omega = pi/factor;
omega2 = pi/factor2;
NN = 8 * factor; %  NN = 8*factor
% define original signal
amp2 = 0   ; % 0.4
theta0 =  0  ;  %  add to price signal   0,  pi/2, pi, 3*pi/2
 for I= 1: NN+1
    zero(I)=0;
    xvector(I) = I-1;
    yvector(I)= sin( omega*xvector(I)   +  theta0 ) + amp2*
sin( omega2*xvector(I) );
  end
  % set parameters of emaaccel
M1=3;
alpha1=2/(M1+1);
M2=6 ;
alpha2=2/(M2+1);
M3=9;
alpha3=2/(M3+1);
startpt =30;  % 30
```

```
% calculate technical indicators on signal
    ema1signal(1) = yvector(1);
  ema2signal(1) = yvector(1);
  macdsignal(1) = ema1signal(1) - ema2signal(1);
  ema3macd(1) = macdsignal(1);
  for I = 2: NN+1
     ema1signal(I) = alpha1 * yvector(I) + (1 - alpha1) * ema1signal(I
- 1);
     ema2signal(I) = alpha2 * yvector(I) + (1 - alpha2) * ema2signal(I
- 1);
     macdsignal(I) = ema1signal(I) - ema2signal(I);
     ema3macd(I) = alpha3 * macdsignal(I) + (1 - alpha3) * ema3macd(I
- 1);
     macdhsignal(I) = macdsignal(I) - ema3macd(I);
  end
  % To calculate buy price and sell price, and profit of emaaccel
  B = 0; % Buy originally set to 0
      Iprofit=1;
     if    macdhsignal(startpt)   >  0  % first data point greater than
0, we do not buy
        Iprofit = 0;
     end
      for I = startpt: NN+1
       if  B == 0  &  macdhsignal(I)  >  0
        I  ,         ybuy = yvector(I)
        B = 1
            else
        if  B == 1  &  macdhsignal(I)  < 0
          I,   ysell = yvector(I)

          switch Iprofit
          case {0}
            profit = 0
     Iprofit=1;
            case{1}
             profit = ( (ysell - ybuy)/2  ) *100
               end
           B = 0
               end
          end
     end
```

```
      figure(1)
        plot(xvector, yvector, 'kx-',  xvector(startpt: NN+1),
macdsignal(startpt : NN+1), 'r+-', xvector(startpt:
NN+1),ema3macd(startpt : NN+1), 'b+-',  xvector, zero, 'k' )
        xlabel('t')
        ylabel('price, ema3-ema6, ema9(ema3-ema6)')

            figure(2)
        plot(xvector, yvector, 'kx-', xvector(startpt: NN+1),
macdhsignal(startpt : NN+1), 'r+-',  xvector, zero, 'k' )
        xlabel('t')
        ylabel('price,  emaacel  of price')
```

D.9 emamema

```
%emamema,  Plot Amplitude and Phase of a fast ema minus a slow ema

clear
NN=240;
intomega=pi/NN;
M1=3 ;  % cf 12 for MACD
alpha1=2/(M1+1);
M2=6 ;  % cf 26 for MACD
alpha2=2/(M2+1);

for I= 1: NN+1
   omegavector(I) = (I-1)*intomega;

    H1vector(I)= alpha1/ ( 1-(1-alpha1)*exp(-i*omegavector(I)));
     mag1(I)=abs(H1vector(I));
     phase1(I)= angle(H1vector(I));

     H2vector(I)= alpha2/ (1-(1-alpha2)*exp(-i*omegavector(I)));
     mag2(I)=abs(H2vector(I));
     phase2(I)= angle(H2vector(I));

     H4vector(I) = H1vector(I) - H2vector(I); %cf MACD
     mag4(I)=abs(H4vector(I));
     phase4(I)= angle(H4vector(I));
     phase4(1) = pi/2;
     barlag4(I) = ( phase4(I) - pi/2 ) / omegavector(I);

       end
```

```
mag1(1) = 1;
phase1(1) = 0;
mag2(1) = 1;
phase2(1) = 0;
mag4(1) = 0;  % fast ema - slow ema

    figure(1)
    plot(omegavector, mag1, 'r+-' , omegavector, mag2, 'bx-' ,
omegavector, mag4, 'k.-' )  %1 fast EMA, 2 slow EMA,  4 fast ema - slow
ema
    xlabel('Circular Frequency (radians)')
    ylabel('Amplitude')
    title('EMA - EMA ')

      figure(2)
    subplot(1, 1, 1)
    plot(omegavector, phase1, 'r+-' , omegavector, phase2, 'bx-' ,
omegavector, phase4, 'k-'  )  %1 fast EMA, 2 slow EMA,  4 fast ema - slow
ema
    xlabel('Circular Frequency (radians)')
    ylabel('Phase (radians)')
     title('EMA - EMA ')

        figure(3)
    plot( omegavector, mag4, 'k-' )  %1 fast EMA, 2 slow EMA,  4 fast
ema - slow ema
    xlabel('Circular Frequency (radians)')
    ylabel('Amplitude')
    title('EMA - EMA ')

      figure(4)
    subplot(1, 1, 1)
    plot( omegavector, phase4, 'k-'  )  %1 fast EMA, 2 slow EMA,  4 fast
ema - slow ema
    xlabel('Circular Frequency (radians)')
    ylabel('Phase (radians)')
     title('EMA - EMA ')

       % to find intersection point of phase4 and omegavector
       for I = 1: NN
                if ( phase4(I) - omegavector(I) ) > 0  & ( phase4(I+1)
- omegavector(I+1) ) < 0
             intersectomega = omegavector(I)
    intersectphase =phase4(I)
          end
       end
```

```
figure(5)
subplot(1, 1, 1)
plot( omegavector, barlag4, 'rx-' )
xlabel('Circular Frequency (radians)')
ylabel('barlag')
title('EMA - EMA ')
```

D.10 emaseveral

```
% emaseveral,  Plot Amplitude and Phase and bar lag of several exponential
moving averages for comparison purpose
clear
NN=60;
intomega=pi/NN;
N1=3;
N2 = 6;
alpha1 = 2/(N1+1);
alpha2 = 2/(N2+1);

for I= 1: NN+1
   omegavector(I) = (I-1)*intomega;

    H1vector(I)= alpha1/ (1 -(1- alpha1)*  exp (-i * omegavector(I) ) ) ;
     mag1(I)=abs(H1vector(I));
     phase1(I)= angle(H1vector(I));
     barlag1(I) = phase1(I) / omegavector(I);

       H2vector(I)=alpha2/ (1 -(1- alpha2)*  exp (-i * omegavector(I) ) ) ;
     mag2(I)=abs(H2vector(I));
     phase2(I)= angle(H2vector(I));
     barlag2(I) = phase2(I) / omegavector(I);

    end

    barlag1(1) = - (N1-1)/2;
    barlag2(1) = - (N2-1)/2;

  figure(1)
  subplot(1, 1, 1)
     plot(omegavector, mag1, 'kx-'  ,  omegavector, mag2, 'k+-' )
     xlabel('Circular Frequency (radians)')
     ylabel('Amplitude')
     title('Exponential Moving Average')
```

```
    figure(2)
    subplot(1, 1, 1)
    plot(omegavector, phase1, 'kx-'  , omegavector, phase2, 'k+-' )
    xlabel('Circular Frequency (radians)')
    ylabel('Phase (radians)')
   title('Exponential Moving Average')

figure(3)
    subplot(1, 1, 1)
    plot(omegavector, barlag1, 'kx-' , omegavector, barlag2, 'k+-')
    xlabel('Circular Frequency (radians)')
    ylabel('bar lag')
     title('Exponential Moving Average')
```

D.11 emasig

```
% emasig,  plot ema of a signal
clear
factor = 9/4;
omega = pi/factor;
NN = 4 * factor;
M1=6;
alpha1=2/(M1+1);
startpt = 5;

  for I= 1: NN+1
     zero(I)=0;
      xvector(I) = I-1;
      yvector(I)= sin( omega*xvector(I));
   end

   emasignal(1) = yvector(1);
   for I = 2: NN+1
      emasignal(I) = alpha1 * yvector(I) + (1 - alpha1) * emasignal(I -
1);
   end

      figure(1)
      plot(xvector, yvector, 'kx-',  xvector(startpt : NN+1),
emasignal(startpt : NN+1), 'k+-',   xvector, zero, 'k' )
      xlabel('t')
      ylabel('price, ema of price')
```

D.12 fftcac40

```
% fftcac40,    plotting signal, magnitude of fft, phase of fft, real of
ifft, and phase of ifft
fft = Fast Fourier Transform, ifft = Inverse Fast Fourier Transform
clear

% CAC 40 from March 6, 2019  to Jun 39, 2019
 yvector = [ 5288  5267 5231  5265  5270  5306  5349  5405  5412  5425
5382  5378  5269  5260  5307  5301  5296  5350  5405  5423  5468  5463
5476  5471  5436  5449  5485  5502  5508  5528  5563  5580  5591  5576
5557  5569  5580  5586  5538  5548  5483  5395  5417  5313  5327  5262
5341  5374  5448  5438  5358  5385  5378  5281  5316  5336  5312  5222
5248  5207  5241  5268  5292  5278  5364  5382  5408  5374  5375  5367
5390  5509  5518  5535  5528  5521  5514  5500  5493  5538  5567  5576
5618  5620  5593  5589  5572  5567  5551  5572  5578  5614  5571  5550
5552  5567  5618  5505  5578  5610  5601  5511  5618  5557  5359  5241
5234  5266  5387  5327  5310  5363  5251  5236  5300  5371  5344
5435   ];
  NN = 117 ; % i.e., 118 data points
  NN = length(yvector) - 1
 for I= 1: NN+1
     zero(I)=0;
      xvector(I) = I-1;

   end
   % To find fft of price
      fftvector =  fft(yvector);
     mag=abs (fftvector);
     phase = angle(fftvector);

      % To find ifft of  fft of price, ifft(fft of price) should equal to
price
     ifftvector = ifft(fftvector);
   real2= real( ifftvector);
     mag2=abs (ifftvector);
     phase2 = angle(ifftvector);

   figure(1)
   subplot(1, 1,1)
          plot(xvector, yvector, 'k+-'  )
      xlabel('n')
      ylabel('price ')
      title(' CAC 40 ')
```

```
figure(2)
subplot(1, 1,1)
 plot(xvector, mag, 'k+',  xvector, zero, 'k' )
 xlabel('n')
  ylabel('magnitude of fft')

  figure(3)
subplot(1, 1,1)
 plot(xvector(2:NN), mag(2:NN), 'k+',  xvector, zero, 'k' )
 xlabel('n')
  ylabel('magnitude of fft, without n = 0')

 figure(4)
  subplot(1, 1,1)
   plot(xvector, phase, 'k+-',  xvector, zero, 'k' )
 xlabel('n')
  ylabel('phase of fft')

 figure(5)
 subplot(1, 1,1)
 plot(xvector, yvector, 'k+-' , xvector, mag2, 'go'  ) % note that mag2
= real2 as the price data do not have imaginary numbers
 xlabel('n')
  ylabel('magnitude of ifft o, price +')

  figure(6)
  subplot(1, 1,1)
   plot(xvector, phase2, 'k+-',  xvector, zero, 'k' )
   xlabel('n')
  ylabel('phse of ifft')
```

D.13 fftftse

```
% fftftse,    plotting signal,  magnitude of fft, phase of fft, real of
ifft, and phase of ifft
clear
% FTSE  from March 1, 19  to Aug 14, 19   115 data point
 yvector = [    7106  7134  7183  7196  7157  7104  7130  7151  7159
```

```
7185  7228  7299  7324  7291  7355  7207  7177  7196  7194  7234  7279
7317  7391  7418  7401  7446  7451  7425  7421  7418  7437  7436  7469
7471  7459  7523  7471  7434  7428  7440  7418  7385  7351  7380  7260
7271  7207  7203  7163  7241  7297  7353  7348  7310  7328  7334  7231
7277  7269  7185  7218  7161  7184  7214  7220  7259  7331  7375  7398
7367  7368  7345  7357  7443  7403  7424  7407  7416  7422  7416  7402
7425  7497  7559  7609  7603  7553  7549  7536  7530  7509  7506  7531
7577  7535  7493  7508  7514  7556  7501  7489  7549  7686  7645  7586
7584  7407  7223  7171  7198  7285  7253  7226  7250  7147   ];
    NN=114;  % i.e., 115 data point
   NN = length(yvector) - 1
 for I= 1: NN+1
     zero(I)=0;
      xvector(I) = I-1;
   end
   % To find fft of price
      fftvector =  fft(yvector);
     mag=abs (fftvector);
     phase = angle(fftvector);
     % To find ifft of  fft of price, ifft(fft of price) should equal to
price
     ifftvector = ifft(fftvector);
   real2= real( ifftvector);
     mag2=abs (ifftvector);
     phase2 = angle(ifftvector);
   figure(1)
   subplot(1, 1,1)
          plot(xvector, yvector, 'k+-'  )
      xlabel('n')
      ylabel('price ')
      title('FTSE 100 ')
     figure(2)
     subplot(1, 1,1)
      plot(xvector, mag, 'k+',  xvector, zero, 'k' )
      xlabel('n')
       ylabel('magnitude of fft')
```

```
figure(3)
subplot(1, 1,1)
plot(xvector(2:NN), mag(2:NN), 'k+', xvector, zero, 'k' )
xlabel('n')
ylabel('magnitude of fft, without n = 0')

figure(4)
subplot(1, 1,1)
plot(xvector, phase, 'k+-', xvector, zero, 'k' )
xlabel('n')
ylabel('phase of fft')

figure(5)
subplot(1, 1,1)
plot(xvector, yvector, 'k+-' , xvector, mag2, 'go' ) % note that mag2
= real2 as the price data do not have imaginary numbers
xlabel('n')
ylabel('magnitude of ifft o, price +')

figure(6)
subplot(1, 1,1)
plot(xvector, phase2, 'k+-', xvector, zero, 'k' )
xlabel('n')
ylabel('phse of ifft')
```

D.14 ffthangseng

```
% ffthangseng, plotting signal, magnitude of fft, phase of fft, real
of ifft, and phase of ifft
clear
%Hang Seng from March 1 2019 to Aug 12, 2019
yvector = [ 28812 28959 28961 29037 28779 28228 28503 28920
28807 28851 29012 29409 29466 29320 29071 29113 28523 28567
28728 28775 29051 29562 29624 29986 29936 30077 30157 30119
29839 29909 29810 30129 30124 29963 29963 29805 29549 29605
29892 29699 29209 29363 29003 28311 28550 28122 28268 28275
27946 27787 27657 27705 27267 27353 27268 27390 27235 27114
26901 26893 26761 26895 26965 27578 27789 27308 27294 27118
27227 27498 28202 28550 28473 28513 28185 28221 28621 28542
28875 28855 28795 28774 28331 28116 28204 28431 28471 28554
28619 28593 28461 28765 28371 28466 28524 28594 28397 28106
28146 27777 27505 26918 26151 25976 25997 26120 25939 25824 ];
```

```
NN=107; % i.e., 108 data point
NN = length(yvector) - 1
for I= 1: NN+1
    zero(I)=0;
    xvector(I) = I-1;
end
% To find fft of price
fftvector = fft(yvector);
mag=abs (fftvector);
phase = angle(fftvector);
% To find ifft of  fft of price, ifft(fft of price) should equal to
price
ifftvector = ifft(fftvector);
real2= real( ifftvector);
mag2=abs (ifftvector);
phase2 = angle(ifftvector);
figure(1)
subplot(1, 1,1)
plot(xvector, yvector, 'k+-' )
xlabel('n')
ylabel('price ')
title('Hang Seng ')

figure(2)
subplot(1, 1,1)
plot(xvector, mag, 'k+',  xvector, zero, 'k' )
xlabel('n')
ylabel('magnitude of fft')

figure(3)
subplot(1, 1,1)
plot(xvector(2:NN), mag(2:NN), 'k+',  xvector, zero, 'k' )
xlabel('n')
ylabel('magnitude of fft, without n = 0')

figure(4)
subplot(1, 1,1)
plot(xvector, phase, 'k+-',  xvector, zero, 'k' )
xlabel('n')
ylabel('phase of fft')
```

```
    figure(5)
    subplot(1, 1,1)
    plot(xvector, yvector, 'k+-' , xvector, mag2, 'go'  ) % note that mag2
= real2 as the price data do not have imaginary numbers
    xlabel('n')

    ylabel('magnitude of ifft o, price +')

    figure(6)
    subplot(1, 1,1)
     plot(xvector, phase2, 'k+-',  xvector, zero, 'k' )
     xlabel('n')
    ylabel('phse of ifft')
```

D.15 fftsinewave

```
% fftsinewave,    plotting Fast Fourier Transform of sine wave, and
Inverse Fast Fourier Transform of Fast Fourier Transform  of sine wave,
which should be the same as the original sine wave
clear
int = 20;
omega = pi/int;
NN = 4 * int - 1;
D = 0;  % D is a constant added to the sine wave, e.g., D  = 2;

  for I= 1: NN+1
     zero(I)=0;
      xvector(I)  = I-1;
      yvector(I)= D +  sin( omega*xvector(I)); % raw signal. e.g., price
   end

      figure(1)
      plot(xvector, yvector, 'r+ ',  xvector, zero, 'k' )
      xlabel('t')
      ylabel('price')

     fftvector =  fft(yvector);
     mag=abs (fftvector);
     phase = angle(fftvector);
```

```
    figure(2)
     plot(xvector, mag, 'r+',  xvector, zero, 'k' ) % plot magnitude of
fft
     xlabel('t')
     ylabel('magnitude of fft')

     figure(3)
      plot(xvector, phase, 'r',  xvector, zero, 'k' ) % plot phase of fft
     xlabel('t')
     ylabel('phase of fft')
     ifftvector = ifft(fftvector);
     real2= real( ifftvector);
    mag2=abs (ifftvector);
    phase2 = angle(ifftvector);

     figure(4)
     plot(xvector, real2, 'r+ ', xvector, yvector,  'go' , xvector, zero,
'k' ) % plot real part of ifft, which is equal to magnitude of ifft, which
should be the same as original price
     xlabel('t')
     ylabel('magnitude of ifft +, price o ')

     figure(5)
      plot(xvector, phase2, 'r',  xvector, zero, 'k' )
     xlabel('t')
     ylabel('phase of ifft')
```

D.16 fftsp500

```
% fftsp500,    plotting signal,  magnitude of fft, phase of fft, real of
ifft, and phase of ifft
clear

% S& P500 from April 24, 2019  to Aug 12, 2019
 yvector = [2927.25  2926.17  2939.88  2943.03  2945.83  2923.73
2917.52  2945.64  2932.47  2884.05  2879.42  2870.72  2881.40  2811.87
2834.41  2850.96  2876.32  2859.53  2840.23  2864.36  2856.27  2822.24
2826.06  2802.39  2783.02  2788.86  2752.06  2744.45  2803.27  2826.15
2843.49  2873.34  2886.73  2885.72  2879.84  2891.64  2886.98  2889.67
2917.75  2926.46  2954.18  2950.46  2945.35  2917.38  2913.78  2924.92
2941.76  2964.33  2973.01  2995.82  2990.41  2975.95  2979.63
2993.07  2999.91  3013.77  3014.30  3004.04  2984.42  2995.11  2976.61
2995.03  3005.47  3019.56  3003.67  3025.86  3020.97  3013.18  2980.38
2953.56  2932.05  2844.74  2881.77  2883.98  2938.09  2918.65
```

```
2882.70 ];
 NN=76; %i.e., 77 data points
 NN = length(yvector) - 1
 for I= 1: NN+1
     zero(I)=0;
      xvector(I) = I-1;
   end
   % To find fft of price
      fftvector = fft(yvector);
     mag=abs (fftvector);
     phase = angle(fftvector);

     % To find ifft of  fft of price, ifft(fft of price) which should equal
to price
     ifftvector = ifft(fftvector);
   real2= real( ifftvector);
     mag2=abs (ifftvector);
     phase2 = angle(ifftvector);

   figure(1)
   subplot(1, 1,1)
          plot(xvector, yvector, 'k+-'  )
      xlabel('n')
      ylabel('price ')
      title('S & P500')

     figure(2)
     subplot(1, 1,1)
      plot(xvector, mag, 'k+',  xvector, zero, 'k' )
      xlabel('n')
       ylabel('magnitude of fft')

       figure(3)
     subplot(1, 1,1)
      plot(xvector(2:NN), mag(2:NN), 'k+',  xvector, zero, 'k' )
      xlabel('n')
       ylabel('magnitude of fft, without n = 0')
```

```
figure(4)
subplot(1, 1,1)
 plot(xvector, phase, 'k+-',  xvector, zero, 'k' )
xlabel('n')
ylabel('phase of fft')

figure(5)
subplot(1, 1,1)
plot(xvector, yvector, 'k+-' , xvector, mag2, 'go'  ) % note that mag2
= real2 as the price data do not have imaginary numbers
xlabel('n')
ylabel('magnitude of ifft o, price +')

figure(6)
subplot(1, 1,1)
 plot(xvector, phase2, 'k+-',  xvector, zero, 'k' )
 xlabel('n')
ylabel('phse of ifft')
```

D.17 hema

```
% hema,   To calculate h(k) of ema,  unit impulse response of
exponential moving average
clear
M3=3;
M6=6;
M9=9;
M12=12;
M26=26;
alpha3 = 2/(M3 +1);
alpha6 = 2/(M6 +1);
alpha9 = 2/(M9 +1);
alpha12 = 2/(M12 +1);
alpha26= 2/(M26 +1);
NN=40;
      for I= 1: NN+1
         kvector(I)=I -1;
    h3vector(I) = alpha3 * (1 - alpha3)^(I-1);
    h6vector(I) = alpha6 * (1 - alpha6)^(I-1);
```

```
    h9vector(I) = alpha9 * (1 - alpha9)^(I-1);
    h12vector(I) = alpha12 * (1 - alpha12)^(I-1);
    h26vector(I) = alpha26 * (1 - alpha26)^(I-1);
    end

    figure(1)
     subplot(1, 1, 1)
    plot(kvector, h3vector, 'ko' , kvector, h6vector, 'kx',kvector,
h9vector, 'k^',kvector, h12vector, 'k*',kvector, h26vector, 'k+' )
    xlabel('k')
    ylabel('Unit sample response, h(k)')
    title('Exponential Moving Average')

    figure(2)
    subplot(1, 1, 1)
    plot(kvector, h3vector, 'r-' , kvector, h6vector, 'b-',kvector,
h9vector, 'g-',kvector, h12vector, 'm-',kvector, h26vector, 'k-' )
    xlabel('k')
    ylabel('Unit sample response, h(k)')
    title('Exponential Moving Average for M =3,6,9,12,26')
```

D.18 macd

```
%macd,  Plot Amplitude and Phase of  MACD
clear
NN= 240; % 240, 14400
intomega=pi/NN;
M1=12;  % 12 for MACD
alpha1=2/(M1+1);
M2=26 ;  % 26 for MACD
alpha2=2/(M2+1);

for I= 1: NN+1
   omegavector(I) = (I-1)*intomega;

    H1vector(I)= alpha1/ ( 1-(1-alpha1)*exp(-i*omegavector(I)));
     mag1(I)=abs(H1vector(I));
     phase1(I)= angle(H1vector(I));

     H2vector(I)= alpha2/ (1-(1-alpha2)*exp(-i*omegavector(I)));
     mag2(I)=abs(H2vector(I));
     phase2(I)= angle(H2vector(I));
```

```
    H4vector(I) = H1vector(I) - H2vector(I); %MACD
    mag4(I)=abs(H4vector(I));
    phase4(I)= angle(H4vector(I));
    phase4(1) = pi/2;
    barlag4(I) = ( phase4(I) - pi/2 ) / omegavector(I);
     end

  mag1(1) = 1;
  phase1(1) = 0;
  mag2(1) = 1;
  phase2(1) = 0;
  mag4(1) = 0;  % MACD

     figure(1)
     plot(omegavector, mag1, 'r+-' , omegavector, mag2, 'bx-' ,
omegavector, mag4, 'k.-' )  %1 fast EMA, 2 slow EMA,  4 MACD
     xlabel('Circular Frequency (radians)')
     ylabel('Amplitude')
     title('MACD')

      figure(2)
     subplot(1, 1, 1)
     plot(omegavector, phase1, 'r+-' , omegavector, phase2, 'bx-'  ,
omegavector, phase4, 'k-'  )  %1 fast EMA, 2 slow EMA,  4 MACD
     xlabel('Circular Frequency (radians)')
     ylabel('Phase (radians)')
      title('MACD')

      % to find intersection point of phase4 and omegavector, Sure and
Unsure Profit Zone
       for I = 1: NN
                if ( phase4(I) - omegavector(I) ) > 0  & ( phase4(I+1)
- omegavector(I+1) ) < 0
            intersectomega = omegavector(I)
     intersectphase =phase4(I)
         end
       end

      figure(3)
      subplot(1, 1, 1)
     plot( omegavector, barlag4, 'kx-'    )
     xlabel('Circular Frequency (radians)')
     ylabel('barlag')
      title('MACD')
```

D.19 macdh

```
%macdh,  Plot Amplitude and Phase of  MACD, signal line, and MACDH

clear
NN=240; %240, larger NN, e.g., 14400, to find intersection point more
accurately, answer: omega = 0.235
intomega=pi/NN;
M1=12 ;
alpha1=2/(M1+1);
M2=26;
alpha2=2/(M2+1);
M3=9;
alpha3=2/(M3+1);

for I= 1: NN+1
   omegavector(I) = (I-1)*intomega;

    H1vector(I)= alpha1/ ( 1-(1-alpha1)*exp(-i*omegavector(I)));
     mag1(I)=abs(H1vector(I));
     phase1(I)= angle(H1vector(I));

     H2vector(I)= alpha2/ (1-(1-alpha2)*exp(-i*omegavector(I)));
     mag2(I)=abs(H2vector(I));
     phase2(I)= angle(H2vector(I));

     H4vector(I) = H1vector(I) - H2vector(I); %MACD
     mag4(I)=abs(H4vector(I));
     phase4(I)= angle(H4vector(I));

     H3vector(I)= alpha3/ ( 1-(1-alpha3)*exp(-i*omegavector(I)));

     H6vector(I) = H3vector(I)*H4vector(I);% signal line
     mag6(I)=abs(H6vector(I));
     phase6(I)= angle(H6vector(I));

     H5vector(I) = H4vector(I) - H6vector(I); % MACDH
     mag5(I)=abs(H5vector(I));
     phase5(I)= angle(H5vector(I));

 end
```

```
  mag1(1) = 1;
  phase1(1) = 0;
  mag2(1) = 1;
  phase2(1) = 0;
  mag4(1) = 0;  % MACD
  phase4(1) = pi/2;
     mag6(1) = 0; % signal line
    phase6(1) = pi/2;
    mag5(1) = 0;  %MACDH
   phase5(1) = pi;

      figure(1)
      plot(omegavector, mag4, 'r+-' , omegavector, mag6, 'bx-' ,
omegavector, mag5, 'k.-' )  % MACD, signal line, MACDH
      xlabel('Circular Frequency (radians)')
      ylabel('Amplitude')
      title('MACDH')

        figure(2)
      subplot(1, 1, 1)
      plot(omegavector, phase4, 'r+-' , omegavector, phase6, 'bx-'  ,
omegavector, phase5, 'k.-'  )   % 4 MACD,   6  signal line,  5 MACDH
      xlabel('Circular Frequency (radians)')
      ylabel('Phase (radians)')
       title('MACDH')

         figure(3)
      subplot(1, 1, 1)
      plot(omegavector,  omegavector, 'k-' , omegavector, phase5, 'k-'  )
%  omegavector, omegavector is the  line plotted to show that there can
be a loss in the trade when phase is less than omega
      xlabel('Circular Frequency (radians)')
      ylabel('Phase (radians)')
       title('MACDH')

       % to find intersection point of phase3 and omegavector
         for I = 1: NN
                     if ( phase5(I) - omegavector(I) ) > 0  & ( phase5(I+1)
- omegavector(I+1) ) < 0
               intersectomega = omegavector(I)
      intersectphase =phase5(I)
            end
         end
```

D.20 macdh1

```
%macdh1,  MACDH with M1 = 1, i.e. price
%Plot Amplitude and Phase of  MACD1, signal line, and MACDH1

clear
NN=240;
intomega=pi/NN;
M1=1; % cf 12 for MACDH
alpha1=2/(M1+1);
M2=26;
alpha2=2/(M2+1);
M3=9;
alpha3=2/(M3+1);

for I= 1: NN+1
   omegavector(I) = (I-1)*intomega;

    H1vector(I)= alpha1/ ( 1-(1-alpha1)*exp(-i*omegavector(I)));
     mag1(I)=abs(H1vector(I));
     phase1(I)= angle(H1vector(I));

     H2vector(I)= alpha2/ (1-(1-alpha2)*exp(-i*omegavector(I)));
     mag2(I)=abs(H2vector(I));
     phase2(I)= angle(H2vector(I));

     H4vector(I) = H1vector(I) - H2vector(I); %MACD1
     mag4(I)=abs(H4vector(I));
     phase4(I)= angle(H4vector(I));

     H3vector(I)= alpha3/ ( 1-(1-alpha3)*exp(-i*omegavector(I)));

     H6vector(I) = H3vector(I)*H4vector(I);% signal line = 6
     mag6(I)=abs(H6vector(I));
     phase6(I)= angle(H6vector(I));

     H5vector(I) = H4vector(I) - H6vector(I); % MACDH1
     mag5(I)=abs(H5vector(I));
     phase5(I)= angle(H5vector(I));
  end

  mag1(1) = 1;
  phase1(1) = 0;
  mag2(1) = 1;
```

```
phase2(1) = 0;
mag4(1) = 0;  % MACD1=4
phase4(1) = pi/2;
   mag6(1) = 0; % signal line
  phase6(1) = pi/2;
  mag5(1) = 0;  %MACDH1=5
 phase5(1) = pi;

 figure(1)
  subplot(1, 1, 1)
    plot(omegavector, mag4, 'r+-' , omegavector, mag6, 'bx-' ,
omegavector, mag5, 'k.-' )
    xlabel('Circular Frequency (radians)')
    ylabel('Amplitude')
    title('MACDH1')

      figure(2)
    subplot(1, 1, 1)
    plot(omegavector, phase4, 'r+-' , omegavector, phase6, 'bx-'  ,
omegavector, phase5, 'k.-'  )   % 4 MACD1,   6  signal line,   5 MACDH1
    xlabel('Circular Frequency (radians)')
    ylabel('Phase (radians)')
     title('MACDH1')
      % to find intersection point of phase5 and omegavector
       for I = 1: NN
                if ( phase5(I) - omegavector(I) ) > 0  & ( phase5(I+1)
- omegavector(I+1) ) < 0
            intersectomega = omegavector(I)
    intersectphase =phase5(I)
         end
       end
```

D.21 macdh1sig

```
% % macdh1sig,  M1 = 1,  plot MACDH1 of a dummy signal, plot signal with
2 frequencies,  plot signal of 1 frequency when amp2 = 0
%  set profit = 0 if first data point of MACDH1 is greater than 0
clear
factor = 6 ; % factor =  20.83, 9, 6.283 , 5, 9/2, 9/3, 9/4
%   check profit,  31.4, 15.7, 10.47, 7.85, 6.28
%   check profit, take approx  30, 15, 10, 8, 6 in book
```

```
factor2 =  2 ; %factor/4;
omega = pi/factor;
omega2 = pi/factor2;
NN = 10 * factor; %  NN = 8*factor, 20*

% define original signal
amp2 = 0. ; % 0.4, 0.25
theta0 = 0 ;  %  add to price signal   0,  pi/2, pi, 3*pi/2
  for I= 1: NN+1
     zero(I)=0;
      xvector(I) = I-1;
      yvector(I)= sin( omega*xvector(I)   +  theta0 ) + amp2*
sin( omega2*xvector(I) );
   end
   % set parameters of MACDH1
M1=1;
alpha1=2/(M1+1);
M2=26;
alpha2=2/(M2+1);
M3=9;
alpha3=2/(M3+1);

startpt =30;  % 30

 % calculate technical indicators on signal
     ema1signal(1) = yvector(1);
   ema2signal(1) = yvector(1);
   macdsignal(1) = ema1signal(1) - ema2signal(1);
   ema3macd(1) = macdsignal(1);
   for I = 2: NN+1
      ema1signal(I) = alpha1 * yvector(I) + (1 - alpha1) * ema1signal(I
- 1);
      ema2signal(I) = alpha2 * yvector(I) + (1 - alpha2) * ema2signal(I
- 1);
      macdsignal(I) = ema1signal(I) - ema2signal(I);
      ema3macd(I) = alpha3 * macdsignal(I) + (1 - alpha3) * ema3macd(I
- 1);
      macdhsignal(I) = macdsignal(I) - ema3macd(I);
   end
      % To calculate buy price and sell price, and profit of MACDH1
   B = 0; % Buy originally set to 0
       Iprofit=1;
      if    macdhsignal(startpt)    >  0  % when first data point is
greater than 0, we do not buy
         Iprofit = 0;
      end
```

```
for I = startpt: NN+1
 if   B == 0  &   macdhsignal(I)    >  0
  I  ,          ybuy = yvector(I)
  B = 1
       else
  if  B == 1   &   macdhsignal(I)  < 0
    I,    ysell = yvector(I)
    switch Iprofit
    case {0}
      profit = 0

     Iprofit=1;
             case{1}
              profit = ( (ysell - ybuy)/2  ) *100
                end
             B = 0
             end
         end
   end
     figure(1)
      plot(xvector, yvector, 'kx-',  xvector(startpt: NN+1),
macdsignal(startpt : NN+1), 'r+-', xvector(startpt:
NN+1),ema3macd(startpt : NN+1), 'b+-',  xvector, zero, 'k' )
      xlabel('t')
      ylabel('price,  macd1, signal line')

           figure(2)
      plot(xvector, yvector, 'kx-',  xvector(startpt: NN+1),
macdhsignal(startpt : NN+1), 'r+-',  xvector, zero, 'k' )
      xlabel('t')
      ylabel('price,  MACDH1  of price')
```

D.22 macdhsig

```
%%macdhsig,  plot MACDH of a dummy signal, plot signal with 2 frequencies,
plot signal of 1 frequency when amp2 = 0
%  set profit = 0 if first data point of MACDH is greater than 0
clear
factor = 6  ; % factor =  20.83, 9, 6.283 , 5, 9/2, 9/3, 9/4
%   check profit,  31.4, 15.7, 10.47, 7.85, 6.28
%   check profit, take approx  30, 15, 10, 8, 6
```

```
factor2 =  factor/4  ;
omega = pi/factor;
omega2 = pi/factor2;
NN = 8 * factor; %  NN = 8*factor

% define original signal
amp2 = 0  ; % 0.4
theta0 = pi/2 ; %  add to price signal   0,  pi/2, pi, 3*pi/2
  for I= 1: NN+1
     zero(I)=0;
      xvector(I) = I-1;
      yvector(I)= sin( omega*xvector(I)   +  theta0 ) + amp2*
sin( omega2*xvector(I) );
   end
   % set parameters of MACDH
M1=12;
alpha1=2/(M1+1);
M2=26;
alpha2=2/(M2+1);
M3=9;
alpha3=2/(M3+1);

startpt =30;  % 30

 % calculate technical indicators on signal
     ema1signal(1) = yvector(1);
   ema2signal(1) = yvector(1);
   macdsignal(1) = ema1signal(1) - ema2signal(1);
   ema3macd(1) = macdsignal(1);
   for I = 2: NN+1
      ema1signal(I) = alpha1 * yvector(I) + (1 - alpha1) * ema1signal(I
- 1);
      ema2signal(I) = alpha2 * yvector(I) + (1 - alpha2) * ema2signal(I
- 1);
      macdsignal(I) = ema1signal(I) - ema2signal(I);
      ema3macd(I) = alpha3 * macdsignal(I) + (1 - alpha3) * ema3macd(I
- 1);
      macdhsignal(I) = macdsignal(I) - ema3macd(I);
   end

   % To calculate buy price and sell price, and profit of MACDH
   B = 0; % Buy originally set to 0

    Iprofit=1;
   if    macdhsignal(startpt)    >  0  % when first data point is
```

```
    greater than 0, we do not buy
            Iprofit = 0;
        end

         for I = startpt: NN+1
          if   B == 0  &   macdhsignal(I)   >  0
           I  ,          ybuy = yvector(I)
           B = 1
                 else
           if  B == 1   &   macdhsignal(I)  < 0
              I,    ysell = yvector(I)

              switch Iprofit
              case {0}
                 profit = 0
        Iprofit=1;
                 case{1}
                  profit = ( (ysell - ybuy)/2  ) *100
                    end

                B = 0
                end
            end
      end

       figure(1)
        plot(xvector, yvector, 'kx-',  xvector(startpt: NN+1),
    macdsignal(startpt : NN+1), 'r+-', xvector(startpt:
    NN+1),ema3macd(startpt : NN+1), 'b+-',  xvector, zero, 'k' )
        xlabel('t')
        ylabel('price, ema12, ema26')

              figure(2)
        plot(xvector, yvector, 'kx-', xvector(startpt: NN+1),
    macdhsignal(startpt : NN+1), 'r+-',  xvector, zero, 'k' )
        xlabel('t')
        ylabel('price,  MACDH  of price')
```

D.23 macdsig

```
%  macdsig,  plot MACD of a dummy signal, plot signal with 2 frequencies,
plot signal of 1 frequency when amp2 = 0
%  set profit = 0 if first data point of macd is greater than 0
```

```
clear
factor = 8 ; % factor = 20.83, 9, 6.283 , 5, 9/2, 9/3, 9/4
%   check profit, 31.4, 15.7, 10.47, 7.85, 6.28
%   check profit, take approx 30, 15, 10, 8, 6

factor2 = factor/4 ;
omega = pi/factor;
omega2 = pi/factor2;
NN = 10 * factor; % NN = 8*factor

% define original signal
amp2 = 0.  ; % 0.4
theta0 = pi/2   ; % add to price signal  0, pi/2, pi, 3*pi/2
  for I= 1: NN+1
     zero(I)=0;
      xvector(I) = I-1;
      yvector(I)= sin( omega*xvector(I)   + theta0 ) + amp2*
sin( omega2*xvector(I) );
   end

      % set parameters of MACD
M1=12;
alpha1=2/(M1+1);
M2=26;
alpha2=2/(M2+1);

startpt =30;  % 30

 % calculate technical indicators on signal
    ema1signal(1) = yvector(1);
   ema2signal(1) = yvector(1);
   for I = 2: NN+1
      ema1signal(I) = alpha1 * yvector(I) + (1 - alpha1) * ema1signal(I
- 1);
      ema2signal(I) = alpha2 * yvector(I) + (1 - alpha2) * ema2signal(I
- 1);
      macdsignal(I) = ema1signal(I) - ema2signal(I);
   end

   % To calculate buy price and sell price, and profit of MACD
   B = 0; % Buy originally set to 0

       Iprofit=1;
      if    macdsignal(startpt)   > 0  % when first data point is
greater than 0, we do not buy
         Iprofit = 0;
      end
```

```
for I = startpt: NN+1
 if  B == 0  &  macdsignal(I)  > 0
  I  ,         ybuy = yvector(I)
  B = 1
        else
  if  B == 1  &  macdsignal(I)  < 0
     I,    ysell = yvector(I)

     switch Iprofit
     case {0}
        profit = 0
Iprofit=1;
        case{1}
         profit = ( (ysell - ybuy)/2  ) *100
           end
       B = 0
        end
   end
end

 figure(1)
   plot(xvector, yvector, 'kx-',  xvector(startpt: NN+1),
emalsignal(startpt : NN+1), 'r+-', xvector(startpt:
NN+1),ema2signal(startpt : NN+1), 'b+-',  xvector, zero, 'k' )
   xlabel('t')
   ylabel('price, ema12, ema26')

        figure(2)
   plot(xvector, yvector, 'kx-',  xvector(startpt: NN+1),
macdsignal(startpt : NN+1), 'r+-',  xvector, zero, 'k' )
   xlabel('t')
   ylabel('price,  MACD  of price')
```

D.24 pmema

```
%pmema,  Plot Amplitude and Phase of  Price minus EMA of price
clear
NN=240;
intomega=pi/NN;
M1=1;  % cf MACD 12
```

```
alpha1=2/(M1+1);
M2= 6   %cf MACD 26
alpha2=2/(M2+1);

for I= 1: NN+1
   omegavector(I) = (I-1)*intomega;

    H1vector(I)= alpha1/ ( 1-(1-alpha1)*exp(-i*omegavector(I)));
     mag1(I)=abs(H1vector(I));
     phase1(I)= angle(H1vector(I));

     H2vector(I)= alpha2/ (1-(1-alpha2)*exp(-i*omegavector(I)));
     mag2(I)=abs(H2vector(I));
     phase2(I)= angle(H2vector(I));

     H4vector(I) = H1vector(I) - H2vector(I); %pmema, cf MACD
     mag4(I)=abs(H4vector(I));
     phase4(I)= angle(H4vector(I));
     phase4(1) = pi/2;

       end

  mag1(1) = 1;
  phase1(1) = 0;
  mag2(1) = 1;
  phase2(1) = 0;
  mag4(1) = 0;  % cf MACD

 figure(1)
      plot( omegavector, mag4, 'k+-  ' )   % Price - EMA of Price
      xlabel('Circular Frequency (radians)')
      ylabel('Amplitude')
      title('   Price - EMA of Price  ')  %   Price - EMA of Price

        figure(2)
      subplot(1, 1, 1)
      plot( omegavector, phase4, 'k+-  ' )   % Price - EMA of Price
      xlabel('Circular Frequency (radians)')
      ylabel('Phase (radians)')
        title('   Price - EMA of Price '  )

        figure(3)
         subplot(1, 1, 1)
      plot( omegavector, phase4, 'k-  '  , omegavector,omegavector, 'k-
```

```
' )  % Price - EMA of Price,plot straight line to find Sure and Unsure
Profit Zone
      xlabel('Circular Frequency (radians)')
      ylabel('Phase (radians) ' )
        title('    Price - EMA of Price '  )

        % to find intersection point of phase3 and omegavector
        for I = 1: NN
                     if ( phase4(I) - omegavector(I) ) > 0  & ( phase4(I+1)
- omegavector(I+1) ) < 0
              intersectomega = omegavector(I)
      intersectphase =phase4(I)
           end
        end

     figure(4)
      plot(omegavector, mag1, 'r+-' , omegavector, mag2, 'bx-' ,
omegavector, mag4, 'k.-' )   %1 fast EMA, 2 slow EMA,  4 fast EMA - slow
EMA
      xlabel('Circular Frequency (radians)')
      ylabel('Amplitude')
      title(' Price - EMA of Price ')

        figure(5)
      subplot(1, 1, 1)
      plot(omegavector, phase1, 'r+-' , omegavector, phase2, 'bx-'  ,
omegavector, phase4, 'k.-'  )   %1 fast EMA, 2 slow EMA,  4  fast EMA -
slow EMA
      xlabel('Circular Frequency (radians)')
      ylabel('Phase (radians)')
        title(' Price - EMA of Price ')
```

D.25 pmemasig

```
%  pmemasig,  plot price minus ema of price  (pmema) of a dummy signal,
plot signal with 2 frequencies,  plot signal of 1 frequency when amp2 =
0
%  set profit = 0 if first data point  pmema is greater than 0
clear
factor = 6  ; % factor =  20.83, 9, 6.283 , 5, 9/2, 9/3, 9/4
%    check profit,  31.4, 15.7, 10.47, 7.85, 6.28
%    check profit, take approx  30, 15, 10, 8, 6

factor2 = factor/4 ;
omega = pi/factor;
```

```
omega2 = pi/factor2;
NN = 8 * factor; % NN = 8*factor

% define original signal
amp2 = 0   ; % 0.4
theta0 = pi/2  ;  %  add to price signal   0,  pi/2, pi, 3*pi/2
  for I= 1: NN+1
     zero(I)=0;
      xvector(I) = I-1;
      yvector(I)= sin( omega*xvector(I)   +  theta0 ) + amp2*
sin( omega2*xvector(I) );
   end
   startpt =30;  % 30

      % set parameters of pmema
M1=1 ;
alpha1=2/(M1+1);
M2= 6 ;

alpha2=2/(M2+1);

 % calculate technical indicators on signal
    ema1signal(1) = yvector(1);
   ema2signal(1) = yvector(1);
   for I = 2: NN+1
      ema1signal(I) = alpha1 * yvector(I) + (1 - alpha1) * ema1signal(I
- 1);
      ema2signal(I) = alpha2 * yvector(I) + (1 - alpha2) * ema2signal(I
- 1);
      macdsignal(I) = ema1signal(I) - ema2signal(I);
   end

      % To calculate buy price and sell price, and profit of pmema
   B = 0; % Buy originally set to 0

       Iprofit=1;
      if    macdsignal(startpt)    >  0  % when first data point is
greater than 0, we do not buy
         Iprofit = 0;
      end

       for I = startpt: NN+1
        if   B == 0  &   macdsignal(I)   >  0
         I  ,          ybuy = yvector(I)
         B = 1
              else
         if  B == 1   &   macdsignal(I)  < 0
            I,    ysell = yvector(I)
```

```
            switch Iprofit
            case {0}
               profit = 0
      Iprofit=1;
               case{1}
                profit = ( (ysell - ybuy)/2  ) *100
                  end

              B = 0
               end
          end
   end

    figure(1)
      plot(xvector, yvector, 'kx-',   xvector(startpt: NN+1),
ema1signal(startpt : NN+1), 'r+-', xvector(startpt:
NN+1),ema2signal(startpt : NN+1), 'b+-',   xvector, zero, 'k' )
      xlabel('t')
      ylabel('price,  ema1 of price, ema2 of price ') %ema1 of price = price
here

            figure(2)
      plot(xvector, yvector, 'kx-',  xvector(startpt: NN+1),
macdsignal(startpt : NN+1), 'r+-',   xvector, zero, 'k' )
      xlabel('t')
      ylabel('price,  (price - ema  of price )  ')
```

D.26 pmsma

```
% pmsma,  Plot Amplitude and Phase of price minus simple moving average
of price

clear
NN=240; %240, 480
intomega=pi/NN;
M1=1  ;  %  1, cf awesome 5

M2=10  %  10, 20, cf awesome  34

for I= 1: NN+1
   omegavector(I)  = (I-1)*intomega;

    H1vector(I)=1/M1*( 1- exp(-i*M1*omegavector(I)) )  /( 1 -
exp(-i*omegavector(I) )  );
     mag1(I)=abs(H1vector(I));
     phase1(I)= angle(H1vector(I));
```

```
H2vector(I)= 1/M2*( 1- exp(-i*M2*omegavector(I)) ) /( 1 -
exp(-i*omegavector(I) ) );
    mag2(I)=abs(H2vector(I));
    phase2(I)= angle(H2vector(I));
    phase2unwrapth(I) = - (M2 -1)/2 * omegavector(I); % theoretical
unwrapped phase, see Science of Financial Market Trading page 156

      H3vector(I)= H1vector(I) - H2vector(I); % 3 = price - SMA of price
    mag3(I)=abs(H3vector(I));
    phase3(I)= angle(H3vector(I));

  end

   phase2unwrap = unwrap(phase2); % matlab function did not unwrap phase2,
and therefore has an error, see Fig 3 which compares phase2unwrap with
phase2unwrapth, the theoretical unwrapped phase
   phaseunwrap = unwrap(phase3); % matlab function, phaseunwrap is exactly
the same as phase3, i.e., does not need to unwrap

 mag(1) = 1;
 phase1(1)=0;
  mag2(1) = 1;
  phase2(1)=0;
   mag3(1) = 0;
 phase3(1) = pi/2;

  for I= 1: NN+1
    barlag (I) = phase3(I)/omegavector(I);
    end

     figure(1)
     plot(omegavector, mag1, 'k+-' , omegavector, mag2, 'kx-' )
     xlabel('Circular Frequency (radians)')
     ylabel('Amplitude')
     title('Simple Moving Average')
```

```
  figure(2)
     plot(omegavector, phase1, 'k+-' , omegavector, phase2, 'kx-'  )
     xlabel('Circular Frequency (radians)')
     ylabel('Phase (radians)')
     title('Simple Moving Average')

      figure(3)
     plot(omegavector, phase2unwrap,'kx', omegavector, phase2unwrapth,
'r-'  )
     xlabel('Circular Frequency (radians)')
     ylabel('Phase (radians)')
     title('Simple Moving Average')

      figure(4)
     plot(omegavector, mag3, 'k-'  )
     xlabel('Circular Frequency (radians)')
     ylabel('Amplitude')
     title(' Price - SMA of Price ')

        figure(5)
     plot(omegavector, phase3, 'k-'  )
     xlabel('Circular Frequency (radians)')
     ylabel('Phase (radians)')
    title(' Price - SMA of Price ')

     figure(6)
      plot(omegavector,phase3,'k-',omegavector,omegavector,'k-'   )
     xlabel('Circular Frequency (radians)')
     ylabel('Phase (radians)')
        title(' Price - SMA of Price ')

    % to find intersection point of phase3 and omegavector
        for I = 1: NN
                    if ( phase3(I) - omegavector(I) ) > 0  & ( phase3(I+1)
- omegavector(I+1) ) < 0
              intersectomega = omegavector(I)
              intersectphase =phase3(I)
  end
```

```
    if ( phase3(I) - omegavector(I) ) < 0  & ( phase3(I+1) -
omegavector(I+1) ) > 0 %for M2 large, e.g., M2 = 100, see text
            intersectomeganegtopos = omegavector(I)
            intersectphasenegtopos =phase3(I)
        end

    end

    figure(7)
    plot(omegavector, phase3, 'k.'  , omegavector, phaseunwrap,
'r-' ) % phaseunwrap - phase3
    xlabel('Circular Frequency (radians)')
    ylabel('Unwrapped Phase (radians)')
    title(' Price - SMA of Price ')

figure(8)
    plot(omegavector, barlag, 'k+-' )
    xlabel('Circular Frequency (radians)')
    ylabel('bars lag)')
   title(' Price - SMA of Price ')
```

D.27 pmsmapmema

```
% pmsmapmema,  Plot Amplitude and Phase of price minus simple moving
average of price and compare with Amplitude and Phase of price -
exponential moving average of price
clear
NN=240; %240, 480
intomega=pi/NN;
M1=1  ;   % cf awesome 5
M2=20  ;  % cf awesome  34

for I= 1: NN+1
  omegavector(I) = (I-1)*intomega;

   H1vector(I)=1/M1*( 1- exp(-i*M1*omegavector(I)) )  /( 1 -
exp(-i*omegavector(I) )  );
    mag1(I)=abs(H1vector(I));
    phase1(I)= angle(H1vector(I));

    H2vector(I)= 1/M2*( 1- exp(-i*M2*omegavector(I)) )  /( 1 -
exp(-i*omegavector(I) )  );
    mag2(I)=abs(H2vector(I));
    phase2(I)= angle(H2vector(I));
```

```
        H3vector(I)= H1vector(I)  - H2vector(I); % pmsma
      mag3(I)=abs(H3vector(I)); % 3 = pmsma
      phase3(I)= angle(H3vector(I));

   end

  mag(1)  = 1;
  phase1(1)=0;
   mag2(1)  = 1;
   phase2(1)=0;
    mag3(1)  = 0;
  phase3(1)  = pi/2;

   % calculate price - ema to compare with price - sma
   M1=1;  % cf MACD 12
 alpha1=2/(M1+1);
 M2=6  ;  %cf MACD 26
 alpha2=2/(M2+1);

 for I= 1: NN+1
    omegavector(I)  = (I-1)*intomega;

     H1vector(I)= alpha1/  ( 1-(1-alpha1)*exp(-i*omegavector(I)));
      mag1e(I)=abs(H1vector(I));
      phase1e(I)= angle(H1vector(I));

      H2vector(I)= alpha2/  (1-(1-alpha2)*exp(-i*omegavector(I)));
      mag2e(I)=abs(H2vector(I));
      phase2e(I)= angle(H2vector(I));

      H4vector(I)  = H1vector(I)  - H2vector(I); %pmema
      mag4e(I)=abs(H4vector(I));  % mag4e = magnitude of pmema
      phase4e(I)= angle(H4vector(I));

        end

   mag1e(1)  = 1;
   phase1e(1)  = 0;
   mag2e(1)  = 1;
   phase2e(1)  = 0;
   phase4e(1)  = pi/2;
   mag4e(1)  = 0;  % pmema

       figure(1)
       plot(omegavector, mag3, 'k-'  , omegavector, mag4e, 'k+-'  )
       xlabel('Circular Frequency (radians)')
       ylabel('Magnitude')
         title(' Price - SMA of Price,   Price - EMA of Price ')
```

```
figure(2)
plot(omegavector, phase3, 'k-' , omegavector, phase4e, 'k+-' )
xlabel('Circular Frequency (radians)')
ylabel('Phase (radians)')
  title(' Price - SMA of Price,  Price - EMA of Price ')
```

D.28 pmsmasig

```
% % pmsmasig, plot price - sma of a dummy signal, plot signal with 2
frequencies, plot signal of 1 frequency when amp2 = 0
% set profit = 0 if first data point of (price - sma of price) is greater
than 0
clear
factor = 15 ; % factor = 30, 15, 10, 8, 6 check profit
%   check profit, 31.4, 15.7, 10.47, 7.85, 6.28

factor2 = factor/4 ;
omega = pi/factor;
omega2 = pi/factor2;
NN = 10 * factor; % NN = 8*factor, N2 = 100  NN = 20*factor

% define original signal
amp2 = 0  ; % 0.4
theta0 =  pi/2  ; % add to price signal  0, pi/2, pi, 3*pi/2
  for I= 1: NN+1
     zero(I)=0;
      xvector(I) = I-1;
      yvector(I)= sin( omega*xvector(I)  + theta0 ) + amp2*
sin( omega2*xvector(I) );
   end

  % set parameters of sma's
N1= 1;
N2=10 ; % 10, 20, 100

 % calculate technical indicators on signal
   for I = N1 : NN+1
      sma1signal(I) = 0;
      for J = 1:N1
         sma1signal(I) = sma1signal(I ) + 1/N1 * yvector(I+1 - J);
         end
   end

     for I = N2 : NN+1
      sma2signal(I) = 0;
      for J = 1:N2
```

```
        sma2signal(I) = sma2signal(I ) + 1/N2 * yvector(I+1 - J);
        end
    end
    for I = N2 : NN+1
      aweosc(I) = sma1signal(I) - sma2signal(I); % calculate price - sma
of price
      end
    end
    % To calculate buy price and sell price, and profit of (price - sma
of price)
    B = 0; % Buy originally set to 0

      Iprofit=1;
      if    aweosc(N2)    >  0  % first data point  greater than 0, we do
not buy
        Iprofit = 0;
      end

      for I = N2: NN+1
       if   B == 0  &   aweosc(I)   >  0
        I  ,          ybuy = yvector(I)
        B = 1
            else
        if  B == 1   &    aweosc(I)  < 0
          I,    ysell = yvector(I)

          switch Iprofit
          case {0}
            profit = 0
      Iprofit=1;
            case{1}
             profit = ( (ysell - ybuy)/2  ) *100

              end
           B = 0
            end
         end
    end

 figure(1)
      plot(xvector, yvector, 'kx-',   xvector(N2: NN+1), sma1signal(N2 :
NN+1), 'r+-', xvector(N2: NN+1),sma2signal(N2 : NN+1), 'b+-',   xvector,
zero, 'k' )
      xlabel('t')
      ylabel('price, sma, sma')
```

```
        figure(2)
    plot(xvector, yvector,'kx-', xvector(N2: NN+1), aweosc(N2 : NN+1),
'r+-',  xvector, zero, 'k' )
    xlabel('t')
    ylabel('price, (price - sma of price ) ')
```

D.29 sinecos

```
% sinecos,  plot price simulated by a sine wave and the slope of the price
with various phase lags from the price signal.  The object of the exercise
is to show that whether profit or loss would be made when a velocity
indicator, which emulates the slope, has a phase lead or lag.
clear
t=40;
f=6/4;
for I= 1: f*t+1
  xvector(I)= 0;
  yvector(I)=0;
  zvector(I)=0;
  zero(I)=0;
end
const = 0;  % 0 , 2
Acos = 1;%  0.8,  usually 1
phaselagcos= pi/2; % pi/2, 0 , -pi/2, pi , -pi ;
  for I = 1: f*t+1
    xvector(I)  = I-1;
    yvector(I)= const +  sin(pi/(t/2) * xvector(I));
    zvector(I)= Acos*  sin(pi/(t/2)  * xvector(I)   + phaselagcos) ; %
sin(omega + pi/2 ) = cos(omega)
    end
    figure(1)
    plot(xvector, yvector , 'r',  xvector, zvector,  'b',  xvector,
zero ,  'k')
    xlabel('t')
    ylabel('price, velocity')
```

D.30 sma

```
% sma,  Plot Amplitude and Phase (wrapped and unwrapped) and bar lag (of
unwrapped phase)  of a simple moving average
clear
NN=180; %N = 10,  NN = 500
%N = 100,  NN = 1000
```

```
intomega=pi/NN;

N = 10; % 6, 100, 50, 20

for I= 1: NN+1
   omegavector(I) = (I-1)*intomega;

    H1vector(I)= (1/N)*( 1 - exp(-i* N *omegavector(I)))/ (1 - exp (-i
* omegavector(I))) ;
     mag1(I)=abs(H1vector(I));
     phase1(I)= angle(H1vector(I)); % wrapped phase
     phase2(I) = - (N-1)/2 * omegavector(I); % unwrapped phase, Science
of financial market trading P156

       barlag(I) = phase2(I) / omegavector(I);

    end

  H1vector(1)= 1 ;
     mag1(1)=abs(H1vector(1));
phase1(1)= angle(H1vector(1)); % wrapped phase

phaseunwrap = unwrap(phase1);% here MATLAB unwrap function does not do
any unwrapping

  figure(1)
  subplot(1, 1, 1)
      plot(omegavector, mag1, 'k-'   )
      xlabel('Circular Frequency (radians)')
      ylabel('Amplitude')
      title('Simple Moving Average')

      figure(2)
      subplot(1, 1, 1)
      plot(omegavector, phase1, 'k+-'   )
      xlabel('Circular Frequency (radians)')
      ylabel('Wrapped Phase (radians)')
    title('Simple Moving Average')

       figure(3)
      subplot(1, 1, 1)
      plot(omegavector, phase2, 'k-'   , omegavector, phaseunwrap,
'r+'  )
      xlabel('Circular Frequency (radians)')
      ylabel('Phase (radians)')
    title('Simple Moving Average')
```

```
        figure(4)
            subplot(1, 1, 1)
            plot(omegavector, barlag, 'r-'  )
            xlabel('Circular Frequency (radians)')
            ylabel('bar lag')
          title('Simple Moving Average')
```

D.31 smasig

```
% smasig,  plot sma of signal
clear
factor =  20;
omega = pi/factor;
NN = 4 * factor;

N = 20;  % N = number of data points used

  for I= 1: NN+1
    zero(I)=0;
     xvector(I) = I-1;
     yvector(I)= sin( omega*xvector(I));
   end

   for I = N: NN+1
     smasignal(I) = 0;
     for J = 1:N
       smasignal(I) = smasignal(I ) + 1/N * yvector(I+1 - J);
       end
   end

     figure(1)
     plot(xvector, yvector, 'kx-',  xvector(N: NN+1), smasignal(N :
NN+1), 'k+-',  xvector, zero, 'k' )
     xlabel('n')
     ylabel('price, sma of price')
```

D.32 smasig2

```
% smasig2,  plot sma of signal with 2 frequencies, plot signal of 1
frequency when amp2 = 0
%  fig 2 plots unwrapped phase
```

```
clear
factor = 9/2  ; % for N =10,factor =  20.83, 9, 6.283 , 5, 9/2, 9/3, 9/4
% N = 10, check profit,  31.4, 15.7, 10.47, 7.85, 6.28
% N = 10  check profit, take approx  30, 15, 10, 8, 6
theta0 = 0 ;  %  add to price signal   0,  pi/2 pi, 3*pi/2
% for N = 100, factor = 99, 66,   99/2
factor2 = 15;
omega = pi/factor;
omega2 = pi/factor2;
NN = 8*factor ; % for N = 10  NN = 8*factor
% for N = 100  NN = 20*factor

N = 10;  % N = number of data points used in SMA,  N = 10, 100

amp2 = 0; % 0.4
  for I= 1: NN+1
     zero(I)=0;
      xvector(I) = I-1;
      yvector(I)= sin( omega*xvector(I)   +  theta0 ) + amp2*
sin( omega2*xvector(I) );
   end

   % To calculate buy price and sell price, and profit
   B = 0; % Buy originally set to 0
   for I = N: NN+1
      smasignal(I) = 0;

      for J = 1:N
         smasignal(I) = smasignal(I ) + 1/N * yvector(I+1 - J);
      end

        if   B == 0  &   (  yvector(I) -  smasignal(I)   ) >  0
         I  ,          ybuy = yvector(I)
         B = 1
             else
         if  B == 1   &     (   yvector(I) - smasignal(I)    ) < 0
             I,    ysell = yvector(I)
             profit = ( (ysell - ybuy)/2  ) *100
             B = 0
              end
          end

   end
```

```
    figure(1)
    plot(xvector, yvector, 'kx-', xvector(N: NN+1), smasignal(N :
NN+1), 'k+-',  xvector, zero, 'k' )
    xlabel('t')
    % calculate unwrapped phase
    sign = 1;
    if factor == 9/2  |  factor == 9/3 %  |  is or
      sign = -1;
      end
     for I = N: NN+1
    smasignalunwrap(I) = sign *smasignal(I)  ;
        end
        % plot price signal and sma of price signal with wrapped
and unwrapped phase
    figure(2)
    plot(xvector, yvector, 'kx-', xvector(N: NN+1), smasignal(N :
NN+1), 'k+-',  xvector(N: NN+1), smasignalunwrap(N : NN+1), 'ro',
xvector, zero, 'k' )
    xlabel('t')
    ylabel('price, sma of price')
    ylabel('price, sma of price')
```

D.33 tradeartif

```
% tradeartif,   trade an artificial signal using different trading
tactics
%  artificial data,  1 sine wave
or sum of 2 sine waves, e.g.,  factor = 25  ;  theta0 = pi  ; factor2
= 4 ; NN = 120;  amp2 = 0.3   ;   amp2 = 0.9
%simulate CAC40,  factor=8,  factor2 = 3
% n = 0  to
clear
tactic =  12  ;  %
% tactic = 1,  sma1msma10
% tactic = 2,  sma1msma20
```

```
% tactic = 3  awesome oscillator
% tactic = 4,  accelerator oscillator
% tactic = 5,  MACD
% tactic = 6, MACDH
% tactic = 7, MACDH1
% tactic = 8 ,  price - ema3 of price
% tactic = 9 ,  price - ema6 of price
% tactic = 10 ,  ema3 of price - ema6 of price
% tactic = 11 ,  emaaccel
% tactic = 12 ,  sine wave with a phase delay to check sampling loss

thetashift =   pi/12  ; % thetashift = arbitrary phase shift of filtered
price signal- phi in buysellprice
startpt = 1;
amp1 = 1 ;
factor = 6  ; % 30, 20,
% N = 10, check profit,  31.4, 15.7, 10.47, 7.85, 6.28
% N = 10  check profit, take approx  30, 15, 10, 8, 6
mu = pi/24 ;% mu to emulate sampling delay,

factor2 = 3 ;  % 3, 4, 5,  3 will get more loss trades
omega = pi/factor;
theta0 =  omega -  mu   ;  %  theta0 can also be set to a certain constant,
e.g., 0,  pi/2,  pi
amp2 = 0.  ; % 0.3,  0.4, 0.2, 0.25
omega2 = pi/factor2;
NN = 20;  %6 * factor; % for N = 10  NN = 8*factor, 120, 20 for tactic
= 12, cf 80 for real data
% for N = 100  NN = 20*factor

  for I= 1: NN+1
     zero(I)=0;
      xvector(I)  = I-1;
      yvector(I)= amp1* sin( omega*xvector(I)   +  theta0 ) + amp2*
sin( omega2*xvector(I) );
   end

 % NN = length(yvector) - 1
 maxprice = max(yvector)
 minprice = min(yvector)
 range=maxprice-minprice
```

```
 for I= 1: NN+1
    zero(I)=0;
     xvector(I) = I-1;

  end

  switch tactic

                 case (1)
    % set parameters of price - simple moving average with N = 10
N1= 1;
N2=10;

 % calculate technical indicators on signal
  for I = N1 : NN+1
     sma1signal(I) = 0;
     for J = 1:N1
        sma1signal(I) = sma1signal(I ) + 1/N1 * yvector(I+1 - J);
        end
  end

    for I = N2 : NN+1
     sma2signal(I) = 0;
     for J = 1:N2
        sma2signal(I) = sma2signal(I ) + 1/N2 * yvector(I+1 - J);
        end
  end

  for I = N2 : NN+1
     pmsma10(I) = sma1signal(I) - sma2signal(I); % calculate  price -
sma10
      techsignal1(I) = sma1signal(I);
      techsignal2(I) = sma2signal(I);
       techsignal(I) = pmsma10(I);
     end
  startpt = N2;

 case (2)
    % set parameters of price - simple moving average with N = 20
N1= 1;
N2=20;

 % calculate technical indicators on signal
  for I = N1 : NN+1
     sma1signal(I) = 0;
```

```
   for J = 1:N1
      sma1signal(I) = sma1signal(I ) + 1/N1 * yvector(I+1 - J);
      end
end
  for I = N2 : NN+1
   sma2signal(I) = 0;
   for J = 1:N2
      sma2signal(I) = sma2signal(I ) + 1/N2 * yvector(I+1 - J);
      end
end
for I = N2 : NN+1
   pmsma(I) = sma1signal(I) - sma2signal(I); % calculate   price - sma10
       techsignal1(I) = sma1signal(I);
       techsignal2(I) = sma2signal(I);
        techsignal(I) = pmsma(I);
      end
startpt = N2;
      case (3)
     % set parameters of awesome oscillator
N1= 5;
N2=34;
 % calculate technical indicators on signal
   for I = N1 : NN+1
      sma1signal(I) = 0;
      for J = 1:N1
         sma1signal(I) = sma1signal(I ) + 1/N1 * yvector(I+1 - J);
         end
   end
     for I = N2 : NN+1
      sma2signal(I) = 0;
      for J = 1:N2
         sma2signal(I) = sma2signal(I ) + 1/N2 * yvector(I+1 - J);
         end
   end
   for I = N2 : NN+1
      aweosc(I) = sma1signal(I) - sma2signal(I); % calculate awesome
oscillator
       techsignal1(I) = sma1signal(I);
       techsignal2(I) = sma2signal(I);
        techsignal(I) = aweosc(I);
      end
      startpt = N2
```

```
  case(4)  % accelerator oscillator
        % set parameters of awesome oscillator and accelerator oscillator
N1= 5;
N2=34;
N3=5;
 % calculate technical indicators on signal
  for I = N1 : NN+1
     sma1signal(I) = 0;
     for J = 1:N1
        sma1signal(I) = sma1signal(I ) + 1/N1 * yvector(I+1 - J);
        end
  end
    for I = N2 : NN+1
     sma2signal(I) = 0;
     for J = 1:N2
        sma2signal(I) = sma2signal(I ) + 1/N2 * yvector(I+1 - J);
        end
  end
  for I = N2 : NN+1
     aweosc(I) = sma1signal(I) - sma2signal(I); % calculate awesome
oscillator

     end
     N2PN3 = N2+N3;
      for I = N2PN3 : NN+1
     signalline(I) = 0;
     for J = 1:N3
        signalline(I) = signalline(I ) + 1/N3 * aweosc(I+1 - J);
        end
  end
  for I = N2PN3 : NN+1
     accelosc (I) = aweosc(I) - signalline(I); %calculate  acelerator
oscillator
      techsignal1(I) = aweosc(I);
     techsignal2(I) = signalline(I);
     techsignal(I) = accelosc(I);
     end
 startpt = N2PN3
     case(5)
   % tactic = 5,  calculate MACD
   M1=12;
 alpha1=2/(M1+1);
```

```
M2= 26;
alpha2=2/(M2+1);
M3=9;
alpha3=2/(M3+1);
startpt = 15;

  ema1signal(1) = yvector(1);
  ema2signal(1) = yvector(1);
  macdsignal(1) = ema1signal(1) - ema2signal(1);
  ema3macd(1) = macdsignal(1);

  for I = 2: NN+1
    ema1signal(I) = alpha1 * yvector(I) + (1 - alpha1) * ema1signal(I
- 1);
    ema2signal(I) = alpha2 * yvector(I) + (1 - alpha2) * ema2signal(I
- 1);
    macdsignal(I) = ema1signal(I) - ema2signal(I);
    ema3macd(I) = alpha3 * macdsignal(I) + (1 - alpha3) * ema3macd(I
- 1);
    macdhsignal(I) = macdsignal(I) - ema3macd(I);

    techsignal1(I) = ema1signal(I);
    techsignal2(I) = ema2signal(I);

    techsignal(I) = macdsignal(I);
  end

case(6)
  % tactic - 6,  calculate MACDH
  M1=12;
alpha1=2/(M1+1);
M2= 26;
alpha2=2/(M2+1);

M3=9;
alpha3=2/(M3+1);
startpt = 15;

  ema1signal(1) = yvector(1);
  ema2signal(1) = yvector(1);
  macdsignal(1) = ema1signal(1) - ema2signal(1);
  ema3macd(1) = macdsignal(1);

  for I = 2: NN+1
    ema1signal(I) = alpha1 * yvector(I) + (1 - alpha1) * ema1signal(I
- 1);
```

```
    ema2signal(I) = alpha2 * yvector(I) + (1 - alpha2) * ema2signal(I
- 1);
    macdsignal(I) = ema1signal(I) - ema2signal(I);
    ema3macd(I) = alpha3 * macdsignal(I) + (1 - alpha3) * ema3macd(I
- 1);
    macdhsignal(I) = macdsignal(I) - ema3macd(I);
    techsignal1(I) = macdsignal(I);
    techsignal2(I) = ema3macd(I);
      techsignal(I) = macdhsignal(I);
  end
 case(7)
  % tactic - 7, calculate MACDH1
  M1=1;
alpha1=2/(M1+1);
M2= 26;
alpha2=2/(M2+1);
M3=9;
alpha3=2/(M3+1);
startpt = 15;
  ema1signal(1) = yvector(1);
  ema2signal(1) = yvector(1);
  macdsignal(1) = ema1signal(1) - ema2signal(1);
  ema3macd(1) = macdsignal(1);
  for I = 2: NN+1
    ema1signal(I) = alpha1 * yvector(I) + (1 - alpha1) * ema1signal(I
- 1);
    ema2signal(I) = alpha2 * yvector(I) + (1 - alpha2) * ema2signal(I
- 1);
    macdsignal(I) = ema1signal(I) - ema2signal(I);
    ema3macd(I) = alpha3 * macdsignal(I) + (1 - alpha3) * ema3macd(I
- 1);
    macdhsignal(I) = macdsignal(I) - ema3macd(I);
    techsignal1(I) = macdsignal(I);
    techsignal2(I) = ema3macd(I);
      techsignal(I) = macdhsignal(I);
  end
case(8)
 % tactic - 8, calculate price minus ema3 of price
  M1=1;
```

```
alpha1=2/(M1+1);
M2= 3;
alpha2=2/(M2+1);

startpt = 15;

   ema1signal(1) = yvector(1);
   ema2signal(1) = yvector(1);
   macdsignal(1) = ema1signal(1) - ema2signal(1);

   for I = 2: NN+1
      ema1signal(I) = alpha1 * yvector(I) + (1 - alpha1) * ema1signal(I
- 1);
      ema2signal(I) = alpha2 * yvector(I) + (1 - alpha2) * ema2signal(I
- 1);
      macdsignal(I) = ema1signal(I) - ema2signal(I);

      techsignal1(I) = ema1signal(I);

      techsignal2(I) = ema2signal(I);

      techsignal(I) = macdsignal(I);

   end

   case(9)
% tactic - 9,  calculate price minus ema6 of price
   M1=1;
alpha1=2/(M1+1);
M2= 6;
alpha2=2/(M2+1);

startpt = 15;

   ema1signal(1) = yvector(1);

   ema2signal(1) = yvector(1);

   macdsignal(1) = ema1signal(1) - ema2signal(1);

   for I = 2: NN+1
      ema1signal(I) = alpha1 * yvector(I) + (1 - alpha1) * ema1signal(I
- 1);
      ema2signal(I) = alpha2 * yvector(I) + (1 - alpha2) * ema2signal(I
- 1);
      macdsignal(I) = ema1signal(I) - ema2signal(I);

      techsignal1(I) = ema1signal(I);

      techsignal2(I) = ema2signal(I);

      techsignal(I) = macdsignal(I);
   end
```

```
  case(10)
  % tactic = 10,  calculate ema3 of price minus ema6 of price
  M1=3;
alpha1=2/(M1+1);
M2= 6;
alpha2=2/(M2+1);
startpt = 15;
  ema1signal(1) = yvector(1);
  ema2signal(1) = yvector(1);
  macdsignal(1) = ema1signal(1) - ema2signal(1);
  for I = 2: NN+1
    ema1signal(I) = alpha1 * yvector(I) + (1 - alpha1) * ema1signal(I
- 1);
    ema2signal(I) = alpha2 * yvector(I) + (1 - alpha2) * ema2signal(I
- 1);
    macdsignal(I) = ema1signal(I) - ema2signal(I);
    techsignal1(I) = ema1signal(I);
    techsignal2(I) = ema2signal(I);
    techsignal(I) = macdsignal(I);
  end
  case(11)
  % tactic = 11,  calculate emaaccel =  (ema3 - ema6) - ema9(ema3 - ema6)
  M1=3 ;
alpha1=2/(M1+1);
M2= 6 ;
alpha2=2/(M2+1);
M3=9  ;
alpha3=2/(M3+1);
startpt = 15;
  ema1signal(1) = yvector(1);
  ema2signal(1) = yvector(1);
  macdsignal(1) = ema1signal(1) - ema2signal(1);
  ema3macd(1) = macdsignal(1);
  for I = 2: NN+1
    ema1signal(I) = alpha1 * yvector(I) + (1 - alpha1) * ema1signal(I
- 1);
    ema2signal(I) = alpha2 * yvector(I) + (1 - alpha2) * ema2signal(I
- 1);
    macdsignal(I) = ema1signal(I) - ema2signal(I);
    ema3macd(I) = alpha3 * macdsignal(I) + (1 - alpha3) * ema3macd(I
- 1);
```

```
        macdhsignal(I) = macdsignal(I) - ema3macd(I);
        techsignal1(I) = macdsignal(I);
        techsignal2(I) = ema3macd(I);
          techsignal(I) = macdhsignal(I);
   end
case(12)
  % sine wave with a phase delay to check sampling loss
    for I= 1: NN+1
     zero(I)=0;
      xvector(I) = I-1;
      techsignal(I) = amp1 *sin( omega*xvector(I)  + theta0 +
thetashift ) + amp2*  sin( omega2*xvector(I) );
   end
   % theoretical calculation
   buytheor = sin ( (fix ( (2*pi - theta0 - thetashift)/omega) +1) * omega
+ theta0 )
 selltheor=  -buytheor
 profittheor = selltheor - buytheor
       end
    end
% To calculate buy price and sell price, and profit of a trading tactic
B = 0; % Buy originally set to 0
totalB = 0;
totalS= 0; %total number of times to  sell
   profit = 0; % set original profit = 0
       for I = startpt: NN
        if     B == 0   & (techsignal(I) <  0    &  techsignal(I + 1) >  0 )
      B = 1;
         totalB = totalB + B
     I  ,          ybuy = yvector(I + 1)  %   n in Figure equal to I printed
here,   e.g., n=19 is equivalent to I+1=20
    Bvector(totalB) = I  ;  % not I +1
         profitvectorB (totalB) = profit;
               else
         if  B == 1   &    ( techsignal(I)  >  0   &  techsignal(I + 1)  <
0 )
            I ,    ysell = yvector(I + 1)
            totalS = totalS + B; %  Number of times of selling
              profitloss(totalS) = ysell - ybuy ; % calculate profit/loss
```

```
of each trade
      profit = profit +  (ysell - ybuy)
      Svector(totalS) = I  ;  % not I +1

      profitvectorS(totalS) = profit;
      B=0;
                 end
              end
         end

    'Number of times selling',  totalS
    profitpercentage = profit/2 * 100

     figure(1)
     subplot(2,1, 1)
        plot(xvector, yvector, 'k+-'  )
       xlabel('n')
       ylabel('price')
             title  ('  Artificial data  ')
       subplot(2,1, 2)

  plot(  xvector(startpt : NN+1), techsignal(startpt : NN+1), 'k.-',
 xvector, zero, 'k' )
        xlabel(' n ')
        switch  tactic
        case(1)
       ylabel(' price - SMA10 of price' )
         case(2)
       ylabel(' price - SMA100 of price' )
         case(3)
       ylabel('awesome osc of price' )
           case(4)
       ylabel('accel osc of price' )
          case(5)
       ylabel('MACD  of price')
    case(6)
       ylabel('MACDH  of price')
         case(7)
       ylabel(' MACDH1  of price')
       case(8)
          ylabel('price -  ema3  of price')
            case(9)
       ylabel('price -  ema6  of price')
   case(10)
       ylabel('ema3 of price  -  ema6  of price')
```

```
case(11)
      ylabel('emaaccel')
case(12)
    ylabel('arbitrary filtered price')

   end

 figure(2)
  subplot(3,1, 1)
       plot(xvector, yvector, 'k+-'  )
      xlabel('  ')
      ylabel('price')
      title ('  Artificial data  ')
      subplot(3,1, 2)

      plot(  xvector(startpt : NN+1), techsignal(startpt : NN+1), 'k+-',
xvector, zero, 'k' )
       xlabel('   ')
       switch  tactic
       case(1)
      ylabel(' price - SMA10 of price' )
        case(2)
      ylabel(' price - SMA20 of price' )
        case(3)
      ylabel('awesome osc of price' )
          case(4)
      ylabel('accel osc of price' )
         case(5)
      ylabel('MACD  of price')
   case(6)
      ylabel('MACDH  of price')
        case(7)
      ylabel(' MACDH1  of price')
      case(8)
         ylabel('price -  ema3  of price')
          case(9)
      ylabel('price -  ema6  of price')
  case(10)
      ylabel('ema3 of price  -  ema6  of price')
case(11)
      ylabel('emaaccel')
    case(12)
    ylabel('arbitrary filtered price')

end
```

```
        subplot(3,1, 3)
       plot( Bvector,  profitvectorB, 'kx' , Svector,  profitvectorS,
'k+' ,  xvector, zero, 'k'  )
      xlabel('n')
      ylabel('total profit ')
      title ('    ')

      figure(3)
  subplot(3,1, 1)
       plot(xvector, yvector, 'k+-'  )
      xlabel('  ')
      ylabel('price')
      title ('  Artificial data  ')

      subplot(3,1, 2)
  plot(  xvector(startpt : NN+1), techsignal(startpt : NN+1), 'k+-',
xvector, zero, 'k' )
       xlabel('   ')
       switch  tactic
       case(1)
      ylabel(' price - SMA10 of price' )
        case(2)
      ylabel(' price - SMA20 of price' )
        case(3)
      ylabel('awesome osc of price' )
          case(4)
      ylabel('accel osc of price' )
         case(5)
      ylabel('MACD  of price')
   case(6)
      ylabel('MACDH  of price')
        case(7)
      ylabel(' MACDH1  of price')
      case(8)
         ylabel('price -  ema3  of price')
           case(9)
      ylabel('price -  ema6  of price')
  case(10)
      ylabel('ema3 of price  -  ema6  of price')
case(11)
   ylabel('emaaccel')
```

```
    case(12)
     ylabel('arbitrary filtered price')
   end
        subplot(3,1, 3)
       plot( Bvector,  profitvectorB, 'kx' , Svector,  profitvectorS,
'k+' ,  Svector,  profitloss, 'go' ,  xvector, zero, 'k'  )
     xlabel('n')
    ylabel('T profit,profit/trade')
     title ('    ')
```

D.34 tradecac40

```
% tradecac40,   trade CAC 40 index using different trading tactics
clear
tactic =  8   ;  %
% tactic = 1,  sma1msma10
% tactic = 2,  sma1msma20
% tactic = 3   awesome oscillator
% tactic = 4,  accelerator oscillator
% tactic = 5,  MACD
% tactic = 6, MACDH
% tactic = 7, MACDH1
% tactic = 8 ,  price - ema3 of price
% tactic = 9 ,  price - ema6 of price
% tactic = 10 ,  ema3 of price - ema6 of price
% tactic = 11 ,  emaaccel

% CAC 40 from March 6, 2019  to Aug 21, 2019,  118 data points
 yvector = [ 5288  5267 5231  5265  5270  5306  5349  5405  5412  5425
5382  5378  5269  5260  5307  5301  5296  5350  5405  5423  5468  5463
5476  5471  5436  5449  5485  5502  5508  5528  5563  5580  5591  5576
5557  5569  5580  5586  5538  5548  5483  5395  5417  5313  5327  5262
5341  5374  5448  5438  5358  5385  5378  5281  5316  5336  5312  5222
5248  5207  5241  5268  5292  5278  5364  5382  5408  5374  5375  5367
5390  5509  5518  5535  5528  5521  5514  5500  5493  5538  5567  5576
5618  5620  5593  5589  5572  5567  5551  5572  5578  5614  5571  5550
5552  5567  5618  5505  5578  5610  5601  5511  5618  5557  5359  5241
5234  5266  5387  5327  5310  5363  5251  5236  5300  5371  5344
5435   ];
```

```
NN = 117;
 % NN = length(yvector) - 1
 maxprice = max(yvector)
 minprice = min(yvector)
 range=maxprice-minprice

  for I= 1: NN+1
     zero(I)=0;
      xvector(I) = I-1;
   end
   switch tactic
       case (1)
     % set parameters of price - simple moving average with N = 10
N1= 1;
N2=10;

 % calculate technical indicators on signal
   for I = N1 : NN+1
      sma1signal(I) = 0;
      for J = 1:N1
         sma1signal(I) = sma1signal(I ) + 1/N1 * yvector(I+1 - J);
         end
   end

     for I = N2 : NN+1
      sma2signal(I) = 0;
      for J = 1:N2
         sma2signal(I) = sma2signal(I ) + 1/N2 * yvector(I+1 - J);
         end
   end

   for I = N2 : NN+1
      pmsma10(I) = sma1signal(I) - sma2signal(I); % calculate  price - 
sma10
       techsignal1(I) = sma1signal(I);
       techsignal2(I) = sma2signal(I);
        techsignal(I) = pmsma10(I);
      end
   startpt = N2;
  case (2)
     % set parameters of price - simple moving average with N = 20
N1= 1;
N2=20;
```

```
% calculate technical indicators on signal
  for I = N1 : NN+1
     sma1signal(I) = 0;
     for J = 1:N1
        sma1signal(I) = sma1signal(I ) + 1/N1 * yvector(I+1 - J);
        end
  end

    for I = N2 : NN+1
     sma2signal(I) = 0;

      for J = 1:N2
         sma2signal(I) = sma2signal(I ) + 1/N2 * yvector(I+1 - J);
         end
   end

   for I = N2 : NN+1
      pmsma(I) = sma1signal(I) - sma2signal(I); % calculate   price - sma10
       techsignal1(I) = sma1signal(I);
       techsignal2(I) = sma2signal(I);
        techsignal(I) = pmsma(I);
      end
startpt = N2;

      case (3)
     % set parameters of awesome oscillator
N1= 5;
N2=34;

 % calculate technical indicators on signal
   for I = N1 : NN+1
      sma1signal(I) = 0;
      for J = 1:N1
         sma1signal(I) = sma1signal(I ) + 1/N1 * yvector(I+1 - J);
         end
   end

     for I = N2 : NN+1
      sma2signal(I) = 0;
      for J = 1:N2
         sma2signal(I) = sma2signal(I ) + 1/N2 * yvector(I+1 - J);
         end
   end
```

```
  for I = N2 : NN+1
     aweosc(I) = sma1signal(I) - sma2signal(I); % calculate awesome
oscillator
      techsignal1(I) = sma1signal(I);
      techsignal2(I) = sma2signal(I);
       techsignal(I) = aweosc(I);
     end

     startpt = N2

  case(4)  % accelerator oscillator
        % set parameters of awesome oscillator and accelerator oscillator
N1= 5;
N2=34;
N3=5;
 % calculate technical indicators on signal
  for I = N1 : NN+1
     sma1signal(I) = 0;
     for J = 1:N1
        sma1signal(I) = sma1signal(I ) + 1/N1 * yvector(I+1 - J);
        end
  end

    for I = N2 : NN+1
     sma2signal(I) = 0;
     for J = 1:N2
        sma2signal(I) = sma2signal(I ) + 1/N2 * yvector(I+1 - J);
        end
  end

  for I = N2 : NN+1
     aweosc(I) = sma1signal(I) - sma2signal(I); % calculate awesome
oscillator

     end

     N2PN3 = N2+N3;
      for I = N2PN3 : NN+1
     signalline(I) = 0;
     for J = 1:N3
        signalline(I) = signalline(I) + 1/N3 * aweosc(I+1 - J);
        end
  end
```

```
   for I = N2PN3 : NN+1
      accelosc (I) = aweosc(I) - signalline(I); %calculate acelerator
oscillator
       techsignal1(I) = aweosc(I);
      techsignal2(I) = signalline(I);
      techsignal(I) = accelosc(I);
      end
 startpt = N2PN3

      case(5)
   % tactic = 5,  calculate MACD
   M1=12;
alpha1=2/(M1+1);
M2= 26;
alpha2=2/(M2+1);

M3=9;
alpha3=2/(M3+1);
startpt = 15;

   ema1signal(1) = yvector(1);
   ema2signal(1) = yvector(1);
   macdsignal(1) = ema1signal(1) - ema2signal(1);
   ema3macd(1) = macdsignal(1);

   for I = 2: NN+1
      ema1signal(I) = alpha1 * yvector(I) + (1 - alpha1) * ema1signal(I
- 1);
      ema2signal(I) = alpha2 * yvector(I) + (1 - alpha2) * ema2signal(I
- 1);
      macdsignal(I) = ema1signal(I) - ema2signal(I);
      ema3macd(I) = alpha3 * macdsignal(I) + (1 - alpha3) * ema3macd(I
- 1);
      macdhsignal(I) = macdsignal(I) - ema3macd(I);
      techsignal1(I) = ema1signal(I);
      techsignal2(I) = ema2signal(I);
      techsignal(I) = macdsignal(I);
   end

case(6)
   % tactic = 6,  calculate MACDH
   M1=12;
alpha1=2/(M1+1);
```

```
M2= 26;
alpha2=2/(M2+1);

M3=9;
alpha3=2/(M3+1);

startpt = 15;

   ema1signal(1) = yvector(1);
   ema2signal(1) = yvector(1);
   macdsignal(1) = ema1signal(1) - ema2signal(1);
   ema3macd(1) = macdsignal(1);

   for I = 2: NN+1
      ema1signal(I) = alpha1 * yvector(I) + (1 - alpha1) * ema1signal(I
- 1);
      ema2signal(I) = alpha2 * yvector(I) + (1 - alpha2) * ema2signal(I
- 1);
      macdsignal(I) = ema1signal(I) - ema2signal(I);
      ema3macd(I) = alpha3 * macdsignal(I) + (1 - alpha3) * ema3macd(I
- 1);
      macdhsignal(I) = macdsignal(I) - ema3macd(I);
      techsignal1(I) = macdsignal(I);
      techsignal2(I) = ema3macd(I);
        techsignal(I) = macdhsignal(I);
   end
 case(7)
   % tactic = 7,  calculate MACDH1
   M1=1;
alpha1=2/(M1+1);
M2= 26;
alpha2=2/(M2+1);
M3=9;
alpha3=2/(M3+1);

startpt = 15;

   ema1signal(1) = yvector(1);
   ema2signal(1) = yvector(1);
   macdsignal(1) = ema1signal(1) - ema2signal(1);
   ema3macd(1) = macdsignal(1);

   for I = 2: NN+1
      ema1signal(I) = alpha1 * yvector(I) + (1 - alpha1) * ema1signal(I
- 1);
```

```
        ema2signal(I) = alpha2 * yvector(I) + (1 - alpha2) * ema2signal(I
- 1);
        macdsignal(I) = ema1signal(I) - ema2signal(I);
        ema3macd(I) = alpha3 * macdsignal(I) + (1 - alpha3) * ema3macd(I
- 1);
        macdhsignal(I) = macdsignal(I) - ema3macd(I);
        techsignal1(I) = macdsignal(I);
        techsignal2(I) = ema3macd(I);
          techsignal(I) = macdhsignal(I);
    end

case(8)
 % tactic - 8, calculate price minus ema3 of price
    M1=1;
alpha1=2/(M1+1);
M2= 3;
alpha2=2/(M2+1);

startpt = 15;

    ema1signal(1) = yvector(1);
    ema2signal(1) = yvector(1);
    macdsignal(1) = ema1signal(1) - ema2signal(1);

    for I = 2: NN+1
        ema1signal(I) = alpha1 * yvector(I) + (1 - alpha1) * ema1signal(I
- 1);
        ema2signal(I) = alpha2 * yvector(I) + (1 - alpha2) * ema2signal(I
- 1);
        macdsignal(I) = ema1signal(I) - ema2signal(I);
        techsignal1(I) = ema1signal(I);
        techsignal2(I) = ema2signal(I);
        techsignal(I) = macdsignal(I);
    end

    case(9)
% tactic - 9, calculate price minus ema6 of price
    M1=1;
alpha1=2/(M1+1);
M2= 6;
alpha2=2/(M2+1);
startpt = 15;
```

```
  ema1signal(1) = yvector(1);
  ema2signal(1) = yvector(1);
  macdsignal(1) = ema1signal(1) - ema2signal(1);

  for I = 2: NN+1
    ema1signal(I) = alpha1 * yvector(I) + (1 - alpha1) * ema1signal(I
- 1);
    ema2signal(I) = alpha2 * yvector(I) + (1 - alpha2) * ema2signal(I
- 1);
    macdsignal(I) = ema1signal(I) - ema2signal(I);
    techsignal1(I) = ema1signal(I);
    techsignal2(I) = ema2signal(I);
    techsignal(I) = macdsignal(I);
  end

  case(10)
  % tactic = 10,  calculate ema3 of price minus ema6 of price
  M1=3;
alpha1=2/(M1+1);
M2= 6;
alpha2=2/(M2+1);
startpt = 15;
  ema1signal(1) = yvector(1);
  ema2signal(1) = yvector(1);
  macdsignal(1) = ema1signal(1) - ema2signal(1);

  for I = 2: NN+1
    ema1signal(I) = alpha1 * yvector(I) + (1 - alpha1) * ema1signal(I
- 1);
    ema2signal(I) = alpha2 * yvector(I) + (1 - alpha2) * ema2signal(I
- 1);
    macdsignal(I) = ema1signal(I) - ema2signal(I);
    techsignal1(I) = ema1signal(I);
    techsignal2(I) = ema2signal(I);
    techsignal(I) = macdsignal(I);
  end

  case(11)
  % tactic = 11,  calculate emaaccel =  (ema3 - ema6) - ema9(ema3 - ema6)
  M1=3 ;
```

```
alpha1=2/(M1+1);
M2= 6 ;
alpha2=2/(M2+1);
M3=9  ;
alpha3=2/(M3+1);

startpt = 15;

   ema1signal(1) = yvector(1);
   ema2signal(1) = yvector(1);
   macdsignal(1) = ema1signal(1) - ema2signal(1);
   ema3macd(1) = macdsignal(1);

   for I = 2: NN+1
      ema1signal(I) = alpha1 * yvector(I) + (1 - alpha1) * ema1signal(I
- 1);
      ema2signal(I) = alpha2 * yvector(I) + (1 - alpha2) * ema2signal(I
- 1);
      macdsignal(I) = ema1signal(I) - ema2signal(I);
      ema3macd(I) = alpha3 * macdsignal(I) + (1 - alpha3) * ema3macd(I
- 1);
      macdhsignal(I) = macdsignal(I) - ema3macd(I);
      techsignal1(I) = macdsignal(I);
      techsignal2(I) = ema3macd(I);
        techsignal(I) = macdhsignal(I);
   end

    end

% To calculate buy price and sell price, and profit of a trading tactic
B = 0; % Buy originally set to 0
totalB = 0;
totalS= 0; %total number of times to  sell
   profit = 0; % set original profit = 0

       for I = startpt: NN
        if     B == 0   & (techsignal(I) <  0    &  techsignal(I + 1) >  0 )

      B = 1;
         totalB = totalB + B
     I  ,          ybuy = yvector(I + 1)  %    n in Figure equal to I printed
here,   e.g., n-19 is equivalent  to I+1-20
     Bvector(totalB) = I  ;  % not I +1
            profitvectorB (totalB) = profit;
             else
```

```
        if  B == 1   &    ( techsignal(I)  >  0   &  techsignal(I + 1)  <
0 )
           I ,     ysell = yvector(I + 1)

          totalS = totalS + B; %  Number of times of selling
           profitloss(totalS) = ysell - ybuy ; % calculate profit/loss
of each trade
           profit0 = ysell - ybuy
      profit = profit +  (ysell - ybuy)
      Svector(totalS) = I  ;  % not I +1

      profitvectorS(totalS) = profit;
      B=0;
                end

                  end
          end
   'Number of times selling',  totalS
   profitpercentage = profit/(maxprice - minprice) * 100

    figure(1)
    subplot(2,1, 1)
      plot(xvector, yvector, 'k+-'  )
     xlabel('n')
     ylabel('price')
            title (' CAC40 ')

     subplot(2,1, 2)
     plot( xvector(startpt : NN+1), techsignal(startpt : NN+1), 'k.-',
xvector, zero, 'k' )
      xlabel(' n ')
      switch  tactic
      case(1)
     ylabel(' price - SMA10 of price' )
       case(2)
     ylabel(' price - SMA100 of price' )
       case(3)
     ylabel('awesome osc of price' )
         case(4)
     ylabel('accel osc of price' )
        case(5)
     ylabel('MACD  of price')
   case(6)
     ylabel('MACDH  of price')
```

```
        case(7)
      ylabel(' MACDH1  of price')
      case(8)
         ylabel('price -  ema3  of price')
           case(9)
      ylabel('price -  ema6  of price')
  case(10)
      ylabel('ema3 of price  -  ema6  of price')
case(11)
      ylabel('emaaccel')
   end
 figure(2)
  subplot(3,1, 1)
       plot(xvector, yvector, 'k+-'  )
      xlabel('  ')
      ylabel('price')
     title ('  CAC40 ')
      subplot(3,1, 2)
      plot(  xvector(startpt : NN+1), techsignal(startpt : NN+1), 'k.-',
xvector, zero, 'k' )
       xlabel('   ')
       switch  tactic
       case(1)
      ylabel(' price - SMA10 of price' )
        case(2)
      ylabel(' price - SMA20 of price' )
        case(3)
      ylabel('awesome osc of price' )
          case(4)
      ylabel('accel osc of price' )
         case(5)
      ylabel('MACD  of price')
   case(6)
      ylabel('MACDH  of price')
        case(7)
      ylabel(' MACDH1  of price')
      case(8)
         ylabel('price -  ema3  of price')
           case(9)
      ylabel('price -  ema6  of price')
```

```
  case(10)
      ylabel('ema3 of price  -  ema6  of price')
case(11)
      ylabel('emaaccel')
   end
        subplot(3,1, 3)
      plot( Bvector,  profitvectorB, 'kx' , Svector,  profitvectorS,
'k+' , xvector, zero, 'k'  )
      xlabel('n')
      ylabel('total profit ')
      title ('   ')

figure(3)
  subplot(3,1, 1)
      plot(xvector, yvector, 'k+-'  )
      xlabel('  ')
      ylabel('price')
      title ('  CAC40 ')

      subplot(3,1, 2)
      plot(  xvector(startpt : NN+1), techsignal(startpt : NN+1), 'k.-',
xvector, zero, 'k' )
       xlabel('   ')
       switch  tactic
       case(1)
      ylabel(' price - SMA10 of price' )
        case(2)
      ylabel(' price - SMA20 of price' )
        case(3)
      ylabel('awesome osc of price' )
          case(4)
      ylabel('accel osc of price' )
         case(5)
      ylabel('MACD  of price')
   case(6)
      ylabel('MACDH  of price')
        case(7)
      ylabel(' MACDH1  of price')
      case(8)
         ylabel('price -  ema3  of price')
```

```
        case(9)
    ylabel('price -  ema6  of price')
  case(10)
    ylabel('ema3 of price  -  ema6  of price')
case(11)
    ylabel('emaaccel')
  end
       subplot(3,1, 3)
      plot( Bvector,  profitvectorB, 'kx' , Svector,  profitvectorS,
'k+' ,  Svector,  profitloss, 'go' ,  xvector, zero, 'k'  )
    xlabel('n')
    ylabel('T profit,profit/trade')
    title ('    ')
```

D.35 tradefηtse

```
% tradeftse,   trade FTSE index using different trading tactics
clear
tactic =  6  ; %
% tactic = 1,  sma1msma10
% tactic = 2,  sma1msma20
% tactic = 3   awesome oscillator
% tactic = 4,  accelerator oscillator
% tactic = 5,  MACD
% tactic = 6, MACDH
% tactic = 7, MACDH1
% tactic = 8 ,  price - ema3 of price
% tactic = 9 ,  price - ema6 of price
% tactic = 10 ,  ema3 of price - ema6 of price
% tactic = 11 ,  emaaccel

% FTSE  from March 1, 19  ro Aug 14, 19  NN =114,  115 data points
 yvector = [    7106  7134  7183  7196  7157  7104  7130  7151  7159
7185  7228  7299  7324  7291  7355  7207  7177  7196  7194  7234  7279
7317  7391  7418  7401  7446  7451  7425  7421  7418  7437  7436  7469
7471  7459  7523  7471  7434  7428  7440  7418  7385  7351   7380  7260
7271  7207  7203  7163  7241  7297  7353  7348  7310  7328  7334  7231
7277  7269  7185  7218  7161  7184  7214  7220  7259  7331  7375  7398
7367  7368  7345  7357  7443  7403  7424  7407  7416  7422  7416  7402
7425  7497  7559  7609  7603  7553  7549  7536  7530  7509  7506  7531
7577  7535  7493  7508  7514  7556  7501  7489  7549  7686  7645  7586
7584  7407  7223  7171  7198  7285  7253  7226  7250  7147   ];
```

```
NN = 114;
 % NN = length(yvector) - 1
maxprice = max(yvector)
minprice = min(yvector)
range=maxprice-minprice
 for I= 1: NN+1
    zero(I)=0;
     xvector(I) = I-1;
  end
  switch tactic
                case (1)
    % set parameters of price - simple moving average with N = 10
N1= 1;
N2=10;
 % calculate technical indicators on signal
  for I = N1 : NN+1
     sma1signal(I) = 0;
     for J = 1:N1
        sma1signal(I) = sma1signal(I ) + 1/N1 * yvector(I+1 - J);
        end
  end
    for I = N2 : NN+1
     sma2signal(I) = 0;
     for J = 1:N2
        sma2signal(I) = sma2signal(I ) + 1/N2 * yvector(I+1 - J);
        end
  end
  for I = N2 : NN+1
     pmsma10(I) = sma1signal(I) - sma2signal(I); % calculate  price -
sma10
      techsignal1(I) = sma1signal(I);
      techsignal2(I) = sma2signal(I);
       techsignal(I) = pmsma10(I);
     end
  startpt = N2;
 case (2)
    % set parameters of price - simple moving average with N = 20
N1= 1;
N2=20;
```

```
% calculate technical indicators on signal
  for I = N1 : NN+1
     sma1signal(I) = 0;
     for J = 1:N1
        sma1signal(I) = sma1signal(I ) + 1/N1 * yvector(I+1 - J);
        end
  end
    for I = N2 : NN+1
     sma2signal(I) = 0;
     for J = 1:N2
        sma2signal(I) = sma2signal(I ) + 1/N2 * yvector(I+1 - J);
        end
  end
  for I = N2 : NN+1
     pmsma(I) = sma1signal(I) - sma2signal(I); % calculate  price - sma10
      techsignal1(I) = sma1signal(I);
      techsignal2(I) = sma2signal(I);
       techsignal(I) = pmsma(I);
     end
startpt = N2;
     case (3)
    % set parameters of awesome oscillator
N1= 5;
N2=34;
 % calculate technical indicators on signal
  for I = N1 : NN+1
     sma1signal(I) = 0;
     for J = 1:N1
         sma1signal(I) = sma1signal(I ) + 1/N1 * yvector(I+1 - J);
         end
   end
     for I = N2 : NN+1
      sma2signal(I) = 0;
      for J = 1:N2
         sma2signal(I) = sma2signal(I ) + 1/N2 * yvector(I+1 - J);
         end
   end
   for I = N2 : NN+1
      aweosc(I) = sma1signal(I) - sma2signal(I); % calculate awesome
 oscillator
```

```
        techsignal1(I) = sma1signal(I);
        techsignal2(I) = sma2signal(I);
         techsignal(I) = aweosc(I);
      end
      startpt = N2
   case(4)  % accelerator oscillator
         % set parameters of awesome oscillator and accelerator oscillator
N1= 5;
N2=34;
N3=5;
 % calculate technical indicators on signal
   for I = N1 : NN+1
      sma1signal(I) = 0;
      for J = 1:N1
         sma1signal(I) = sma1signal(I ) + 1/N1 * yvector(I+1 - J);
         end
   end
     for I = N2 : NN+1
      sma2signal(I) = 0;
      for J = 1:N2
         sma2signal(I) = sma2signal(I ) + 1/N2 * yvector(I+1 - J);
         end
   end
   for I = N2 : NN+1
      aweosc(I) = sma1signal(I) - sma2signal(I); % calculate awesome
oscillator

      end

      N2PN3 = N2+N3;
       for I = N2PN3 : NN+1
      signalline(I) = 0;
      for J = 1:N3
         signalline(I) = signalline(I ) + 1/N3 * aweosc(I+1 - J);
         end
   end
   for I = N2PN3 : NN+1
      accelosc (I) = aweosc(I) - signalline(I); %calculate  acelerator
oscillator
       techsignal1(I) = aweosc(I);
      techsignal2(I) = signalline(I);
      techsignal(I) = accelosc(I);
      end
```

```
 startpt = N2PN3
     case(5)
   % tactic - 5,  calculate MACD
   M1=12;
alpha1=2/(M1+1);
M2= 26;
alpha2=2/(M2+1);

M3=9;
alpha3=2/(M3+1);

startpt = 15;

   ema1signal(1) = yvector(1);
   ema2signal(1) = yvector(1);
   macdsignal(1) = ema1signal(1) - ema2signal(1);
   ema3macd(1) = macdsignal(1);

   for I = 2: NN+1
      ema1signal(I) = alpha1 * yvector(I) + (1 - alpha1) * ema1signal(I
- 1);
      ema2signal(I) = alpha2 * yvector(I) + (1 - alpha2) * ema2signal(I
- 1);
      macdsignal(I) = ema1signal(I) - ema2signal(I);
      ema3macd(I) = alpha3 * macdsignal(I) + (1 - alpha3) * ema3macd(I
- 1);
      macdhsignal(I) = macdsignal(I) - ema3macd(I);
      techsignal1(I) = ema1signal(I);
      techsignal2(I) = ema2signal(I);
      techsignal(I) = macdsignal(I);
   end
case(6)
   % tactic - 6,  calculate MACDH
   M1=12;
alpha1=2/(M1+1);
M2= 26;
alpha2=2/(M2+1);

M3=9;
alpha3=2/(M3+1);

startpt = 15;
   ema1signal(1) = yvector(1);
   ema2signal(1) = yvector(1);
   macdsignal(1) = ema1signal(1) - ema2signal(1);
   ema3macd(1) = macdsignal(1);
```

```
  for I = 2: NN+1
     ema1signal(I) = alpha1 * yvector(I) + (1 - alpha1) * ema1signal(I
- 1);
     ema2signal(I) = alpha2 * yvector(I) + (1 - alpha2) * ema2signal(I
- 1);
     macdsignal(I) = ema1signal(I) - ema2signal(I);
     ema3macd(I) = alpha3 * macdsignal(I) + (1 - alpha3) * ema3macd(I
- 1);
     macdhsignal(I) = macdsignal(I) - ema3macd(I);
     techsignal1(I) = macdsignal(I);
     techsignal2(I) = ema3macd(I);
       techsignal(I) = macdhsignal(I);
  end

 case(7)
  % tactic - 7,  calculate MACDH1
  M1=1;
alpha1=2/(M1+1);
M2= 26;
alpha2=2/(M2+1);
M3=9;
alpha3=2/(M3+1);
startpt = 15;
  ema1signal(1) = yvector(1);
  ema2signal(1) = yvector(1);
  macdsignal(1) = ema1signal(1) - ema2signal(1);
  ema3macd(1) = macdsignal(1);

  for I = 2: NN+1
     ema1signal(I) = alpha1 * yvector(I) + (1 - alpha1) * ema1signal(I
- 1);
     ema2signal(I) = alpha2 * yvector(I) + (1 - alpha2) * ema2signal(I
- 1);
     macdsignal(I) = ema1signal(I) - ema2signal(I);
     ema3macd(I) = alpha3 * macdsignal(I) + (1 - alpha3) * ema3macd(I
- 1);
     macdhsignal(I) = macdsignal(I) - ema3macd(I);
     techsignal1(I) = macdsignal(I);
     techsignal2(I) = ema3macd(I);
       techsignal(I) = macdhsignal(I);
  end
```

```
case(8)
 % tactic = 8,  calculate price minus ema3 of price
  M1=1;
alpha1=2/(M1+1);
M2= 3;
alpha2=2/(M2+1);

startpt = 15;

  ema1signal(1) = yvector(1);
  ema2signal(1) = yvector(1);
  macdsignal(1) = ema1signal(1) - ema2signal(1);

  for I = 2: NN+1
    ema1signal(I) = alpha1 * yvector(I) + (1 - alpha1) * ema1signal(I
- 1);
    ema2signal(I) = alpha2 * yvector(I) + (1 - alpha2) * ema2signal(I
- 1);
    macdsignal(I) = ema1signal(I) - ema2signal(I);
    techsignal1(I) = ema1signal(I);
    techsignal2(I) = ema2signal(I);
    techsignal(I) = macdsignal(I);
  end

  case(9)
% tactic = 9,  calculate price minus ema6 of price
  M1=1;
alpha1=2/(M1+1);
M2= 6;
alpha2=2/(M2+1);

startpt = 15;

  ema1signal(1) = yvector(1);
  ema2signal(1) = yvector(1);
  macdsignal(1) = ema1signal(1) - ema2signal(1);

  for I = 2: NN+1
    ema1signal(I) = alpha1 * yvector(I) + (1 - alpha1) * ema1signal(I
- 1);
    ema2signal(I) = alpha2 * yvector(I) + (1 - alpha2) * ema2signal(I
- 1);
    macdsignal(I) = ema1signal(I) - ema2signal(I);
    techsignal1(I) = ema1signal(I);
    techsignal2(I) = ema2signal(I);
    techsignal(I) = macdsignal(I);
  end
```

```
  case(10)
  % tactic = 10,  calculate ema3 of price minus ema6 of price
  M1=3;
alpha1=2/(M1+1);
M2= 6;
alpha2=2/(M2+1);

startpt = 15;

  ema1signal(1) = yvector(1);
  ema2signal(1) = yvector(1);
  macdsignal(1) = ema1signal(1) - ema2signal(1);

  for I = 2: NN+1
    ema1signal(I) = alpha1 * yvector(I) + (1 - alpha1) * ema1signal(I
- 1);
    ema2signal(I) = alpha2 * yvector(I) + (1 - alpha2) * ema2signal(I
- 1);
    macdsignal(I) = ema1signal(I) - ema2signal(I);

    techsignal1(I) = ema1signal(I);

    techsignal2(I) = ema2signal(I);

    techsignal(I) = macdsignal(I);
  end
  case(11)
  % tactic = 11,  calculate emaaccel =  (ema3 - ema6) - ema9(ema3 - ema6)
  M1=3 ;
alpha1=2/(M1+1);
M2= 6 ;
alpha2=2/(M2+1);
M3=9  ;
alpha3=2/(M3+1);

startpt = 15;

  ema1signal(1) = yvector(1);
  ema2signal(1) = yvector(1);
  macdsignal(1) = ema1signal(1) - ema2signal(1);
  ema3macd(1) = macdsignal(1);

  for I = 2: NN+1
    ema1signal(I) = alpha1 * yvector(I) + (1 - alpha1) * ema1signal(I
- 1);
    ema2signal(I) = alpha2 * yvector(I) + (1 - alpha2) * ema2signal(I
- 1);
    macdsignal(I) = ema1signal(I) - ema2signal(I);
```

```
    ema3macd(I) = alpha3 * macdsignal(I) + (1 - alpha3) * ema3macd(I
- 1);
    macdhsignal(I) = macdsignal(I) - ema3macd(I);
    techsignal1(I) = macdsignal(I);
    techsignal2(I) = ema3macd(I);
     techsignal(I) = macdhsignal(I);
  end
   end
% To calculate buy price and sell price, and profit of a trading tactic
B = 0; % Buy originally set to 0
totalB = 0;
totalS= 0; %total number of times to  sell
  profit = 0; % set original profit = 0
     for I = startpt: NN
      if    B == 0  & (techsignal(I) <  0   &  techsignal(I + 1) >  0 )
    B = 1;
      totalB = totalB + B
   I  ,         ybuy = yvector(I + 1)  %   n in Figure equal to I printed
here,  e.g., n=19 is equivalent to I+1=20
   Bvector(totalB) = I  ;  % not I +1
          profitvectorB (totalB) = profit;
           else
      if  B == 1  &   ( techsignal(I)  >  0  &  techsignal(I + 1)  <
0 )
        I ,    ysell = yvector(I + 1)
      totalS = totalS + B; %  Number of times of selling
        profitloss(totalS) = ysell - ybuy ; % calculate profit/loss
of each trade
        profit0 = ysell - ybuy
    profit = profit +  (ysell - ybuy)
    Svector(totalS) = I  ;  % not I +1
    profitvectorS(totalS) = profit;
    B=0;
            end
                end
      end
  'Number of times selling', totalS
  profitpercentage = profit/(maxprice - minprice) * 100
```

```
    figure(1)
    subplot(2,1, 1)
       plot(xvector, yvector, 'k+-' )
      xlabel('n')
      ylabel('price')
            title (' FTSE 100 ')
      subplot(2,1, 2)
      plot( xvector(startpt : NN+1), techsignal(startpt : NN+1), 'k.-',
xvector, zero, 'k' )
       xlabel(' n ')
       switch tactic
       case(1)
      ylabel(' price - SMA10 of price' )
        case(2)
      ylabel(' price - SMA100 of price' )
        case(3)
      ylabel('awesome osc of price' )
          case(4)
      ylabel('accel osc of price' )
         case(5)
      ylabel('MACD  of price')
   case(6)
      ylabel('MACDH  of price')
        case(7)
      ylabel(' MACDH1  of price')
      case(8)
         ylabel('price -  ema3  of price')
           case(9)
      ylabel('price -  ema6  of price')
  case(10)
      ylabel('ema3 of price  -  ema6  of price')
case(11)
      ylabel('emaaccel')

   end
 figure(2)
  subplot(3,1, 1)
       plot(xvector, yvector, 'k+-' )
      xlabel('  ')
      ylabel('price')
       title (' FTSE 100 ')
      subplot(3,1, 2)
```

```
      plot(  xvector(startpt : NN+1), techsignal(startpt : NN+1), 'k.-',
xvector, zero, 'k' )
       xlabel('   ')
       switch  tactic
       case(1)
      ylabel(' price - SMA10 of price' )
        case(2)
      ylabel(' price - SMA20 of price' )
        case(3)
      ylabel('awesome osc of price' )
          case(4)
      ylabel('accel osc of price' )
         case(5)
      ylabel('MACD  of price')
   case(6)
      ylabel('MACDH  of price')
        case(7)
      ylabel(' MACDH1  of price')
      case(8)
         ylabel('price -  ema3  of price')
           case(9)
      ylabel('price -  ema6  of price')
  case(10)
      ylabel('ema3 of price  -  ema6  of price')
case(11)
      ylabel('emaaccel')
   end
         subplot(3,1, 3)
       plot( Bvector,  profitvectorB, 'kx' , Svector,  profitvectorS,
'k+' , xvector, zero, 'k'  )
      xlabel('n')
      ylabel('total profit ')
      title ('    ')

figure(3)
  subplot(3,1, 1)

       plot(xvector, yvector, 'k+-'  )
      xlabel('  ')
      ylabel('price')
        title ('  FTSE 100  ')

      subplot(3,1, 2)

      plot(  xvector(startpt : NN+1), techsignal(startpt : NN+1), 'k.-',
```

```
xvector, zero, 'k' )
      xlabel('  ')
      switch  tactic
      case(1)
     ylabel(' price - SMA10 of price' )
      case(2)
     ylabel(' price - SMA20 of price' )
      case(3)
     ylabel('awesome osc of price' )
        case(4)
     ylabel('accel osc of price' )
       case(5)
     ylabel('MACD  of price')
   case(6)
     ylabel('MACDH  of price')
      case(7)
     ylabel(' MACDH1  of price')
     case(8)
        ylabel('price -  ema3  of price')
         case(9)
     ylabel('price -  ema6  of price')
  case(10)
     ylabel('ema3 of price  -  ema6  of price')
case(11)
     ylabel('emaaccel')
   end
        subplot(3,1, 3)
       plot( Bvector,  profitvectorB, 'kx' , Svector,  profitvectorS,
'k+' ,  Svector, profitloss, 'go' , xvector, zero, 'k'  )
     xlabel('n')
     ylabel('T profit,profit/trade')
     title ('   ')
```

D.36 tradehangseng

```
% tradehangseng,    trade Hang Seng index using different trading tactics
clear
tactic =  2   ;  %6, cf 9
% tactic = 1,  sma1msma10
% tactic = 2,  sma1msma20
% tactic = 3   awesome oscillator
```

```
% tactic = 4,  accelerator oscillator
% tactic = 5,  MACD
% tactic = 6, MACDH
% tactic = 7, MACDH1
% tactic = 8 ,  price - ema3 of price
% tactic = 9 ,  price - ema6 of price
% tactic = 10 ,  ema3 of price - ema6 of price
% tactic = 11 ,  emaaccel

NN = 107;  % Hang seng from March 1, 2019  to Aug 12, 2019, 108 data points
 yvector = [  28812  28959  28961  29037  28779  28228  28503  28920
28807  28851  29012  29409  29466  29320  29071  29113  28523  28567
28728  28775  29051  29562  29624  29986  29936  30077  30157  30119
29839  29909  29810  30129  30124  29963  29963  29805  29549  29605
29892  29699  29209  29363  29003  28311  28550  28122  28268  28275
27946  27787  27657  27705  27267  27353  27268  27390  27235  27114
26901  26893  26761  26895  26965  27578  27789  27308  27294  27118
27227  27498  28202  28550  28473  28513  28185  28221  28621   28542
28875  28855  28795  28774  28331  28116  28204   28431  28471  28554
28619  28593  28461  28765  28371  28466  28524  28594  28397  28106
28146  27777  27505  26918  26151  25976  25997  26120  25939  25824  ];

  % NN = length(yvector) - 1
 maxprice = max(yvector)
 minprice = min(yvector)
 range=maxprice-minprice

  for I= 1: NN+1
     zero(I)=0;
      xvector(I) = I-1;
   end
   switch tactic
               case (1)
    % set parameters of price - simple moving average with N = 10
    N1= 1;
    N2=10;
     % calculate technical indicators on signal
       for I = N1 : NN+1
          sma1signal(I) = 0;
          for J = 1:N1
             sma1signal(I) = sma1signal(I ) + 1/N1 * yvector(I+1 - J);
             end
       end
```

```
    for I = N2 : NN+1
     sma2signal(I) = 0;
     for J = 1:N2
        sma2signal(I) = sma2signal(I ) + 1/N2 * yvector(I+1 - J);
        end
  end

  for I = N2 : NN+1
     pmsma10(I) = sma1signal(I) - sma2signal(I); % calculate  price -
sma10

      techsignal1(I) = sma1signal(I);
      techsignal2(I) = sma2signal(I);
       techsignal(I) = pmsma10(I);

     end

  startpt = N2;

 case (2)
    % set parameters of price - simple moving average with N = 20
N1= 1;
N2=20;

 % calculate technical indicators on signal
  for I = N1 : NN+1
     sma1signal(I) = 0;
     for J = 1:N1
        sma1signal(I) = sma1signal(I ) + 1/N1 * yvector(I+1 - J);
        end
  end

    for I = N2 : NN+1
     sma2signal(I) = 0;
     for J = 1:N2
        sma2signal(I) = sma2signal(I ) + 1/N2 * yvector(I+1 - J);
        end
  end

  for I = N2 : NN+1
     pmsma(I) = sma1signal(I) - sma2signal(I); % calculate  price - sma10
      techsignal1(I) = sma1signal(I);
      techsignal2(I) = sma2signal(I);
       techsignal(I) = pmsma(I);
     end
 startpt = N2;
```

```
    case (3)
    % set parameters of awesome oscillator
N1= 5;
N2=34;

 % calculate technical indicators on signal
  for I = N1 : NN+1
    sma1signal(I) = 0;
    for J = 1:N1
      sma1signal(I) = sma1signal(I ) + 1/N1 * yvector(I+1 - J);
      end
  end

   for I = N2 : NN+1
    sma2signal(I) = 0;
    for J = 1:N2
      sma2signal(I) = sma2signal(I ) + 1/N2 * yvector(I+1 - J);
      end
  end

  for I = N2 : NN+1
    aweosc(I) = sma1signal(I) - sma2signal(I); % calculate awesome
oscillator
     techsignal1(I) = sma1signal(I);
     techsignal2(I) = sma2signal(I);
      techsignal(I) = aweosc(I);
    end
    startpt = N2
  case(4)  % accelerator oscillator
      % set parameters of awesome oscillator and accelerator oscillator
N1= 5;
N2=34;
N3=5;

 % calculate technical indicators on signal
  for I = N1 : NN+1
    sma1signal(I) = 0;
    for J = 1:N1
      sma1signal(I) = sma1signal(I ) + 1/N1 * yvector(I+1 - J);
      end
  end
```

```
    for I = N2 : NN+1
     sma2signal(I) = 0;
     for J = 1:N2
        sma2signal(I) = sma2signal(I ) + 1/N2 * yvector(I+1 - J);
        end
  end

  for I = N2 : NN+1
     aweosc(I) = sma1signal(I) - sma2signal(I); % calculate awesome
oscillator
     end
     N2PN3 = N2+N3;
      for I = N2PN3 : NN+1
     signalline(I) = 0;
     for J = 1:N3
        signalline(I) = signalline(I ) + 1/N3 * aweosc(I+1 - J);
        end
  end

  for I = N2PN3 : NN+1
     accelosc (I) = aweosc(I) - signalline(I); %calculate acelerator
oscillator
      techsignal1(I) = aweosc(I);
     techsignal2(I) = signalline(I);
     techsignal(I) = accelosc(I);
     end
 startpt = N2PN3

     case(5)

  % tactic = 5,  calculate MACD
  M1=12;
alpha1=2/(M1+1);
M2= 26;
alpha2=2/(M2+1);

M3=9;
alpha3=2/(M3+1);

startpt = 15;

   ema1signal(1) = yvector(1);
   ema2signal(1) = yvector(1);
   macdsignal(1) = ema1signal(1) - ema2signal(1);
   ema3macd(1) = macdsignal(1);
```

```
  for I = 2: NN+1
    ema1signal(I) = alpha1 * yvector(I) + (1 - alpha1) * ema1signal(I
- 1);
    ema2signal(I) = alpha2 * yvector(I) + (1 - alpha2) * ema2signal(I
- 1);
    macdsignal(I) = ema1signal(I) - ema2signal(I);
    ema3macd(I) = alpha3 * macdsignal(I) + (1 - alpha3) * ema3macd(I
- 1);
    macdhsignal(I) = macdsignal(I) - ema3macd(I);
    techsignal1(I) = ema1signal(I);
    techsignal2(I) = ema2signal(I);
    techsignal(I) = macdsignal(I);
  end
case(6)
  % tactic = 6,  calculate MACDH
  M1=12;
alpha1=2/(M1+1);
M2= 26;
alpha2=2/(M2+1);

M3=9;
alpha3=2/(M3+1);

startpt = 15;

  ema1signal(1) = yvector(1);
  ema2signal(1) = yvector(1);
  macdsignal(1) = ema1signal(1) - ema2signal(1);
  ema3macd(1) = macdsignal(1);

  for I = 2: NN+1
    ema1signal(I) = alpha1 * yvector(I) + (1 - alpha1) * ema1signal(I
- 1);
    ema2signal(I) = alpha2 * yvector(I) + (1 - alpha2) * ema2signal(I
- 1);
    macdsignal(I) = ema1signal(I) - ema2signal(I);
    ema3macd(I) = alpha3 * macdsignal(I) + (1 - alpha3) * ema3macd(I
- 1);
    macdhsignal(I) = macdsignal(I) - ema3macd(I);
    techsignal1(I) = macdsignal(I);
    techsignal2(I) = ema3macd(I);
     techsignal(I) = macdhsignal(I);
  end
```

```
 case(7)
   % tactic = 7,  calculate MACDH1
   M1=1;
alpha1=2/(M1+1);
M2= 26;
alpha2=2/(M2+1);

M3=9;
alpha3=2/(M3+1);

startpt = 15;

   ema1signal(1) = yvector(1);
   ema2signal(1) = yvector(1);
   macdsignal(1) = ema1signal(1) - ema2signal(1);
   ema3macd(1) = macdsignal(1);

   for I = 2: NN+1
      ema1signal(I) = alpha1 * yvector(I) + (1 - alpha1) * ema1signal(I
- 1);
      ema2signal(I) = alpha2 * yvector(I) + (1 - alpha2) * ema2signal(I
- 1);
      macdsignal(I) = ema1signal(I) - ema2signal(I);
      ema3macd(I) = alpha3 * macdsignal(I) + (1 - alpha3) * ema3macd(I
- 1);
      macdhsignal(I) = macdsignal(I) - ema3macd(I);

      techsignal1(I) = macdsignal(I);
      techsignal2(I) = ema3macd(I);
        techsignal(I) = macdhsignal(I);
   end

case(8)
 % tactic = 8,  calculate price minus ema3 of price
   M1=1;
alpha1=2/(M1+1);
M2= 3;
alpha2=2/(M2+1);

startpt = 15;

   ema1signal(1) = yvector(1);
   ema2signal(1) = yvector(1);
   macdsignal(1) = ema1signal(1) - ema2signal(1);

   for I = 2: NN+1
      ema1signal(I) = alpha1 * yvector(I) + (1 - alpha1) * ema1signal(I
- 1);
```

```
      ema2signal(I) = alpha2 * yvector(I) + (1 - alpha2) * ema2signal(I
- 1);
      macdsignal(I) = ema1signal(I) - ema2signal(I);
      techsignal1(I) = ema1signal(I);
      techsignal2(I) = ema2signal(I);
      techsignal(I) = macdsignal(I);
   end

   case(9)
% tactic - 9,  calculate price minus ema6 of price
   M1=1;
alpha1=2/(M1+1);
M2= 6;
alpha2=2/(M2+1);
startpt = 15;
   ema1signal(1) = yvector(1);
   ema2signal(1) = yvector(1);
   macdsignal(1) = ema1signal(1) - ema2signal(1);

   for I = 2: NN+1
      ema1signal(I) = alpha1 * yvector(I) + (1 - alpha1) * ema1signal(I
- 1);
      ema2signal(I) = alpha2 * yvector(I) + (1 - alpha2) * ema2signal(I
- 1);
      macdsignal(I) = ema1signal(I) - ema2signal(I);
      techsignal1(I) = ema1signal(I);
      techsignal2(I) = ema2signal(I);
      techsignal(I) = macdsignal(I);
   end
   case(10)
   % tactic - 10,  calculate ema3 of price minus ema6 of price
   M1=3;
alpha1=2/(M1+1);
M2= 6;
alpha2=2/(M2+1);
startpt = 15;
   ema1signal(1) = yvector(1);
   ema2signal(1) = yvector(1);
   macdsignal(1) = ema1signal(1) - ema2signal(1);
```

```
  for I = 2: NN+1
    ema1signal(I) = alpha1 * yvector(I) + (1 - alpha1) * ema1signal(I
- 1);
    ema2signal(I) = alpha2 * yvector(I) + (1 - alpha2) * ema2signal(I
- 1);
    macdsignal(I) = ema1signal(I) - ema2signal(I);
    techsignal1(I) = ema1signal(I);
    techsignal2(I) = ema2signal(I);
    techsignal(I) = macdsignal(I);
  end

  case(11)
  % tactic = 11,  calculate emaaccel =  (ema3 - ema6) - ema9(ema3 - ema6)
  M1=3 ;
alpha1=2/(M1+1);
M2= 6 ;
alpha2=2/(M2+1);
M3=9  ;
alpha3=2/(M3+1);

startpt = 15;

  ema1signal(1) = yvector(1);
  ema2signal(1) = yvector(1);
  macdsignal(1) = ema1signal(1) - ema2signal(1);
  ema3macd(1) = macdsignal(1);

  for I = 2: NN+1
    ema1signal(I) = alpha1 * yvector(I) + (1 - alpha1) * ema1signal(I
- 1);
    ema2signal(I) = alpha2 * yvector(I) + (1 - alpha2) * ema2signal(I
- 1);
    macdsignal(I) = ema1signal(I) - ema2signal(I);
    ema3macd(I) = alpha3 * macdsignal(I) + (1 - alpha3) * ema3macd(I
- 1);
    macdhsignal(I) = macdsignal(I) - ema3macd(I);
    techsignal1(I) = macdsignal(I);
    techsignal2(I) = ema3macd(I);
      techsignal(I) = macdhsignal(I);
  end

   end
```

```
% To calculate buy price and sell price, and profit of a trading tactic
B = 0; % Buy originally set to 0
totalB = 0;
totalS= 0; %total number of times to  sell
  profit = 0; % set original profit = 0
     for I = startpt: NN
      if    B == 0  & (techsignal(I) <  0   &  techsignal(I + 1) >  0 )
    B = 1;
      totalB = totalB + B
    I  ,         ybuy = yvector(I + 1) %   n in Figure equal to I printed
here,   e.g., n=19 is equivalent to I+1=20
    Bvector(totalB) = I  ; % not I +1
          profitvectorB (totalB) = profit;
           else
       if B == 1   &    ( techsignal(I)  >  0   &  techsignal(I + 1)  <
0 )
         I ,    ysell = yvector(I + 1)
       totalS = totalS + B; %  Number of times of selling
         profitloss(totalS) = ysell - ybuy ; % calculate profit/loss
of each trade
         profit0 = ysell - ybuy
    profit = profit +  (ysell - ybuy)
    Svector(totalS) = I  ; % not I +1
    profitvectorS(totalS) = profit;
    B=0;
            end
               end
        end
  'Number of times selling',  totalS
  profitpercentage = profit/(maxprice - minprice) * 100
   figure(1)
   subplot(2,1, 1)
     plot(xvector, yvector, 'k+-'  )
    xlabel('n')
    ylabel('price')
         title (' Hang Seng  ')
    subplot(2,1, 2)
    plot(  xvector(startpt : NN+1), techsignal(startpt : NN+1), 'k.-',
xvector, zero, 'k' )
```

```
    xlabel(' n ')
    switch  tactic
    case(1)
   ylabel(' price - SMA10 of price' )
     case(2)
   ylabel(' price - SMA100 of price' )
     case(3)
   ylabel('awesome osc of price' )
       case(4)
   ylabel('accel osc of price' )
      case(5)
   ylabel('MACD  of price')
case(6)
   ylabel('MACDH  of price')
     case(7)
   ylabel(' MACDH1  of price')
   case(8)
      ylabel('price -  ema3  of price')
        case(9)
   ylabel('price -  ema6  of price')
  case(10)
      ylabel('ema3 of price  -  ema6  of price')
case(11)
      ylabel('emaaccel')

   end

 figure(2)

  subplot(3,1, 1)

       plot(xvector, yvector, 'k+-'  )
      xlabel('  ')
      ylabel('price')
       title  (' Hang Seng  ')

      subplot(3,1, 2)

      plot(  xvector(startpt : NN+1), techsignal(startpt : NN+1), 'k.-',
xvector, zero, 'k' )
       xlabel('   ')
       switch  tactic
       case(1)
      ylabel(' price - SMA10 of price' )
        case(2)
      ylabel(' price - SMA20 of price' )
```

```
        case(3)
      ylabel('awesome osc of price' )
          case(4)
      ylabel('accel osc of price' )
         case(5)
      ylabel('MACD  of price')
   case(6)
      ylabel('MACDH  of price')
        case(7)
      ylabel(' MACDH1  of price')
      case(8)
         ylabel('price -  ema3  of price')
           case(9)
      ylabel('price -  ema6  of price')
  case(10)
      ylabel('ema3 of price  -  ema6  of price')
case(11)
      ylabel('emaaccel')
   end
         subplot(3,1, 3)
       plot( Bvector,  profitvectorB, 'kx' , Svector,  profitvectorS,
'k+' ,  xvector, zero, 'k'  )
      xlabel('n')
      ylabel('total profit ')
      title ('    ')

figure(3)
  subplot(3,1, 1)
       plot(xvector, yvector, 'k+-'  )
      xlabel('  ')
      ylabel('price')
          title (' Hang Seng  ')

      subplot(3,1, 2)
      plot(  xvector(startpt : NN+1), techsignal(startpt : NN+1), 'k.-',
xvector, zero, 'k' )
       xlabel('   ')
       switch  tactic
       case(1)
      ylabel(' price - SMA10 of price' )
        case(2)
      ylabel(' price - SMA20 of price' )
        case(3)
      ylabel('awesome osc of price' )
```

```
      case(4)
   ylabel('accel osc of price' )
     case(5)
   ylabel('MACD  of price')
case(6)
   ylabel('MACDH  of price')
    case(7)
   ylabel(' MACDH1  of price')
   case(8)
      ylabel('price -  ema3  of price')
        case(9)
      ylabel('price -  ema6  of price')
  case(10)
      ylabel('ema3 of price  -  ema6  of price')
case(11)
      ylabel('emaaccel')
   end
        subplot(3,1, 3)
       plot( Bvector,  profitvectorB, 'kx' , Svector,  profitvectorS,
'k+' ,  Svector, profitloss, 'go' , xvector, zero, 'k'  )
      xlabel('n')
      ylabel('T profit,profit/trade')
      title ('    ')
```

D.37 tradesp500

```
% tradesp500,   trade S & P 500 index using different trading tactics
%  S&P500   from April 24, 19  to Aug 12, 19
% n = 0 corresponds to April 24, 19,  n = 76 corresponds to Aug 12. 19
clear
tactic =  1  ;  %
% tactic = 1,  sma1msma10
% tactic = 2,  sma1msma20
% tactic = 3  awesome oscillator
% tactic = 4,  accelerator oscillator
% tactic = 5,  MACD
% tactic = 6, MACDH
```

```
% tactic = 7, MACDH1
% tactic = 8 , price - ema3 of price
% tactic = 9 , price - ema6 of price
% tactic = 10 , ema3 of price - ema6 of price
% tactic = 11 , emaaccel

NN = 76; % S& P500 from April 24, 2019 to Aug 12, 2019, 77 data points
% NN = Number of data points - 1
 yvector = [2927.25 2926.17 2939.88 2943.03 2945.83 2923.73
2917.52 2945.64 2932.47 2884.05 2879.42 2870.72 2881.40 2811.87
2834.41 2850.96 2876.32 2859.53 2840.23 2864.36 2856.27 2822.24
2826.06 2802.39 2783.02 2788.86 2752.06 2744.45 2803.27 2826.15
2843.49 2873.34 2886.73 2885.72 2879.84 2891.64 2886.98 2889.67
2917.75 2926.46 2954.18 2950.46 2945.35 2917.38 2913.78 2924.92
2941.76 2964.33 2973.01 2995.82 2990.41 2975.95  2979.63
2993.07 2999.91 3013.77 3014.30 3004.04 2984.42 2995.11 2976.61
2995.03 3005.47 3019.56 3003.67 3025.86 3020.97 3013.18 2980.38
2953.56 2932.05 2844.74 2881.77 2883.98 2938.09 2918.65
2882.70 ];

 % NN = length(yvector) - 1
 maxprice = max(yvector)
 minprice = min(yvector)
 range=maxprice-minprice

  for I= 1: NN+1
     zero(I)=0;
      xvector(I) = I-1;
   end
   switch tactic
               case (1)
     % set parameters of price - simple moving average with N = 10
N1= 1;
N2=10;

 % calculate technical indicators on signal
   for I = N1 : NN+1
      sma1signal(I) = 0;
      for J = 1:N1
         sma1signal(I) = sma1signal(I ) + 1/N1 * yvector(I+1 - J);
         end
end
```

```
  for I = N2 : NN+1
   sma2signal(I) = 0;
   for J = 1:N2
        sma2signal(I) = sma2signal(I ) + 1/N2 * yvector(I+1 - J);
        end
  end

  for I = N2 : NN+1
     pmsma10(I) = sma1signal(I) - sma2signal(I); % calculate  price -
sma10
      techsignal1(I) = sma1signal(I);
      techsignal2(I) = sma2signal(I);
       techsignal(I) = pmsma10(I);
     end
  startpt = N2;

 case (2)
    % set parameters of price - simple moving average with N = 20
N1= 1;
N2=20;
 % calculate technical indicators on signal
  for I = N1 : NN+1
     sma1signal(I) = 0;
     for J = 1:N1
        sma1signal(I) = sma1signal(I ) + 1/N1 * yvector(I+1 - J);
        end
  end

    for I = N2 : NN+1
     sma2signal(I) = 0;
     for J = 1:N2
        sma2signal(I) = sma2signal(I ) + 1/N2 * yvector(I+1 - J);
        end
  end

  for I = N2 : NN+1
     pmsma(I) = sma1signal(I) - sma2signal(I); % calculate  price - sma10
      techsignal1(I) = sma1signal(I);
      techsignal2(I) = sma2signal(I);
       techsignal(I) = pmsma(I);
     end
```

```
startpt = N2;
      case (3)
     % set parameters of awesome oscillator
N1= 5;
N2=34;

 % calculate technical indicators on signal
   for I = N1 : NN+1
      sma1signal(I) = 0;
      for J = 1:N1
         sma1signal(I) = sma1signal(I ) + 1/N1 * yvector(I+1 - J);
         end
   end

     for I = N2 : NN+1
      sma2signal(I) = 0;
      for J = 1:N2
         sma2signal(I) = sma2signal(I ) + 1/N2 * yvector(I+1 - J);
         end
   end

   for I = N2 : NN+1
      aweosc(I) = sma1signal(I) - sma2signal(I); % calculate awesome
oscillator
       techsignal1(I) = sma1signal(I);
       techsignal2(I) = sma2signal(I);
        techsignal(I) = aweosc(I);
      end

      startpt = N2
   case(4)  % accelerator oscillator
         % set parameters of awesome oscillator and accelerator oscillator
N1= 5;
N2=34;
N3=5;

 % calculate technical indicators on signal
   for I = N1 : NN+1
      sma1signal(I) = 0;
      for J = 1:N1
         sma1signal(I) = sma1signal(I ) + 1/N1 * yvector(I+1 - J);
         end
end
```

```
     for I = N2 : NN+1
      sma2signal(I) = 0;
      for J = 1:N2
         sma2signal(I) = sma2signal(I ) + 1/N2 * yvector(I+1 - J);
         end
   end

   for I = N2 : NN+1
      aweosc(I) = sma1signal(I) - sma2signal(I); % calculate awesome
oscillator
      end

      N2PN3 = N2+N3;
       for I = N2PN3 : NN+1
      signalline(I) = 0;
      for J = 1:N3
         signalline(I) = signalline(I ) + 1/N3 * aweosc(I+1 - J);
         end
   end

   for I = N2PN3 : NN+1
      accelosc (I) = aweosc(I) - signalline(I); %calculate acelerator
oscillator
       techsignal1(I) = aweosc(I);
      techsignal2(I) = signalline(I);
      techsignal(I) = accelosc(I);
      end
 startpt = N2PN3

      case(5)
      % tactic = 5,  calculate MACD
   M1=12;
alpha1=2/(M1+1);
M2= 26;
alpha2=2/(M2+1);

M3=9;
alpha3=2/(M3+1);
startpt = 15;
```

```
  ema1signal(1) = yvector(1);
  ema2signal(1) = yvector(1);
  macdsignal(1) = ema1signal(1) - ema2signal(1);
  ema3macd(1) = macdsignal(1);

  for I = 2: NN+1
    ema1signal(I) = alpha1 * yvector(I) + (1 - alpha1) * ema1signal(I
- 1);
    ema2signal(I) = alpha2 * yvector(I) + (1 - alpha2) * ema2signal(I
- 1);
    macdsignal(I) = ema1signal(I) - ema2signal(I);
    ema3macd(I) = alpha3 * macdsignal(I) + (1 - alpha3) * ema3macd(I
- 1);
    macdhsignal(I) = macdsignal(I) - ema3macd(I);
    techsignal1(I) = ema1signal(I);
    techsignal2(I) = ema2signal(I);
    techsignal(I) = macdsignal(I);
  end

case(6)
  % tactic = 6, calculate MACDH
  M1=12;
alpha1=2/(M1+1);
M2= 26;
alpha2=2/(M2+1);
M3=9;
alpha3=2/(M3+1);
startpt = 15;

  ema1signal(1) = yvector(1);
  ema2signal(1) = yvector(1);
  macdsignal(1) = ema1signal(1) - ema2signal(1);
  ema3macd(1) = macdsignal(1);

    for I = 2: NN+1
      ema1signal(I) = alpha1 * yvector(I) + (1 - alpha1) * ema1signal(I
  - 1);
      ema2signal(I) = alpha2 * yvector(I) + (1 - alpha2) * ema2signal(I
  - 1);
      macdsignal(I) = ema1signal(I) - ema2signal(I);
      ema3macd(I) = alpha3 * macdsignal(I) + (1 - alpha3) * ema3macd(I
  - 1);
```

```
      macdhsignal(I) = macdsignal(I) - ema3macd(I);

      techsignal1(I) = macdsignal(I);

      techsignal2(I) = ema3macd(I);

        techsignal(I) = macdhsignal(I);

   end

 case(7)

   % tactic = 7, calculate MACDH1

   M1=1;

alpha1=2/(M1+1);

M2= 26;

alpha2=2/(M2+1);

M3=9;

alpha3=2/(M3+1);

startpt = 15;

   ema1signal(1) = yvector(1);
   ema2signal(1) = yvector(1);
   macdsignal(1) = ema1signal(1) - ema2signal(1);
   ema3macd(1) = macdsignal(1);

   for I = 2: NN+1
      ema1signal(I) = alpha1 * yvector(I) + (1 - alpha1) * ema1signal(I
- 1);
      ema2signal(I) = alpha2 * yvector(I) + (1 - alpha2) * ema2signal(I
- 1);
      macdsignal(I) = ema1signal(I) - ema2signal(I);
      ema3macd(I) = alpha3 * macdsignal(I) + (1 - alpha3) * ema3macd(I
- 1);
      macdhsignal(I) = macdsignal(I) - ema3macd(I);

      techsignal1(I) = macdsignal(I);

      techsignal2(I) = ema3macd(I);

        techsignal(I) = macdhsignal(I);

   end

case(8)

 % tactic = 8, calculate price minus ema3 of price

   M1=1;

alpha1=2/(M1+1);

M2= 3;
alpha2=2/(M2+1);
```

```
startpt = 15;

   ema1signal(1) = yvector(1);
   ema2signal(1) = yvector(1);
   macdsignal(1) = ema1signal(1) - ema2signal(1);

   for I = 2: NN+1
      ema1signal(I) = alpha1 * yvector(I) + (1 - alpha1) * ema1signal(I
- 1);
      ema2signal(I) = alpha2 * yvector(I) + (1 - alpha2) * ema2signal(I
- 1);
      macdsignal(I) = ema1signal(I) - ema2signal(I);
      techsignal1(I) = ema1signal(I);
      techsignal2(I) = ema2signal(I);
      techsignal(I) = macdsignal(I);
   end

   case(9)
% tactic - 9,  calculate price minus ema6 of price
   M1=1;
alpha1=2/(M1+1);
M2= 6;
alpha2=2/(M2+1);
startpt = 15;

   ema1signal(1) = yvector(1);
   ema2signal(1) = yvector(1);
   macdsignal(1) = ema1signal(1) - ema2signal(1);

   for I = 2: NN+1
      ema1signal(I) = alpha1 * yvector(I) + (1 - alpha1) * ema1signal(I
- 1);
      ema2signal(I) = alpha2 * yvector(I) + (1 - alpha2) * ema2signal(I
- 1);
      macdsignal(I) = ema1signal(I) - ema2signal(I);
      techsignal1(I) = ema1signal(I);
      techsignal2(I) = ema2signal(I);
      techsignal(I) = macdsignal(I);
   end
```

```
  case(10)
  % tactic = 10,  calculate ema3 of price minus ema6 of price
  M1=3;
alpha1=2/(M1+1);
M2= 6;
alpha2=2/(M2+1);

startpt = 15;

  ema1signal(1) = yvector(1);
  ema2signal(1) = yvector(1);
  macdsignal(1) = ema1signal(1) - ema2signal(1);

  for I = 2: NN+1
    ema1signal(I) = alpha1 * yvector(I) + (1 - alpha1) * ema1signal(I
- 1);
    ema2signal(I) = alpha2 * yvector(I) + (1 - alpha2) * ema2signal(I
- 1);
    macdsignal(I) = ema1signal(I) - ema2signal(I);

    techsignal1(I) = ema1signal(I);

    techsignal2(I) = ema2signal(I);

    techsignal(I) = macdsignal(I);
  end
  case(11)
  % tactic = 11,  calculate emaaccel =  (ema3 - ema6) - ema9(ema3 - ema6)
  M1=3 ;
alpha1=2/(M1+1);
M2= 6 ;
alpha2=2/(M2+1);
M3=9  ;
alpha3=2/(M3+1);

startpt = 15;

  ema1signal(1) = yvector(1);
  ema2signal(1) = yvector(1);
  macdsignal(1) = ema1signal(1) - ema2signal(1);
  ema3macd(1) = macdsignal(1);
```

```
  for I = 2: NN+1
    ema1signal(I) = alpha1 * yvector(I) + (1 - alpha1) * ema1signal(I
- 1);
    ema2signal(I) = alpha2 * yvector(I) + (1 - alpha2) * ema2signal(I
- 1);
    macdsignal(I) = ema1signal(I) - ema2signal(I);
    ema3macd(I) = alpha3 * macdsignal(I) + (1 - alpha3) * ema3macd(I
- 1);
    macdhsignal(I) = macdsignal(I) - ema3macd(I);
    techsignal1(I) = macdsignal(I);
    techsignal2(I) = ema3macd(I);
      techsignal(I) = macdhsignal(I);
  end

   end

% To calculate buy price and sell price, and profit of a trading tactic
B = 0; % Buy originally set to 0
totalB = 0;
totalS= 0; %total number of times to  sell

  profit = 0; % set original profit - 0

     for I = startpt: NN
      if    B == 0  & (techsignal(I) <  0   &  techsignal(I + 1) >  0 )

    B = 1;
      totalB = totalB + B
   I  ,        ybuy = yvector(I + 1)  %   n in Figure equal to I printed
here,   e.g., n-19 is equivalent to I+1=20
   Bvector(totalB) = I  ;  % not I +1
          profitvectorB (totalB) = profit;
           else
      if  B == 1  &   ( techsignal(I)  >  0  &  techsignal(I + 1)  <
0 )
        I ,    ysell = yvector(I + 1)
       totalS = totalS + B; %  Number of times of selling
        profitloss(totalS) = ysell - ybuy ; % calculate profit/loss
of each trade
```

```
        profit0 = ysell - ybuy
    profit = profit +  (ysell - ybuy)
    Svector(totalS) = I  ;  % not I +1

    profitvectorS(totalS) = profit;
    B=0;
              end
                 end
        end

  'Number of times selling',  totalS
  profitpercentage = profit/(maxprice - minprice) * 100

   figure(1)

   subplot(2,1, 1)

     plot(xvector, yvector, 'k+-'  )
    xlabel('n')
    ylabel('price')
         title ('  S & P500  ')

    subplot(2,1, 2)
    plot(  xvector(startpt : NN+1), techsignal(startpt : NN+1), 'k.-',
xvector, zero, 'k' )
     xlabel(' n ')
     switch  tactic
     case(1)
    ylabel(' price - SMA10 of price' )
      case(2)
    ylabel(' price - SMA100 of price' )
      case(3)
    ylabel('awesome osc of price' )
        case(4)
    ylabel('accel osc of price' )
       case(5)
    ylabel('MACD  of price')
  case(6)
    ylabel('MACDH  of price')
      case(7)
    ylabel(' MACDH1  of price')
```

```
case(8)
ylabel('price - ema3 of price')
case(9)
ylabel('price - ema6 of price')
case(10)
ylabel('ema3 of price - ema6 of price')
case(11)
ylabel('emaaccel')

end


figure(2)
subplot(3,1, 1)
plot(xvector, yvector, 'k+-' )
xlabel(' ')
ylabel('price')
title (' S & P500 ')

subplot(3,1, 2)

plot( xvector(startpt : NN+1), techsignal(startpt : NN+1), 'k.-',
xvector, zero, 'k' )
xlabel(' ')
switch tactic
case(1)
ylabel(' price - SMA10 of price' )
case(2)
ylabel(' price - SMA20 of price' )
case(3)
ylabel('awesome osc of price' )
case(4)
ylabel('accel osc of price' )
case(5)
ylabel('MACD of price')
case(6)
ylabel('MACDH of price')
case(7)
ylabel(' MACDH1 of price')
```

```
      case(8)
         ylabel('price -  ema3  of price')
           case(9)
      ylabel('price -  ema6  of price')
  case(10)
      ylabel('ema3 of price  -  ema6  of price')
case(11)
      ylabel('emaaccel')
   end

         subplot(3,1, 3)
       plot( Bvector,  profitvectorB, 'kx' , Svector,  profitvectorS,
'k+' ,  xvector, zero, 'k'  )
      xlabel('n')
      ylabel('total profit ')
      title ('    ')

figure(3)

  subplot(3,1, 1)

       plot(xvector, yvector, 'k+-'  )
      xlabel('  ')
      ylabel('price')
       title ('  S & P500  ')

      subplot(3,1, 2)

      plot(  xvector(startpt : NN+1), techsignal(startpt : NN+1), 'k.-',
xvector, zero, 'k' )
       xlabel('   ')
       switch  tactic
       case(1)
      ylabel(' price - SMA10 of price' )
        case(2)
      ylabel(' price - SMA20 of price' )
        case(3)
      ylabel('awesome osc of price' )
          case(4)
      ylabel('accel osc of price' )
```

```
        case(5)
      ylabel('MACD  of price')
   case(6)
      ylabel('MACDH  of price')
        case(7)
      ylabel(' MACDH1  of price')
      case(8)
         ylabel('price -  ema3  of price')
           case(9)
      ylabel('price -  ema6  of price')
  case(10)
      ylabel('ema3 of price  -  ema6  of price')
case(11)
      ylabel('emaaccel')
   end

         subplot(3,1, 3)
        plot( Bvector,  profitvectorB, 'kx' , Svector,  profitvectorS,
'k+' ,  Svector,  profitloss, 'go' , xvector, zero, 'k'  )
      xlabel('n')
      ylabel('T profit,profit/trade')
      title ('    ')
```

D.38 unsure

```
%unsure, to plot profit percentage versus mu, the phase shift of the price
signal due to sampling.

 clear
 % omega and phi are given
 omega = pi/6
 phi =  pi/4   % phi - phase lead of velocity indicator, e.g., pi/2
 N = 1440;
 NN = 2*N;
 piint = 2*pi/NN;
```

```
for I= 1: NN+1
   zero(I)=0;
    muvector(I) = -pi +(I-1)*piint;
    theta0vector(I) = omega - muvector(I);
    nbuyvector(I) = fix( (2*pi - theta0vector(I) - phi)/omega ) + 1 ;
    buypricevector(I)  = sin (  nbuyvector(I) *omega +
theta0vector(I)  ) ;
    profitvector(I)= -2*buypricevector(I);
    profitpervector(I) = profitvector(I)/2*100;
   end

   %draw figure
   figure(1)
    subplot(1,1, 1)

       plot ( muvector, zero, 'k-', muvector, profitpervector, 'k.-'  )
      xlabel(' mu ')
      ylabel(' profit percentage ')
      title ('  Artificial data  ')
```

Bibliography

Antoniou, I., Ivanov, V.V., Ivanov, V.V., Zrelov, P.V.: On the log-normal distribution of stock market data. Phys. A. **331**, 617–638 (2004)

Appel, G.: Winning Market Systems: 83 Ways to Beat the Market. Traders Press, Greenville (1991)

Aziz, A.: How to Day Trade for a Living: A beginner's Guide to Trading Tools and Tactics, Money Mangement, Discipline and Trading Psychology, 3rd edn. CreateSpace Independent Publishing Platform, Scotts Valley (2016)

Bernstein, J.: Cycles of Profit. HarperBusiness, New York (1991)

Brigham, E.O.: The Fast Fourier Transform. Prentice-Hall, Englewood Cliffs (1974)

Broesch, J.D.: Digital Signal Processing Demystified. LLH Technology Publishing, Eagle Rock (1997)

Casti, J.L.: Complexification. Harper Perennial, New York (1995)

Casti, J.L.: Would-be Worlds. Wiley, Hoboken (1997)

Chan, H.F.C., Lee, S.T.H., Wong, W.K.: Technical Analysis and Financial Asset Forecasting: From Simple Tools to Advanced Techniques. World Scientific, Singapore (2014)

Crapa, G.: Intra-Day Trading Tactics: Pristine.com's Strategies for Seizing Short-Term Opportunities. Wiley, Hoboken (2007)

Crapa, G.: Trading Tools and Tactics, +Website: Reading the Mind of the Market. Wiley, Hoboken (2011)

Ehlers, J.F.: MESA and Trading Market Cycles. Wiley, Hoboken (1992)

Ehlers, J.F.: Rocket Science for Traders. Wiley, Hoboken (2001)

Ehlers, J.F.: Cycle Analytics for Traders. Wiley, Hoboken (2013)

Elder, A.: Trading for a Living. Wiley, Hoboken (1993)

Elder, A.: Come into My Trading Room. Wiley, Hoboken (2002)

D. K. Mak, *Trading Tactics in the Financial Market*, Management for Professionals,
https://doi.org/10.1007/978-3-030-70622-7

Elder, A.: The New Trading for a Living. Wiley, Hoboken (2014)

Freund, J.E.: Mathematical Statistics. Prentice Hall, Upper Saddle River (1992)

Grimes, A.: The Art and Science of Technical Analysis: Market Structure, Price Action, and Trading Strategies. Wiley, Hoboken (2012)

Halliday, D., Resnick, R., Walker, J.: Fundamentals of Physics, 7th edn. Wiley, Hoboken (2004)

Hamming, R.W.: Digital Filters, 3rd edn. Dover Publications, Garden City (1989)

Hanselman, D., Littlefield, B.: The Student Edition of MATLAB, Version 5 User's Guide. Prentice Hall, Upper Saddle River (1997)

Hayes, M.H.: Digital Signal Processing, Schaum's Outlines. McGraw-Hill, Upper Saddle River (1999)

Hubbard, B.B.: The World According to Wavelets, 2nd edn. A. K. Peters, Ltd., Natick (1998)

Johnson, N.F., Jeffries, P., Hui, P.M.: Financial Market Complexity. Oxford University Press, Oxford (2003)

Kaplan, W.: Advanced Calculus. Addison-Wesley, Boston (1959)

Kirkpatrick II, C., Dahlquist, J.: Technical Analysis : The Complete Resource for Technicians, 3rd edn. FT Press, Upper Saddle River (2015)

Lillo, F., Mantegna, R.N.: Power-law relaxation in a complex system: Omori law after a financial market crash. Phys. Rev. E. **68**, 016119-1–016119-5 (2003)

Lo, A.W., MacKinlay, A.C.: A Non-Random Walk down Wall Street. Princeton University Press, Princeton (1999)

Lynch, W.: Day Trading Investing: For Your Financial Freedom. A Practical Guide to Strategies, Methods, Tools and Tactics. Learn the Trading Psychology and How to Manage Your Money. Independently Published (2020)

Lyons, R.G.: Understanding Digital Signal Processing. Addison-Wesley, Boston (1997)

Mak, D.K.: Science of Financial Market Trading. World Scientific, Singapore (2003)

Mak, D.K.: Mathematical Techniques in Financial Market Trading. World Scientific, Singapore (2006)

Mandelbrot, B.B.: The Fractal Geometry of Nature. W. H. Freeman and Company, New York (1983)

Mandelbrot, B.B.: Fractals and Scaling in Finance. Springer, New York (1997)

Mantegna, R.N., Stanley, H.E.: Scaling behaviour in the dynamics of an economic index. Nature. **376**, 46–49 (1995)

Mantegna, R.N., Stanley, H.E.: An Introduction to Econophysics, Correlations and Complexity in Finance. Cambridge University Press, Cambridge (2000)

Meyer, P.L.: Introductory Probability and Statistical Applications. Addison-Wesley, Boston (1965)

Michael, F., Johnson, M.D.: Financial market dynamics. Phys. A. **320**, 525–534 (2002)

Miner: High Probability Trading Strategies: Entry to Exit Tactics for the Forex, Futures,and Stock Markets. Wiley, Hoboken (2008)

Murphy, J.: The visual investors: How to spot market trends. Wiley, Hoboken (1996)

Oppenheim, A.V., Schafer, R.W., Buck, J.R.: Discrete-Time Signal Processing, 2nd edn. Prentice-Hall, Englewood Cliffs (1999)

Penfold, B.: The Universal Principles of Successful; Trading: Essential Knowledge for All Traders in All Markets. Wiley, Hoboken (2010)

Penfold, B.: The Universal Tactics of Successful Trend Trading: Finding Opportunity in Uncertainty. Wiley, Hoboken (2020)

Penn, D.: The Three Secrets to trading Momentum Indicators. Marketplace Books, Troy (2010)

Person, J.L.: A complete Guide to Technical Trading Tactics: How to Profit using Pivot Points, Candlesticks and Other Indicators. Wiley, Hoboken (2004)

Prechter Jr., R.R., Frost, A.J.: Elliott Wave Principle. New Classic Library, Gainesville (1990)

Pring, M.J.: Technical Analysis Explained, The Successful Investor's Guide to Spotting Investment Trends and Turning Points, 3rd edn. McGraw-Hill, New York (1991)

Proakis, J.G., Manolakis, D.G.: Digital Signal Processing, Principles, Algorithms and Applications, 3rd edn. Prentice-Hall, Englewood Cliffs (1996)

Protter, M.H., Morrey Jr., C.B.: Calculus with Analytic Geometry. Addison-Wesley, Boston (1963)

Sornette, D.: Why Stock Markets Crash. Princeton University Press, Princeton (2003)

Stanley, H.E., Mantegna, R.N.: Introduction to Econophysics: Correlations and Complexity in Finance. Cambridge University Press, Cambridge (2007)

Strang, G., Nguyen, T.: Wavelets and Filter Banks, Revised edn. Wellesley-Cambridge Press, Wellesley (1997)

Tsallis, C., Bukman: Anomalous diffusion in the presence of external forces: exact time-dependent solutions and their thermostatistical basis. Phys. Rev. E. **54**, R2197–R2200 (1996)

Waldrop, M.M.: Complexity. Simon & Schuster, New York (1992)

Williams, B.: Trading Chaos: Applying Expert Techniques to Maximize Your Profits (A Marketplace Book), 1st edn. Wiley, Hoboken (1995)

Williams, B.: New Trading Dimensions: How to Profit from Chaos in Stocks, Bonds, and Commodities. Wiley, Hoboken (1998)

Williams, B., Gregory-Williams: Trading Chaos: Maximize Profits with Proven Technical Techniques, 2nd edn. Wiley, Hoboken (2004)

Index

A
Acceleration, 1, 2, 24–27, 78, 89, 90, 92, 94, 98
Acceleration indicators, 1, 2, 27, 69, 70, 78, 80, 81, 89, 90, 94, 98–100, 103, 108, 112, 114, 122, 123, 126
Accelerator oscillator (AC), 37, 73–83, 98, 99, 107–108, 116, 122, 123
Amplitudes, 5, 9, 12, 16, 30, 31, 34–40, 42, 44–48, 50, 51, 53, 59–65, 67, 69, 70, 73–75, 77–80, 82, 86, 87, 89, 90, 92–94, 99, 103, 104, 107, 117, 119, 120, 123, 125, 129, 140
Awesome oscillator (AO), 37, 73–83, 98–100, 106–108, 116, 122, 123, 125, 126, 139

B
Band-pass filter, 86, 89, 91, 100, 101, 111, 116, 123
Bar lag, 138, 141, 143
Bears, 88, 89
Bulls, 88, 89

C
CAC 40 index, 114, 115
Calculus, 5, 6, 24, 126
Circular frequencies, 6, 12, 16, 18, 19, 30, 61, 86, 87, 90, 91, 94, 100, 103, 104, 108, 109, 112, 114, 115, 127, 128, 132, 133
Concave down, 24–26
Concave up, 24–26
Convolution, v, 20–22, 111, 117, 126
Cosine wave, 6, 7
Cycles, 5–8, 30, 32, 104, 125

D
Derivative, 6, 8
Discrete time Fourier transform, 16, 30

E
EMAACCEL, 69–71, 98, 99, 116, 157–159
Exponent moving average (EMA), 29, 57–61, 63, 64, 66–69, 78, 85–95, 97, 98, 119–123, 126, 141–143

F
Filters, 1, 32, 59, 85, 86, 89–91, 93, 99, 102, 114, 116, 126
Fourier series, 5
Fourier transform, 85, 86, 89, 103–105, 108, 109, 112, 114, 115
Frequencies, 6, 8, 12, 23–24, 29–32, 34, 35, 37, 39, 42, 44, 45, 47–50, 52–55, 57, 59, 61, 63, 64, 66–69, 71, 73–83, 85–95, 99–117, 119, 120, 122–127, 132, 137, 139, 141, 142
FTSE 100 index, 109, 110, 112

G
Genetic algorithm, 4

H
Hang seng index, 105–109
High pass filters, 45, 61, 89–91, 93, 102, 114

I
Impulse response, 59

D. K. Mak, *Trading Tactics in the Financial Market*, Management for Professionals,
https://doi.org/10.1007/978-3-030-70622-7

Indicators, 1, 2, 9, 12, 21, 29–32, 37, 47, 52, 53, 55, 57, 62, 66, 68–70, 73, 77, 81, 85, 87–92, 94, 95, 98–100, 103, 105, 119, 120, 125, 126

L

Loss zones, 12, 22–23, 46, 68, 70, 77, 81, 83, 87, 91, 98–100, 114, 116, 119, 122–124, 126, 127, 132–136
Low pass filters, 29, 57, 85, 86, 89

M

Models, 2, 4
Momentum, 73, 78
Moving average, 29–31, 40, 55, 57–71, 78, 85–95, 97, 123, 125, 126, 141–143
Moving average convergence divergence (MACD), 2, 85–95, 98–114, 116, 119–123, 125, 126, 142, 174–175
Moving average convergence divergence histogram (MACDH), 2, 69, 78, 85–95, 98–102, 110–111, 113, 114, 116, 117, 122, 123, 126, 176–177
Moving average convergence divergence histogram1 (MACDH1), 92–95, 98, 99, 113–114, 116, 178–179

N

Neural network, 4
Nyquist (sampling) theorem, 104

O

Operators, 1

P

Periods, 5–10, 24, 30, 39, 73, 78, 98, 125, 143
Phases, 6, 9–13, 15–24, 27, 29–37, 40, 41, 43, 44, 46–55, 57, 59–66, 68–71, 73–83, 86–95, 98–101, 103, 104, 107, 108, 111, 116, 119–136, 138–142
Profit zones, 12, 17–19, 22, 47, 52, 53, 55, 62, 66, 77, 87, 91–93, 98–100, 119, 122–124, 126–132

R

Random, 3, 125

S

Sampling, 12–24, 104, 127, 129–132, 134–136
Sampling delay, 16, 19, 49, 55, 62, 66, 119, 120, 126, 127, 132
Second derivative, 24
Signals, 5, 9–12, 15–21, 23, 27, 30–32, 34–37, 45, 47–50, 52, 53, 55, 78, 83, 85–91, 93–95, 99, 100, 103–105, 108, 109, 112, 114, 115, 119, 123–136, 138, 139, 141, 143
Simple moving average (SMA), 29–55, 57, 73, 74, 78, 97, 119, 123, 126, 137–140
Sine waves, 2, 3, 5–10, 12, 15, 16, 24–26, 32, 34–39, 47, 48, 52, 54, 62–64, 66, 68, 69, 71, 77, 78, 82, 83, 87, 88, 92, 94, 95, 104, 105, 127, 129, 132
Skipped convolution, 20–22, 111, 117, 126
Slope of a slope, 1, 24–26
Slopes, 1, 5–8, 24–26, 125, 141
S&P 500 index, 100
Sure loss zone, 23, 127, 133, 136
Sure profit zones, 19–20, 49, 50, 52, 53, 55, 62, 66, 68, 70, 71, 77, 81, 83, 87, 91, 93, 98–100, 108, 116, 119, 122, 124, 126, 127, 130–132
Systems, 2, 22, 30, 124

T

Technical analysis, 1–4
Timeframe, 4, 21, 126
Time lag, 30
Trading tactics, 1–4, 37, 44–55, 61–71, 73, 77, 82, 87, 92, 94, 97–117, 119–127
Trending indicators, 29
Trends, 2, 29, 122
Turning points, 5–27

U

Unit sample response, 30, 32, 59
Unsure loss zone, 23, 127, 133–135
Unsure profit zones, 19–20, 49, 50, 52, 53, 55, 62, 66, 68, 70, 77, 81, 83, 87, 91, 98, 99, 102, 106, 119, 126–130
Unwrapped phases, 32–44, 46, 52, 53, 76, 77, 80, 82, 138, 139

V

Velocity, 1, 2, 6–9, 12, 21, 23–27, 29, 45, 47, 48, 61–63, 73, 85–95, 97, 98, 103, 108, 112, 114, 125

Velocity indicators, 1, 2, 8–12, 15–17, 19, 21–24, 27, 29, 45, 47–49, 52–54, 61–64, 66, 68–71, 73, 77, 78, 81–83, 85–95, 97–100, 119, 122–129, 132, 133, 138

W

Waves, 2, 7, 8, 125
Wrapped phases, 32–35, 37–41, 43, 45, 46, 52, 53, 75–77, 80, 81, 120, 122, 139